W9-ATQ-378

12

1980s Project Studies/Council on Foreign Relations

STUDIES AVAILABLE

SOVIET-AMERICAN RELATIONS IN THE 1980s:
Superpower Politics and East-West Trade
Studies by Lawrence T. Caldwell and William Diebold, Jr.

INDUSTRIAL POLICY AS AN INTERNATIONAL ISSUE
William Diebold, Jr.

GROWTH POLICIES AND THE INTERNATIONAL ORDER
Lincoln Gordon

CHALLENGES TO INTERDEPENDENT ECONOMIES:
The Industrial West in the Coming Decade
Studies by Robert J. Gordon and Jacques Pelkmans

SHARING GLOBAL RESOURCES
Studies by Ruth W. Arad and Uzi B. Arad, Rachel McCulloch and José Piñera, and Ann L. Hollick

AFRICA IN THE 1980s:
A Continent in Crisis
Studies by Colin Legum, I. William Zartman, and Steven Langdon and Lynn K. Mytelka

BEYOND THE NORTH-SOUTH STALEMATE
Roger D. Hansen

ENHANCING GLOBAL HUMAN RIGHTS
Studies by Jorge I. Domínguez, Nigel S. Rodley, Bryce Wood, and Richard Falk

OIL POLITICS IN THE 1980s:
Patterns of International Cooperation
Øystein Noreng

SIX BILLION PEOPLE:
Demographic Dilemmas and World Politics
Studies by Georges Tapinos and Phyllis T. Piotrow

THE MIDDLE EAST IN THE COMING DECADE:
From Wellhead to Well-being?
Studies by John Waterbury and Ragaei El Mallakh

REDUCING GLOBAL INEQUITIES
Studies by W. Howard Wriggins and Gunnar Adler-Karlsson

RICH AND POOR NATIONS IN THE WORLD ECONOMY
Studies by Albert Fishlow, Carlos F. Díaz-Alejandro, Richard R. Fagen, and Roger D. Hansen

CONTROLLING FUTURE ARMS TRADE
Studies by Anne Hessing Cahn and Joseph J. Kruzel, Peter M. Dawkins, and Jacques Huntzinger

DIVERSITY AND DEVELOPMENT IN SOUTHEAST ASIA:
The Coming Decade
Studies by Guy J. Pauker, Frank H. Golay, and Cynthia H. Enloe

NUCLEAR WEAPONS AND WORLD POLITICS:
Alternatives for the Future
Studies by David C. Gompert, Michael Mandelbaum, Richard L. Garwin, and John H. Barton

CHINA'S FUTURE:
Foreign Policy and Economic Development in the Post-Mao Era
Studies by Allen S. Whiting and Robert F. Dernberger

ALTERNATIVES TO MONETARY DISORDER
Studies by Fred Hirsch and Michael W. Doyle and by Edward L. Morse

NUCLEAR PROLIFERATION:
Motivations, Capabilities, and Strategies for Control
Studies by Ted Greenwood and by Harold A. Feiveson and Theodore B. Taylor

INTERNATIONAL DISASTER RELIEF:
Toward a Responsive System
Stephen Green

Soviet-American Relations in the 1980s

E
183.8
.R9
C29

Soviet-American Relations in the 1980s

SUPERPOWER POLITICS AND EAST-WEST TRADE

LAWRENCE T. CALDWELL

WILLIAM DIEBOLD, JR.

Introduction by John C. Campbell

1980s Project/Council on Foreign Relations

McGRAW-HILL BOOK COMPANY

New York   St. Louis   San Francisco
Auckland   Bogotá   Hamburg   Johannesburg   London   Madrid
Mexico   Montreal   New Delhi   Panama   Paris   São Paulo
Singapore   Sydney   Tokyo   Toronto

Tennessee Tech. Library
Cookeville, Tenn.

314037

Copyright © 1981 by the Council on Foreign Relations, Inc. All rights reserved. Printed in the United States of America. No part of this publication may be reproduced, stored in a retrieval system, or transmitted, in any form or by any means, electronic, mechanical, photocopying, recording, or otherwise, without the prior written permission of the publisher.

The Council on Foreign Relations, Inc., is a nonprofit and nonpartisan organization devoted to promoting improved understanding of international affairs through the free exchange of ideas. Its membership of about 1,700 persons throughout the United States is made up of individuals with special interest and experience in international affairs. The Council has no affiliation with and receives no funding from the United States government.

The Council publishes the journal *Foreign Affairs* and, from time to time, books and monographs that in the judgment of the Council's Committee on Studies are responsible treatments of significant international topics worthy of presentation to the public. The 1980s Project is a research effort of the Council; as such, 1980s Project Studies have been similarly reviewed through procedures of the Committee on Studies. As in the case of all Council publications, statements of fact and expressions of opinion contained in 1980s Project Studies are the sole responsibility of their authors.

Thomas E. Wallin and Tita Gillespie were the editors for the Council on Foreign Relations. Thomas Quinn and Michael Hennelly were the editors for McGraw-Hill Book Company. Christopher Simon was the designer. Teresa Leaden supervised the production. This book was set in Times Roman by Offset Composition Services, Inc.
Printed and bound by R.R. Donnelley and Sons.

Library of Congress Cataloging in Publication Data

Caldwell, Lawrence T
Soviet-American relations in the 1980s.

(1980s project/Council on Foreign Relations)
Bibliography: p.
Includes index.
1. United States—Foreign relations—Russia.
2. Russia—Foreign relations—United States.
3. United States—Foreign relations—1945–
4. Russia—Foreign relations—1945–   I. Diebold,
William, joint author. II. Title. III. Series:
Council on Foreign Relations. 1980s Project/Council on
Foreign Relations.
E183.8.R9C29   327.47'073   79–20183
ISBN-0-07-009615-5
ISBN 0-07-009616-3 pbk.

1 2 3 4 5 6 7 8 9 R R D R R D 8 0 6 5 4 3 2 1

Contents

EAST EUROPEAN COUNTRIES IN THE WORLD ECONOMY

William Diebold, Jr.

LIST OF TABLES

LIST OF FIGURES

Foreword: The 1980s Project

The political and economic relationships between the United States and the Soviet Union are so central to global stability and welfare that no effort to think about the future of international society can fail to focus on them. The studies in this volume on the Soviet Union's role in international affairs, on the potential for American influence over the course of Soviet foreign policy, and on growth in East-West economic interactions are part of a stream of studies commissioned by the 1980s Project of the Council on Foreign Relations. Each 1980s Project study analyzes issues that are likely to be of international concern during the next 10 to 20 years.

The ambitious purpose of the 1980s Project is to examine important political and economic problems not only individually but in relationship to one another. Some studies or books produced by the Project will primarily emphasize the interrelationship of issues. In the case of other, more specifically focused studies, a considerable effort has been made to write, review, and criticize them in the context of more general Project work. Each Project study is thus capable of standing on its own; at the same time it has been shaped by a broader perspective.

The 1980s Project had its origin in the widely held recognition that many of the assumptions, policies, and institutions that have characterized international relations during the past 30 years are inadequate to the demands of today and the foreseeable demands of the period between now and 1990 or so. Over the course of the next decade, substantial adaptation of institutions and behavior will be needed to respond to the changed circumstances of the 1980s and beyond. The Project seeks to identify those future conditions and the kinds of adaptation they might require. It is not the Project's purpose to arrive at a single or exclusive set of goals. Nor does it focus upon the foreign policy or national interests of the United States alone. Instead, it seeks to identify goals that are compatible with the perceived interests of most states, despite differences in ideology and in level of economic development.

The published products of the Project are aimed at a broad readership, including policy makers and potential policy makers and those who would influence the policy-making process, but are confined to no single nation or region. The authors of Project studies were therefore asked to remain mindful of interests broader than those of any one society and to take fully into account the likely realities of domestic politics in the principal societies involved. All those who have worked on the Project, however, have tried not to be captives of the status quo; they have sought to question the inevitability of existing patterns of thought and behavior that restrain desirable change and to look for ways in which those patterns might in time be altered or their consequences mitigated.

The 1980s Project is at once a series of separate attacks upon a number of urgent and potentially urgent international problems and also a collective effort, involving a substantial number of persons in the United States and abroad, to bring those separate approaches to bear upon one another and to suggest the kinds of choices that might be made among them. The Project involves more than 300 participants. A small central staff and a steering Coordinating Group have worked to define the questions and to assess the compatibility of policy prescriptions. Nearly 100 authors, from more than a dozen countries, have been at work on separate studies. Ten working groups of specialists and generalists have been convened to subject the Project's studies to critical scrutiny and to help in the process of identifying interrelationships among them.

The 1980s Project is the largest single research and studies effort the Council on Foreign Relations has undertaken in its 55-year history, comparable in conception only to a major study of the postwar world, the War and Peace Studies, undertaken by the Council during the Second World War. At that time, the impetus of the effort was the discontinuity caused by worldwide conflict and the visible and inescapable need to rethink, replace, and supplement many of the features of the international system that had prevailed before the war. The discontinuities in today's world are less obvious and, even when occasionally quite visible—as in the abandonment of gold convertibility and fixed monetary parities—only briefly command the spotlight of public attention. That new institutions and patterns of behavior are needed in many areas is widely acknowledged, but the sense of need is less urgent—existing institutions have not for the most part dramatically failed and collapsed. The tendency, therefore, is to make do with outmoded arrangements and to improvise rather than to undertake a basic analysis of the problems that lie before us and of the demands that those problems will place upon all nations.

The 1980s Project is based upon the belief that serious effort and integrated forethought can contribute—indeed, are indispensable—to progress in the next decade toward a more humane, peaceful, productive, and just world. And it rests upon the hope that participants in its deliberations and readers of Project publications—whether or not they agree with an author's point of view—may be helped to think more informedly about the opportunities and the dangers that lie ahead and the consequences of various possible courses of future action.

The 1980s Project has been made possible by generous grants from the Ford Foundation, the Lilly Endowment, the Andrew W. Mellon Foundation, the Rockefeller Foundation, and the German Marshall Fund of the United States. Neither the Council on Foreign Relations nor any of those foundations is responsible for statements of fact and expressions of opinion contained in publications of the 1980s Project; they are the sole responsibility of the individual authors under whose names they appear. But the

Council on Foreign Relations and the staff of the 1980s Project take great pleasure in placing those publications before a wide readership both in the United States and abroad.

The 1980s Project

1980s PROJECT WORKING GROUPS

During 1975 and 1976, ten Working Groups met to explore major international issues and to subject initial drafts of 1980s Project studies to critical review. Those who chaired Project Working Groups were:

Cyrus R. Vance, Working Group on Nuclear Weapons and Other Weapons of Mass Destruction

Leslie H. Gelb, Working Group on Armed Conflict

Roger Fisher, Working Group on Transnational Violence and Subversion

Rev. Theodore M. Hesburgh, Working Group on Human Rights

Joseph S. Nye, Jr., Working Group on the Political Economy of North-South Relations

Harold Van B. Cleveland, Working Group on Macroeconomic Policies and International Monetary Relations

Lawrence C. McQuade, Working Group on Principles of International Trade

William Diebold, Jr., Working Group on Multinational Enterprises

Eugene B. Skolnikoff, Working Group on the Environment, the Global Commons, and Economic Growth

Miriam Camps, Working Group on Industrial Policy

1980s PROJECT STAFF

Persons who have held senior professional positions on the staff of the 1980s Project for all or part of its duration are:

Miriam Camps	*Catherine Gwin*
William Diebold, Jr.	*Roger D. Hansen*
Tom J. Farer	*Edward L. Morse*
David C. Gompert	*Richard H. Ullman*

Richard H. Ullman was Director of the 1980s Project from its inception in 1974 until July 1977, when he became Chairman of the Project Coordinating Group. Edward L. Morse was Executive Director from July 1977 until June 1978. At that time, Catherine Gwin, 1980s Project Fellow since 1976, took over as Executive Director.

PROJECT COORDINATING GROUP

The Coordinating Group of the 1980s Project had a central advisory role in the work of the Project. Its members as of June 30, 1978, were:

Carlos F. Díaz-Alejandro
Richard A. Falk
Tom J. Farer
Edward K. Hamilton
Stanley Hoffmann
Gordon J. MacDonald
Bruce K. MacLaury

Bayless Manning
Theodore R. Marmor
Ali Mazrui
Michael O'Neill
Stephen Stamas
Fritz Stern
Allen S. Whiting

Until they entered government service, other members included:

W. Michael Blumenthal
Richard N. Cooper
Samuel P. Huntington

Joseph S. Nye, Jr.
Marshall D. Shulman

COMMITTEE ON STUDIES

The Committee on Studies of the Board of Directors of the Council on Foreign Relations is the governing body of the 1980s Project. The Committee's members as of June 1, 1979, were:

Barry E. Carter
Robert A. Charpie
Stanley Hoffmann
Henry A. Kissinger
Walter J. Levy

Robert E. Osgood
Stephen Stamas
Philip Geyelin
Marina v. N. Whitman

James A. Perkins (Chairman)

Soviet-American Relations in the 1980s

Introduction: The Role of the Soviet Union in World Politics in the 1980s

John C. Campbell

One need be no historical determinist to conclude that for better or worse the position and policies of the Soviet Union will have a great deal to do with the shape of the world order that will emerge in the 1980s. Soviet conduct may hold the key to whether that world order is one dominated by a continuing military confrontation, or one in which there is growing Soviet participation in cooperative international arrangements for common benefit. Those may not be clearcut alternatives, of course; the eventuality may be somewhere in between and may contain elements of both. But Moscow's general choice of direction will be all-important.

The countries of the West and of the Third World would do well to make no predetermination of what that choice might be. They should look to their defenses, but not be mesmerized by the Soviet threat; they should offer cooperation, but not be lulled by false hopes of what détente will bring. They do not have to gear their own policies to what the Soviets may be saying or doing. On hundreds of political and economic questions they can make decisions and build institutions to suit their own interests without looking over their shoulder at Moscow. They can create conditions, consciously or unconsciously, that will limit the Soviet Union's choices or otherwise influence its conduct. The United States, more than any other, can affect the role the U.S.S.R. plays in world politics, just as Soviet decisions will affect the role played by the United States.

This relationship is often put forward in the form of the simple proposition that since the two superpowers are the only states which can blow each other up, and the rest of the world as well, they must concentrate their foreign policies on their bilateral relations, especially the strategic dimension. The facts of military power and the strategic balance have imposed themselves as a central element in such order as the world has had in the past three decades, as well as the principal threat to it. The "system," if it can be called that, based first on American strategic superiority and later on what has been called *parity* or *essential equivalence,* has had sufficient stability for the avoidance of nuclear war.

There is no guarantee that it will continue to do so. First, it is possible that the Soviets, if they build up their strategic nuclear power to the point where they have, or believe they have, superiority over the United States, might take greater risks of nuclear war. Their military doctrine and planning, like ours, envisage the waging of a nuclear war; it is not unthinkable. Second, the possibility of war occurring by miscalculation or accident, in conditions of hair-trigger preparedness on both sides for a massive counterstrike, cannot be ruled out. Third, technology will continue to stimulate the arms competition, change the character of the military equation, and perhaps destroy its stability. Fourth, the powers of decision rest with the two governments alone, each making its own calculations as to the possession and use of weapons of mass destruction. As long as these huge arsenals of weapons are at the disposal of two rival powers, they and the world must live under the threat that they may be used.

Below the level of strategic power, moreover, there will be many situations involving the threat or use of force by one or the other superpower in areas of the world where they are in competition. We do not have to reach precise conclusions regarding such situations to accept the plausibility of their occurrence and the dangers to peace they will bring. The strategic balance, whether or not it provides a reliable deterrent to nuclear war, may actually encourage military moves in local areas; the balance of power in such areas may be an uncertain one and, therefore, not a bar to adventurism; and risks taken for limited gain may in fact be risks of nuclear war because they set in motion an uncontrolled train of events.

These prospects can induce doomsday thinking. Many a voice has warned that the world's governments, and especially the two superpowers, must bring about substantial nuclear disarmament and control within the next decade or resign themselves to the destruction of civilized life. President Carter has taken account of the world's fears in stating his own aim of banishing nuclear weapons from the face of the earth. Yet the contrast between the urgency of such pleas and the glacial progress of the American–Soviet Strategic Arms Limitation Talks (SALT) and the near-total absence of results in other negotiations for the reduction of arms or force levels puts the question starkly.

One could justify devoting a study of Soviet-American relations, or of the place of the U.S.S.R. in the world order of the 1980s, solely to a search for the ways and means of controlling nuclear weapons.* We can assume that that search will go on, on the part of governments, international organizations, and private institutions and individuals. We cannot assume that it will be successful. It is questionable how far Western governments can go in bargaining about force levels and numbers of weapons and means of verification and control, which are matters of ultimate security, without regard to the political drives, economic needs, and ideological attitudes that make up the Soviet Union's relations with the outside world. Superpower status, on a par with the United States, is and will continue to be a central aim of Soviet conduct. The question is how the Soviet leadership will pursue that aim.

There is a Western concept of international order which is challenged both by the communist powers and by the Third World. There is a Soviet concept of international order, at least in Soviet official doctrine, which requires the victory of socialism over imperialism and capitalism. It is pointless to try to reconcile

*The nuclear relationship between the United States and the Soviet Union is the subject of another 1980s Project volume, *Nuclear Weapons and World Politics,* David C. Gompert et al., McGraw-Hill, for the Council on Foreign Relations/1980s Project, New York, 1977.

those legal and doctrinal concepts, and much more important to see how in practical terms the United States and the U.S.S.R. can regulate their political and economic relations, reduce risks of conflict, and widen fruitful cooperation. We can recognize that Soviet doctrine envisages "peaceful coexistence" as a desirable state of relations with the West for the present, without prejudice to the Soviet view of the ultimate future. For both sides the question is how a period of peaceful coexistence can be used.

Lawrence Caldwell and William Diebold, who address these general questions in this volume, do not give clear and categorical answers; indeed, no one can. But their analyses do point in a definite direction. They see an evolving Soviet Union which, by a combination of choice and circumstance, becomes more engaged in the world economy and also, in playing the game of great-power competition and ideological struggle, may be brought to abide by certain—though still undefined and unagreed-upon—rules. They look at ways in which the mixture of cooperation and conflict, which is the pattern of East-West relations today, may be pushed toward an increase of cooperation and a reduction of conflict.

The pattern of the 1980s will be shaped, on the Soviet side, by the character of the regime and its general approach to the outside world, by the forces in Soviet society and the problems they pose to the Soviet leadership, and by external developments that affect Soviet decisions. Such external developments include Western policies, deliberate or not, which the Soviet leaders must take into account in making decisions.

II

As Caldwell makes clear, those leaders themselves will change soon, certainly before the mid-1980s. The change will be significant because it will bring about more or less simultaneously a shift at the very top, a thorough turnover in the Politburo, and a generational shift in the political elite both at the center and in the union republics. Whether these changes are accompanied by a struggle for power such as to warrant the description of

4

"succession crisis" may be less important than the fact of the change in generations. Those who were a part of the system through the Stalin purges and the Second World War are passing from the scene, to be replaced by a group of leaders whose careers have been shaped by the environment of the Soviet Union in the Khrushchev and Brezhnev years.

To predict which individuals will occupy the top positions would be too speculative to be useful, although we know the names of those now on the threshold of membership in the Politburo and of the few likely to be in contention for the post of General Secretary. More important than the individuals will be the character of the leadership, the approach to domestic problems, and the outlook on the world. The Brezhnev regime has been conservative, bureaucratic, relatively immobile in domestic affairs, and rather cautious in foreign policy, stressing détente with the West although willing to undertake venturesome initiatives in Africa. It has rejected the reforming spirit and impulsive experimentation of Khrushchev without attempting a return to the full-scale repression and arbitrary personal rule of Stalin. It is probable that with a new leadership the pendulum will swing toward bolder innovation and change in domestic affairs, for the simple reason that problems the Brezhnev regime has avoided or postponed will demand it. Whether Soviet foreign policy will be more dynamic and aggressive is an open question.

The Soviet system provides no regular procedures for the transfer of political power and no fixed period of office for the man at the top. The uncertainties of a period of succession may make for competition of ideas and of institutional interests, and thus for shifts in policy. But the supremacy of the Communist Party and the very weight of the party machinery place limits on the competition for leadership and on the policies that can be followed. Besides, the Soviet government is a ponderous, bureaucratic machine made up of thousands of persons with vested interests in keeping things more or less as they are. The experience of the past decade, despite the rise of Brezhnev to a position of primacy among his colleagues in the Politburo, seems to have solidified the process of collegial decision making and diminished the possibility of a single leader's ever again wielding the personal authority of a Stalin or even of a Khrushchev.

The party professionals, the security apparatus (KGB), and the military-industrial complex may have their constituencies contending for shares of power, but the struggle is within a system they all accept and must uphold. The military establishment may conceivably take an even more prominent role than it has now. It is a safe guess that the military will have first claim on resources, as it has in the Brezhnev period, but that does not mean that the influence of the military leaders will be thrown on the side of immobility at home or of aggressive policies abroad. They will be interested, above all, in the consolidation and recognition of superpower status of the U.S.S.R. and in an efficient economy that supports a position of strength.

Nothing can be said for certain about the new generation of leadership except that it will be young (as Soviet leaders go), less burdened by the Stalinist past, confident in the Soviet future, and better acquainted with the outside world than any leaders since the time of Lenin. This profile does not tell us what the nature and directions of policy will be: whether rigid or moderate in relations with the United States; more ready to expand economic relations with the rest of the world, or less so; repressive or permissive in handling Eastern Europe; bold and interventionist in the Third World or staying within the limits of normal relations and the international equilibrium.

These questions will have their answers only when we see what the leadership's economic priorities are, what positions are taken in international negotiations, and what new gloss is put on the concept of peaceful coexistence. Lawrence Caldwell sees a continuing division and debate in the Soviet regime and in Soviet society, in which the forces of orthodoxy and conservatism are arrayed against those of modernization. In the former category one may place those whose highest concerns are the security and continuity of the political system, and who look at all proposals for reform from that viewpoint. In the latter are those more willing to experiment in the interest of efficiency, more prepared to rely on incentives and less on control. There may be some correspondence between these attitudes on domestic matters and those held on foreign relations, with those desiring to move toward a more efficient economy looking to foreign trade and credits as a means of getting there.

III

Soviet Russia is often described by Western writers as the last of the great imperialist powers. The representatives of Communist China have their own term, "social imperialists," for the Russians. Whatever the terminology, Soviet practice over the years since World War II has included physical domination, by a military presence or the threat of it, of those nations of Eastern Europe that are part of the Soviet security system; attempts, at one time or another, to push the boundaries of that system further outward by bringing other countries on the periphery of this empire (such as Finland, Yugoslavia, Albania, Greece, Turkey, and Iran) under its control; pressure on Western Europe to weaken its ties with America and limit its ability to adopt policies inimical to Soviet interests; and exploitation of relations with certain Third World countries to enhance the global power position of the U.S.S.R. The Soviet Union will no doubt continue to be an imperialist power in all these respects. New leadership will not cease to regard control of Eastern Europe as vital to the security of the U.S.S.R. itself, nor will it give up efforts to impose its will on border countries, keep pressure on Western Europe, overawe China, and seek new client states in the Third World.

The formidable military power of the Soviet Union compels the rest of the world to take such manifestations of Soviet imperialism seriously, especially since the buildup of Soviet armaments in the 1970s may be expected to go on into the 1980s. Military power begets counterpower, however, and if no effective limits are placed on the arms race, the United States, its NATO allies, and China will continue to build up their own forces.

By their concentration on military strength the Soviets will quite possibly induce the hostile encirclement and two-front threat they most fear. Of the world's five centers of industrial and actual or potential military power (North America, Western

7

Europe, the U.S.S.R., Japan, and China), four may be brought together in formal or informal alliance against the fifth, the U.S.S.R., largely because the latter's power and policies are seen as a common danger.

Needless to say, the threat of such a combination could play on the ever-present paranoia in the minds of Soviet leaders, leading to irrational international behavior dangerous to peace. On the other hand, we should not underestimate the salutary effect of a global balance that tends to deprive the Soviet Union of the military instrument as a means of forcing basic changes in its favor. This may seem a prescription for an uncontrolled arms race at a time when all the world's real interest calls for negotiated disarmament. But negotiated disarmament will not be possible until the Soviet government itself is prepared to limit the use of military power, for political ends, and that may be only when its leaders, as rational men, are convinced it is not worth the risk and the cost. Where actual military conflict is concerned, the Soviet leadership has been rational and reasonably circumspect throughout the entire period since World War II. This should be no less true in the 1980s.

Once one looks beyond the military factor, the weight of the Soviet Union in world affairs is quite modest for a country of its size, population, resources, and industrial development. Virtually self-sufficient economically, it has the advantage of not being dependent on foreign countries for key resources, but its small share of the world's trade and nonparticipation in international economic and financial institutions reduce the influence it can have on the economic decisions of other governments. There are two exceptions. The first is the group of countries of Eastern Europe, plus Mongolia and Cuba, associated with the U.S.S.R. in the Council for Mutual Economic Assistance, whose close economic relations result from, and in turn help to buttress, Soviet political control; this group could be enlarged in the 1980s. The second is the group of countries, shifting in its makeup, with which the Soviet Union has made extensive bilateral arrangements (including commodity deals, easy credits, military aid, and technical assistance) covering a substantial segment of their national economies. Such arrangements may bring economic advantages to the Soviet Union, or they may represent economic loss; the point is that the motivation on the Soviet side is primarily political or military. The Soviet authorities have to decide in all these cases whether the present and potential gains are worth the economic cost.

The economic side of Soviet international relations, sometimes distorted by political strategy, is relatively simple. Trade with other countries is tied to the government's economic plan: what is needed for the plan and not available at home is imported, and exports are a means of paying for the imports, either by barter or in hard currency. In addition to discussing the familiar problems of fitting a state-trading economy into a world system of largely market economies, William Diebold's essay clarifies the serious limitations on what the Soviet economy offers to the rest of the world outside Eastern Europe. Some of its exports are wanted by other countries—for some years now it has been a significant source of oil and gas for Western Europe. In general, however, its international economic power is not comparable to its military power.

The other side of the picture is what international trade and financial relations can contribute to the Soviet economy and its growth. As the Soviet leaders try to see the patterns of the 1980s, they must be aware that basic problems exist in agriculture, energy, industrial growth, manpower, productivity, and technology, and that they or their successors will face critical decisions. Will they choose to turn inward, to autarky, in order to reduce reliance on the capitalist world? Or will their choice be to increase ties with the West, to avail themselves of the capital and technology necessary to develop the country's resources and maintain the desired rate of economic growth?

We can draw now a rough picture of the economic problems of the Soviet Union in the 1980s because most of them have already begun to appear and are systemic: a slowdown in the industrial growth rate; inability to develop energy resources rapidly enough to meet the rising demand for the home market and for export; failure to produce at home new technology comparable to that available in the West; and continuing inability of Soviet agriculture to avoid occasional years of short harvests

9

requiring massive imports of grains. Other problems can be predicted from the demographic charts, which point to serious shortages of labor in the coming years. These shortages will appear especially in the more developed sections of the country, which means that the economy will have to depend increasingly on the population of the less developed, non-Russian republics. That situation may have serious political as well as economic implications if there is rising nationalism among non-Russian nationalities.

One of the most serious of future Soviet economic problems, and certainly the most publicized and discussed in the West, may well be that of energy. The U.S.S.R. is now the world's biggest producer of oil, but it is also a voracious consumer, and its ability to supply its own needs through the 1980s has been seriously questioned. Not that vast resources of oil and gas do not exist in the subsoil of the U.S.S.R.; they do, but most of them are in remote areas of Siberia and will require tremendous capital expenditures and much time before they can be brought on stream. First to suffer will be Soviet oil exports to Eastern Europe, which are important for political reasons, and to the West, which are needed to bring in hard currency. The Soviet Union can be counted on to make tremendous efforts not to become dependent on foreign sources of energy, but it still seems likely that at some point in the 1980s it will become a net importer of oil. The question is whether that prospect presages new Soviet policies of cooperation with other consuming countries or with producing areas such as the Middle East, or possibly an aggressive policy aimed at control of Middle East oil.

The choices facing the Soviet government in coping with its economic problems will lie in internal and in foreign policy, and in both cases the decisions will be political as well as economic. On the domestic side attempts at remedies may include shifting priorities, cutting consumption, or increasing automation. But solutions may be found only through such modifications in the system of the command economy as decentralization of management decisions, increased incentives, experimentation, and profitability; in short, the same types of reforms that have modified central planning in Yugoslavia, Hungary, and other socialist countries. But aside from the inertia of the Soviet system, with its automatic resistance to change, the high officials of party and government have strong political reasons for not relaxing controls that would accompany or grow out of economic reform. The experience of Eastern Europe appears to them more as a chilling lesson than as an example.

A key question for the 1980s is whether the Kremlin will regard internal reform and expansion of external relations as alternative or as complementary ways of overcoming its economic dilemmas. Several years ago, in a policy decision that was confirmed at the Twenty-Fourth Party Congress in 1971, the Soviet high command decided to turn to the West for the capital goods and technology needed to revive the lagging growth rate and speed the transition from the age of steel to that of computers. That decision has been one of the premises of the declared policy of peaceful coexistence and offers of expanded trade and industrial and scientific cooperation to the United States, Western Europe, and Japan. With the United States the policy has run into roadblocks in the form of political mistrust and restrictive United States legislation, and the proposed large-scale projects for the development of Soviet energy resources have not been consummated. But the Soviet government has left no doubt, not just by declarations but by the contracts concluded mainly with European and Japanese firms, that its commitment to the policy is real and will go on into the 1980s.

The two authors of this volume address the foregoing questions, and the issues of Western policy related to them, with a combination of economic analysis and political judgment. William Diebold stresses the limits of Soviet participation in the world economic system, which is essentially a private-trading system despite the major role played by governments and which does not easily accommodate state-run economies; but even such limited participation, including particularly new forms of industrial cooperation found desirable on both sides, can become an integral element in the Soviet economy. Lawrence Caldwell fits his economic analysis into a wider argument that the United States and other Western nations have an interest in strengthening the hand of the moderate forces, the "modernizers," in

11

the Soviet system, and can do so through economic and other policies.

One conclusion for the 1980s that comes through clearly from known data and reasonable projections is that the Soviets will be burdened with serious problems in planning, organizing, and running their economy and that they will not succeed by depending only on their own "socialist world." The turn to the developed nations of the West for cooperation is not a temporary tactic but a long-term necessity. The relationship will be reciprocal and will give bargaining power to both sides. Although the state-run economy on the Soviet side is better situated tactically for bargaining, the relative needs of the U.S.S.R. will be greater, thus conferring some advantage on the West. The relationship is not likely to be susceptible to direct pressures or demands by the West for significant political concessions. But it may well affect the way the Soviet Union conducts itself on the international scene, and not only in economic matters.

IV

In assessing the place of the Soviet Union in the world of the 1980s the authors of this volume have been relatively conservative. Others have posed such questions as whether the U.S.S.R. can survive until 1984, and whether it can avoid war with China. The future is bound to produce surprises, although probably not so calamitous as those. How many prophets foresaw the Soviet-Chinese break of the 1950s? Yet conservatism in prophecy seems justified in view of the profoundly conservative nature of the Soviet regime itself and the slowness with which the system changes, although startling reversals of specific policies may take place from time to time. The Soviets will not cease to test the limits of their relationship with the West. Yet the entire record of Soviet policy over many changes of leadership shows an absence of recklessness, a close calculation of what is possible and what is not.

If there is one consistent theme in Soviet conduct over the past 25 years, it is its claim to act, and to be treated, as a superpower equal to the United States. That 25 years ago the Soviet Union was not in fact equal, according to many indices of power, only increased the intensity of its claim and the emphasis the Kremlin placed on the one kind of power, military, in which it could most closely compete. The buildup of strategic arms to the point of parity and of naval and air power with a global reach was perhaps less significant as a threat to the world's security than for the psychological effect it has had, and will continue to have, on Soviet assertions and defense of Soviet interests in a hundred different ways all over the world: in standing up to America generally, in pressing Europe to shun anti-Soviet policies, in combatting Chinese influence in Asia or forcing a change in China itself, or in seeking military positions and client states in the Third World.

A Soviet Union intent on self-assertion, with military power as its main claim to greatness and principal instrument of policy, will not be an easy partner in creating and maintaining a secure and moderate world order in the 1980s. Such a world order cannot be static, but one of its main functions will be to contain the destructive effects of change, in which Soviet cooperation cannot be assumed. Yet we need not assume the worst, and knowledge of the magnitude of the problem should make it possible to think rationally about it.

One can look at the outlines of a future international order from many angles, as the variety of books emerging from the 1980s Project of the Council on Foreign Relations will attest. From the particular standpoint of where the Soviet Union comes into the picture, it may be useful to stress three aspects: (a) military deterrence, to deny the Soviets direct use of their armed forces; (b) constructive attack on problems of the developed and developing worlds, to minimize Soviet opportunities to exploit them; and (c) practical consultation and cooperation to expand areas of common interest between the U.S.S.R. and the rest of the world.

The first, deterrence, might also be called "containment," and evokes unpleasant memories of the cold war. It should not matter what the labels and the memories are. The important point is that, in the search for new cooperative relationships, deterrence of military action be maintained. For strategic power the importance of deterrence is self-evident. For the balance of power in Europe and in Northeast Asia, and for the many "gray areas" of the world where the Soviets might be tempted to take military action, it may be less apparent but just as urgent. The world can no longer afford military adventures on the part of the big powers, whether by the Soviet Union, the United States, or China.

Military deterrence is a proposition that raises many questions, including American military commitments to allies. How can military action be ruled out, but still retained as a credible deterrent to others? As to possible—or acceptable—Soviet military action, what about Eastern Europe? Has it not already been recognized de facto as a sphere of influence in which the U.S.S.R. can intervene at will? What about a Soviet armed incursion into, say Afghanistan, to defend that country's communist government against internal opponents? What about a Soviet commitment of forces, at the invitation of African governments, to the fight against South Africa, or the sending of combat forces, in the guise of advisers, to the help of an embattled regime in Ethiopia or Angola? There will be difficult cases such as these. But it is worth noting that deterrence has worked in the past. Since World War II the Soviet Union has not sent armed forces into action beyond its frontiers, except into its Eastern European preserve (and a brief and limited experiment in Egypt in 1970–1972). The risks have been too high, and they must be kept high by the maintenance of a balance of power. Others have a part to play, but the main burden of that aspect of world order falls on the United States.

The second aspect is that of building more durable and mutually acceptable relationships among nations outside the Soviet Union, particularly between the developed and the developing. Perhaps it would be more accurate to call the task one of the management of disorder rather than the building of a new order, for it will involve extraordinary political and psychological as well as economic adjustments on both sides to overcome the effects of past exploitation and discrimination by developed countries and of bitterness, false hopes, and inflated claims of developing countries, in addition to the real conflicts of interest that will persist.

How so-called North-South questions are dealt with over the

14

next ten years may be decisive in determining whether a viable international order emerges at all, and they are especially difficult where North-South and East-West issues intersect. The U.S.S.R. and its socialist allies could make a positive material contribution to this effort, although it would be a marginal one in view of the weaknesses of the Soviet economy. The most important contribution they could make would be to refrain from disrupting the world order, for in that respect their capabilities are considerable. These include propaganda playing on the theme of the common struggle of the socialist world and the Third World against the imperialists; arms shipments, which can be disruptive both within receiving countries and in regional balances of power (as is the case with American or other arms shipments); selective economic aid for Soviet political purposes; and taking sides in conflicts that can imperil world peace and vastly complicate the task of building a more stable international system. The pattern is known from past and present Soviet actions in Southeast Asia, the Middle East, the Horn of Africa, and elsewhere. It is not difficult to forecast its continuation wherever the conditions may be inviting, as they probably will be in one of the most explosive areas, southern Africa.

Now the Soviets cannot be prevented from playing that game. Others cannot close off the Third World from the exercise of Soviet influence. They cannot deter arms sales, treaties of friendship, political deals, or aid to guerrillas in the same way that they can deter armed aggression. These are instruments of policy not used exclusively by the Soviet Union. The salient question is whether Soviet policies may be kept within certain limits in their encouragement of violence and war and their disruption of efforts to enhance regional stability and economic progress, and above all, whether the Soviets can be prevented from establishing positions where they threaten the independence of other nations or the security of the West.

It is a lesson of the past 20 years that the United States and its Western allies cannot successfully frustrate such policies by engaging the Soviets in a game of move and countermove, directly contesting their gains, seeking strategic positions to outflank theirs, and lining up local governments as allies, all with little regard for the prevailing political currents in the Third World

15

and conceptions of their own interests held by those countries. From the 1950s into the 1970s those political currents, strong on anticolonialism and liberation, were generally running against the West and enabled the Soviet Union to make such gains as it did during those years. The experience was not all favorable, either for the Soviets or for the new friends whom they won, some of them only temporarily. In the 1980s it is likely that the leaders and peoples of the Third World, with a few exceptions, will see the U.S.S.R. as just another great power, its ideology irrelevant, its economic attraction minimal, and its tendency to dominate more real than that of the tired democracies of the West. At that time, also, the new generation of leadership in the Third World should be less transfixed by the issues and dogmas of the struggle for independence, more willing to work out with the developed countries the basis of a mutually beneficial relationship.

The 1980s will require changes in Western approaches to regional security as well as to economic relations. Specific situations will exist, of course, such as that between Israel and its Arab neighbors (whether or not negotiated settlements are broadened and sustained), that will require direct American commitments, but in the Third World generally the West should pay heed to the strength of the idea of nonalignment and not hand it over as an issue to the Russians; should accept and encourage regional security arrangements and organizations excluding outside powers, even if the weakness of such organizations is apparent; and should act in time to prevent a crystallization of Third World sentiment and policy against the West on issues such as those of southern Africa.

No American or Western policies will be able to neutralize Soviet intrusions and influence in the Third World, and it is not necessary that they should. Those areas will produce enough disputes and revolutionary ferment to provide Moscow with opportunities; local governments and political movements will be looking for arms or other outside help to defeat their adversaries or to save "the revolution." The West may also have to act in immediate situations to protect its interests. But gains won by opportunism are likely to be temporary. The most successful long-term policies will be those that recognize the views and

16

interests, the balances and regional arrangements, of the specific countries, without trying to impose on them alignments with outside powers or a system conceived by one superpower or the other or by both.

This last point brings us to the third aspect of the place of the U.S.S.R. in the international order of the 1980s: what can be done with the Soviets by way of consultation, cooperation, joint efforts; in short, the further development of détente in the direction of entente. The United States would not serve itself or others well if it joined with the U.S.S.R. in attempts to dictate to the rest of the world, an idea that has appealed at times to the Kremlin, at least as a temporary expedient. That is not to say that consultation and common action will not be necessary both to defuse incipient or actual crises and to establish and maintain patterns of peaceful conduct. The principles agreed upon, or at least put on paper, at the Nixon-Brezhnev meetings of 1972–1974 represented a start, but a decline in consultation has accompanied the more general decline of détente. There will be good reason in the years ahead to recover lost ground and move forward.

The two aspects of world order discussed earlier emphasized the adversary relationship with the Soviet Union: the need to deter the use of military force and the need to work out relations with other nations in constructive ways that would deny the U.S.S.R. opportunities for intervention and disruption. Policies to achieve those ends should not mean containment in the sense of isolation or exclusion. On the contrary, we have every interest in having the U.S.S.R. participate in the world order, not staying sullenly on the periphery and recognizing no order but its own. The more we can encourage that participation, the less tension there should be in the military realm.

The insistence of the Soviet Union on being treated as a world power has already been stressed. This is not something to be feared or fought by the West, except as it may represent an attempt to project military power, but to be welcomed because it reflects the growing reality of interdependence. While the two superpowers do not have the right to dictate the destiny of other nations, they do have an obligation to make sure that the interaction of their own competing policies with the affairs of others does not become too dangerous to all. They have, in other words, a common interest in the management of interdependence, in working out through consultation and in anticipation of critical situations a clearer understanding of where their respective interests lie and some mutually acceptable rules of the game.

The issue is broader than the management of crises or the avoidance of war. The Soviet Union, regardless of fundamental ideological differences, has become more involved in the world system than it has in the past in many ways other than by its military might. It is involved because of the increasing complexity and needs of its own society. As contacts with other countries are multiplied, they take on a life of their own other than the purely tactical. Thus, there will be forms of the Soviet presence in various areas of the world, of Soviet participation in evolving international relationships, that should be encouraged. Such involvement puts the Soviet leadership continuously to the test of responsible conduct.

One reason for the difficulties of reaching agreements on arms limitation in SALT and other negotiations is the absence of a sufficiently broad political and economic relationship to sustain the immensely complex decisions on matters affecting ultimate security and survival. It was sound politics and sound diplomacy, in the moves toward détente in the early 1970s, to proceed simultaneously with SALT agreements and with efforts toward expanded economic cooperation and political discourse.

These elements in the relationship of the U.S.S.R. to the rest of the world should take on increased significance in the coming decade. Without them, the management of military power may be more difficult and dangerous. In many specific economic matters likely to demand international decisions, or new agreements or institutions—in areas such as food supply, energy, access to certain raw materials, exploitation of the oceans, and preservation of the environment—the participation of the Soviet Union may be necessary both for its own interests and for those of others. It is worth noting that the authors of the two studies which follow, both solidly analytical and not given to wishful thinking, see positive possibilities here for a firmer and more enduring association of the Soviet Union and other socialist countries with the First and Third worlds in a viable international order.

The Future of Soviet-American Relations

Lawrence T. Caldwell

ONE

The Soviet-American Relationship and the International System

CONFLICT AND COOPERATION

Relations between the United States and the Soviet Union will continue to be vitally important throughout the 1980s. Although other issues will press more insistently for the attention of political leaders in both nations, and although the security of each will be increasingly affected by other actors in world affairs, the unavoidable primacy of this one relationship will remain unaltered. Soviet-American bilateral relations will, quite possibly, slip out of focus for extended periods and may be jolted back into focus by occasional crises. But the relationship will remain absolutely important.

The strategic and conventional military power of these two states guarantees that the quality of their relationship will be a central preoccupation of foreign policy makers in both capitals. Decisions made in Moscow and Washington will continue to determine Soviet and American survival and that of the rest of the world as well. That military power is the unavoidable reality. It acts like a gyroscope to pull the attention of American and Soviet political leaders back to this one relationship no matter how powerful the claims of other issues for policy decisions.

This one foreign policy relationship, then, inevitably combines elements of conflict and cooperation. Marshall Shulman, in his

EDITOR'S NOTE: Appendices related to this study appear at the end of the volume.

lectures before the Council on Foreign Relations a decade ago, argued that limitations had been placed by political realities on the adversative nature of the Soviet-American relationship, and he has continued to call attention to the mix of cooperative and competitive elements in the relationship.[1] Cooperation has characterized the modest achievements in arms limitation, in economic relations, and, increasingly, in some functional areas like space, environmental quality, and cultural exchange. But competition has continued in both strategic and conventional arms, in the global effort by each power to increase its political influence and to contain the influence of the adversary, and in persistent efforts on each side to affect the ideological character of the other's political system, most recently in the struggle over human rights. These elements of cooperation and conflict will continue throughout the 1980s, and the choices for policy pertain to the desirable mix of them.

Competition in Soviet-American relations stems from two fundamental sources. First, there is the fact of great-power rivalry. The size and power of the U.S.S.R. and the United States inevitably cause their interests to overlap, thus inducing conflicts. Second, the two societies are fundamentally different. People are accustomed to the ideological explanation of those differences—communist versus democratic-capitalist. But that difference overlays more fundamental divergences of political culture. Centuries of autocracy, of peasant isolation from metropolitan Russia, of creating the appearance of strength to camouflage internal weaknesses—these traditions would conflict with the Puritan and Enlightenment origins of American culture even if there were no communist regime in Moscow or if there were one in Washington. The fact is that both populations, even the largest segments of the elite in each country, are largely ignorant of, and perhaps indifferent to, the other culture. Thus, cooperative re-

---

[1]Marshall D. Shulman, *Beyond the Cold War,* Yale University Press, New Haven, 1966; "What Does Security Mean Today?," *Foreign Affairs,* July 1971, pp. 607–618; "Toward a Western Philosophy of Coexistence," ibid., October 1973, pp. 35–58; his testimony before a House subcommittee, October 26, 1977, U.S. Congress, 95th Congress, First Session, Subcommittee on Europe and the Middle East, *Hearings,* Washington, D.C., 1978.

lations, when they are cultivated by the leaderships (as in the 1969–1973 period), always rest on tenuous grounds. Other political forces—often for reasons extraneous to U.S.-Soviet relations—can upset the relationship by drawing on the reservoir of mistrust, ignorance, and misperception far more easily than those who favor cooperation can create the conditions for it.

Furthermore, these two basic sources of conflict may be reinforced by another, more transitory problem in the 1980s: the appearance of new political leaders in both countries, for whom the lessons of war will be more remote and whose political experience will have been less affected by questions of Soviet-American relations than was the experience of Khrushchev and Brezhnev, Truman, Eisenhower, Kennedy, Johnson, and Nixon. The process by which the determination to maintain a delicate peace might atrophy need not be insidious. It seems far more likely to occur by natural domestic political processes. Perhaps the transfer of power to President Jimmy Carter illustrates the danger. After a period of pronounced emphasis on Soviet-American relations, it is natural for an "outsider" to stress other issues in obtaining the political spotlight. We have no reason to expect that this same process does not occur within the U.S.S.R., where no claimant to succeed Brezhnev, certainly not among the younger members of the Politburo, would dare presume to intrude on the foreign policy issues so carefully marked out by him as his special domain. When new leadership arrives it is almost by definition likely to have other policy preoccupations and expertise. That need not be a bad thing, but it almost certainly will create instability in American-Soviet relations during a period of probing and education.

It is certain, therefore, that conflict will persist in relations between the United States and the Soviet Union. On the other hand, cooperation is unavoidable. At a minimum, these two powers must cooperate to survive and to ensure that civilized life survives as well. This objective, of course, implies cooperation only in the most primitive and reduced terms. There are those in both societies who favor no more cooperation than is required to avoid nuclear holocaust. But no one can be certain just how much cooperation will guarantee even this limited objective.

Therefore, for most members of the political leaderships in Moscow and Washington, cooperation implies not only the negative goal of keeping the missiles "buttoned up," but also an active search for ways of reducing the risk that political conflict might lead to military confrontation. This extended vision of the requirements for cooperation implies a common interest in nurturing a stable international system. Thus, between the United States and the Soviet Union, cooperation and conflict are not absolute qualities. On the contrary, cooperative and conflictive interests are spread along a spectrum, and the proportion of each in foreign policy at any moment is the subject of intense political struggle in both countries. My instinct is that the possibilities for cooperation are greater than have yet been realized.

The discussion of Soviet-American relations in the pages that follow stresses the bilateral relationship only. No matter how rationally that relationship might be managed, the political leaderships in Moscow and Washington have limited control over international politics. The international system itself is becoming more complex. The dynamics of the Soviet-American relationship will interact symbiotically with changes in the system as a whole.

SOVIET–AMERICAN POWER AND
THE INTERNATIONAL SYSTEM

One of the fundamental ironies of the international political system in the last quarter of the twentieth century is that although American and Soviet power seems reduced, global military power, in fact, remains fundamentally bipolar. On the one hand, the hegemony these two powers exercised over their respective alliances eroded dramatically during the 1960s. New issues have arisen to change the East–West focus of world affairs and the substantive concerns of foreign ministries. New actors have appeared to diminish the importance of nation-states in the international political system. Yet, in an important sense bipolarity persists, and the failure to understand that, or to keep it sharply in mind, constitutes one of the great dangers of the coming decade. The Soviet Union and the United States retain military power on a scale greatly disproportionate to that of all other actors in the international system, and most other "significant" military powers are in some critical way militarily dependent on one or the other of them.

This has importance far beyond the strategic "balance of terror" between the U.S.S.R. and the United States. Something of a facile assumption has been made in many quarters that the constraints of their effective strategic parity and of their conflicting ideological and political interests will hold. Two challenges to this assumption pose threats to international stability.

First, many actors—from significant military powers like Israel and Syria to subnational terrorist groups—assume that the Soviet and American stalemate will inhibit superpower intervention in local conflicts. But each is improving its capability to intervene, and the evidence of Vietnam, Angola, and even Entebbe brings the assumed inhibition into question. Within Washington and Moscow, it appears that little urgency is felt to restrain the production, deployment, and transfer of the conventional weapons with which most local conflicts are decided. Political competition takes precedence over the risks of military conflict. African states and movements have become more prone to employ military means for political ends, and the United States and the U.S.S.R. have not shown great restraint in choosing and backing clients. NATO has behaved in the mutual force reduction talks as if alliance management were more important than reducing the risks of military confrontation in Europe. Cuba has intervened in Africa. Radical leftists and terrorists have continued to act as if the military power of states were incapable of counteraction.

Second, there is a danger that the leaders and citizens of the United States and the U.S.S.R. may come to accept strategic stability as a given rather than as a delicate combination of military, political, and psychological factors whose stability must be worked at to be maintained. The familiarity of strategic stability may atrophy the determination to avoid crises. Thus the system of constraints that has grown out of effective strategic parity might erode, and the complacent assumption that it will continue to form the basis of a stable international system threatens to deprive world affairs of the imagination and creative statesmanship that peace requires.

The pattern of American-Soviet relations may change, and international politics will change with it. It makes little sense to anticipate the shape of the 1980s without considering the possibility of fundamental alterations in this relationship. Soviet and American inhibitions against the use of force might actually weaken in one of three ways.

The Possibility of Increased American–Soviet Collaboration

The combination of strategic parity and the conflict of political interests between the superpowers has probably produced some inhibitions to their use of force, and has freed smaller actors to dominate crises. It need not be supposed that political conflict between the United States and the Soviet Union will disappear, however, to imagine ways in which superpower interaction may work in the 1980s to reduce the leverage of these smaller actors on the international system. For example, the U.S.S.R. and the United States each retain the power to convert the terms of any international crisis. At a minimum they hold the option, admittedly often "irrational," to raise almost any issue to a superpower confrontation. Any such escalation by either would imply large risks of drawing in the other, and the reciprocal effect, of course, would be to alter the stakes of the original issue profoundly. Once the superpowers are drawn in, there follows a natural imperative to compromise, and the goals of the original actors are not likely to be achieved.

Persistent frustration with other actors who seem to defy the mutual interests of Moscow and Washington may possibly produce collective use of their power. Terrorism, access to resources, international arms transfers, nuclear proliferation, or even the implementation of United Nations Resolutions in regional crises where the two powers agree—all of these might represent areas for increased collaboration during the next decade. In an era of strategic and conventional military parity, in-

26

stances of tacit abstention by one superpower may increase, freeing the other to assert its interests with military power. Spheres of influence may be extended through a system of constraints that will free both powers to use limited military power in the pursuit of their individual interests. Collaboration will almost certainly continue to be the exception, not the rule, of superpower behavior with respect to third parties in the international system, but cooperation between them may well reduce the independence of some actors in the international system and weaken the inhibitions against the use of force by one or both of the superpowers against third parties.

Changes in Military Technology and the Inhibition to Use Force

The dynamics of the Soviet and American military balance seem far more certain to erode the system of constraints against the use of force than to foster collaboration. But actors in the international system who count on Soviet-American inhibitions against employing their forces may find that *any* development that weakens these constraints actually increases superpower interference in their affairs and reduces their own capacity to employ violent means to achieve political ends. Thus, technological changes in the primary military balance may make both Washington and Moscow far more nervous about the consequences of open military conflict almost anywhere on the globe and increase their incentive to intervene or to enforce political compromises. As technology makes the military balance more ambiguous, the dangers of inadvertent superpower confrontation may increase. The result, of course, may be war, but it also may be reinforcement of possibilities for superpower collaboration in avoiding the risks of war and in restricting the leverage that third parties have to draw them into it.

Nonetheless, it seems virtually certain that changes in weapons technology and the evolution of Soviet and American strategic forces during the 1980s will make the central military balance more ambiguous. Miniaturization of components, improvements in ballistic missile mobility and accuracy, terrain-matching guidance, cruise missiles—all of these technological developments

27

will complicate the military relationship between the United States and the U.S.S.R. in two significant ways. First, at least in the short run, negotiated arms control will become more difficult. Advocates of arms control have been disappointed with the experience of the 1960s and early 1970s. They have argued that SALT I in particular has not placed effective constraints on the development of weapons systems. But these negotiations did close off some destabilizing lines of development—for example, the ABM—and did proscribe certain other areas of potential conflict, such as atmospheric testing and some uses of space. In these respects, the discussions provided some political control over the course of arms competition, increased political confidence, and created a forum for mutual education. Technology presently coming into superpower arsenals makes verification of agreements more difficult, and may place unbearable strain on political cooperation, fueling the arms race even further.

Second, those same technological developments in delivery systems, when coupled with parallel ones in warheads—like precision-guided munitions, or the "smart bombs," used in Vietnam—may blur the distinction between conventional and nuclear weapons and reduce the inhibition to cross the nuclear threshold. The interchangeability of "tactical" and "strategic" delivery systems and of "conventional" and "tactical nuclear" warheads will certainly complicate arms control. Whether it will also reduce the constraints against the use of force remains to be seen, but the possibility of such an outcome is sufficient to require that analysts of Soviet-American relations attempt to anticipate the consequences.

Finally, some developments in conventional weapons systems themselves seem to point to a possible erosion of Soviet and American restraint against the use of force in international affairs. These developments can be viewed as the "globalization" of superpower military capabilities. Of course the United States has been a global power for a long time. But, partly as a response to American capabilities, partly as a response to the Soviet perception of the Vietnam war, and partly as a tangential development of its efforts to counter sea-based American strategic forces, the Soviet Union has now acquired a considerable capacity to project military force around the world. This capability is new, and its effect will be one of the serious uncertainties of the superpower relationship in the 1980s.

The deployments of the Soviet Union's KIEV aircraft carrier and the American TARAWA LHA (landing helicopter assault ship—five of which are to be built by the United States Navy) in July 1976 symbolized this development and increased the capacity of both powers to project military force into local conflicts. A new era of "races to the beaches" may thus emerge, and the power that first establishes a presence on the ground in support of effective local clients will place an unacceptable burden of escalation on the other. In several ways, then, the constraints against the use of limited military power may actually erode during a period of persistent and mutually acknowledged strategic parity.

The Likelihood of Persistent Political Conflict

Thus, increased American-Soviet collaboration against third parties in the international system does not require that we imagine the elimination of conflicting political and economic interests between them. On the contrary, those conflicts will certainly persist, and the serious threat to the peaceful and stable international system will almost certainly be from technological ambiguities in the central military balance and from the outright adversary relationship between the two. Three sources of international conflict, particularly, seem most to threaten the delicate political and military balance on which the Soviet and American inhibition against the use of force has rested.

First, no characteristic of the 1970s is quite so striking as the persistence of ideological opposition between socialism on the one hand and the pluralist democracies and capitalist economies on the other. The Soviet leadership has built its détente policy on the explicit contention that ideological conflict increases as state relations improve. Partly because of the perception that the communist regimes might be threatened by extensive exposure of their populations to the "decadent" influences of the West and partly because of complicated bureaucratic stresses within the Kremlin, the Brezhnev leadership has emphasized that détente will not be achieved at the price of abandoning the "revolutionary struggle," especially in the Third World. The Carter administration's emphasis on "human rights" is an interesting obverse of the same phenomenon. Both tendencies demonstrate the persistence of ideological antagonism between communist and noncommunist impulses.

These ideologies are no longer monolithic, and it is implicit in the process of détente that their interaction become more complex. Within the West there has developed a mounting challenge to the values of individualism and consumerism, and to conceptions of material progress and competitive psychology. These are complicated intellectual currents, and certainly they do not all move in the direction of collectivist or communal values, but some do. These constitute fissures within Western society that reproduce some features of the ideological confrontation between East and West. Moreover, much of the brave and exciting dissent inside the U.S.S.R. has moved away from state socialism and toward affirmation of individualist values. Thus, ideological conflict between the United States and the Soviet Union persists along classic lines, but also intrudes into their domestic societies. These lines of contention may reinforce one another and increase Soviet-American conflict. Especially with respect to the "national liberation" and "revolutionary" processes, ideological conflict between them continues to be pregnant with possibilities for the use of military force in securing or protecting interests. On the other hand, the cleavages of ideological conflict that also extend to the societies themselves may, in the future, promote internal instabilities that will also exacerbate the dangers of military conflict between them.

Second, these ideological conflicts, of course, do not take place in a bipolar context alone. They reflect, and are reflected in, larger historical processes on a global scale. Political instability in Africa, Asia, Latin America, and the Middle East—to say nothing of Europe and North America—often forms along the same fissures. Late in the twentieth century it is apparent that Third World conflict is a far more complicated process than it sometimes appeared in the early days of decolonialization. Na-

tionalism, tribal rivalry, the aspirations of economic development, a sense of injustice about the past, confrontation between
elitist and egalitarian values—all of these promise political and
economic instability. Because of the superpower rivalry, and
because some of the cleavages in the Third World seem to parallel
the superpowers' conflicting ideological values, it would be uto-
pian to suppose that the United States and the U.S.S.R. will not
be drawn into conflicts in Asia, Africa, or Latin America. Thus,
conflicting Third World interests will continue to pose the danger
of superpower confrontation and military conflict. Such a confrontation would be the inverse of the proposition that the United
States and the Soviet Union might actually collaborate to "disci-
pline" miscreant actors in the international system, but it would
erode existing restraints on the use of force by the Soviet Union
and the United States.

Third, international stability will be affected by the continuing
demands for redistribution of global wealth. It is difficult to predict just how this force in international affairs will affect American-Soviet relations. Both are consumer and materialist cultures,
both are developed and largely white, both have strong roots in
European and Christian traditions. Moreover, they are both certain to resist reductions in their standards of living. Their habits
of material progress will alter slowly. Still, the demands for redistribution may create additional occasions for political conflict
between them. For the United States, at least, the issue will be
an internal political issue of growing importance, one which could
affect the whole of American foreign policy. Soviet-American
competition for global resources—both to assure access for one-
self as well as to deny them to the other—will certainly characterize the 1980s more than the period since World War II, and,
quite possibly, lead to the use of military force.

Therefore, powerful forces will be at work in the international
system during the 1980s that will threaten the stability of Soviet-
American relations and the inhibitions to the use of force between
them. By this argument I do not intend to create a pessimistic
or fatalistic picture. On the contrary, my intention is to stress
the delicacy of the political and economic relationship between

31

the United States and the Soviet Union and the necessity to nurture the traditions of restraint in relations between them.

Besides, American foreign policy toward the Soviet Union critically affects the United States' capability to solve other problems and conduct relations with other states. Despite the obvious importance of the Soviet-American relationship, other claims on the time and resources of the political leaderships in both countries will compete more actively with this central security relationship. For that reason America must be especially clearheaded about its objectives in relations with the U.S.S.R.

CONCLUSION: THE PROBLEM OF POWER— MOSCOW AND WASHINGTON

The political, economic, and especially the military power of the Soviet Union and the United States will affect the international system of the 1980s, then, in a number of decisive ways. These two countries will continue to be the primary military powers, on whose actions will hinge the fate of world peace and on whom most other powers will be militarily dependent—either explicitly for matériel or implicitly for the maintenance of political conditions in which their own interests might be sought or preserved. Their political rivalry will retain its potential for being extended into any conflict anywhere on the globe. Their economic strength will continue to be decisive. And the character of the emerging pattern of economic relations will depend in critical ways on how they set their national priorities as well as how they respond to demands for a redistribution of the world's income and wealth. The power of each will also continue to be a central preoccupation of the other. Everything that either the Soviet or American leadership chooses to do in the 1980s will be affected by the fact of the other's power. No significant domestic goals can be achieved without reference to the relationship between these two adversaries. This locks them into inevitable partnership.

The possibilities of American responses to the challenges of the 1980s at home and abroad, then, derive in substantial part from the character of this country's relationship with the Soviet

Union. A relatively hostile relationship would create apprehension in Washington and might well promote the interests of persons and bureaucracies whose priorities are defense spending and ideological conflict with the U.S.S.R. Such an environment would diminish the influence of persons and bureaucracies with other interests—say, education, or urban development, or environmental protection. The same holds for Moscow. Soviet-American relations interact inevitably and symbiotically with the whole political complexion of each country. Furthermore, the domestic political effects of a relationship characterized by hostility are cumulative. An exacerbation of conflict at a given moment creates policies and promotes personalities more inclined to view the relationship in a conflictive manner in a later period. Conflict engenders conflict. Perhaps cooperation will promote cooperation.

While the complexity of political phenomena makes impossible reliable and precise prediction of what the Soviet leadership or what Soviet politics might be like in the 1980s, some political conditions that will have an impact on the nature of Soviet power can be predicted. In thinking about American policy for the 1980s, it is prudent to make projections of some critical elements in Soviet power.

American discussion of the Soviet Union during the 1970s has demonstrated a natural, but ultimately untenable, double fantasy. First, much of the discussion of Soviet military power has supposed that the United States retains the option of military superiority. This illusion often accompanies the most well-meaning devotion to American national interests and security. For example, observations of improvements in Soviet naval capabilities are often accompanied by calls for countering improvements in the United States Navy as if these could guarantee "sea control" in the World War II sense or in the sense implicit in the naval balance during the 1950s, when the U.S.S.R. was simply a land power. It may be sensible to increase the budget of the United States Navy or to alter its priorities, but it is not sensible to do so with the expectation that these increments or changes will produce unchallenged lines of trans-oceanic communications. Navy programs can affect the relative balance; they cannot guarantee meaningful superiority. Similarly, even people who normally favor arms control often find themselves slipping into the habit of addressing the strategic balance in terms of American "superiority." Their argument posits that SALT I or II should somehow be more palatable because the United States has an edge in forward-based systems (FBS), or multiple independently targeted reentry vehicles (MIRV), or cruise missiles. Of course, these systems may constitute military advantages in certain scenarios. The Soviets have advantages in other scenarios. This fact is the meaning of asymmetry. But American superiority is a thing of the past. To argue that it is necessary, or to imply that it somehow constitutes grounds for adopting one or another defense or arms control strategy is to harbor an illusion. Such an illusion, of course, may also provide the basis of future conflict between the United States and the Soviet Union.

A parallel illusion can be found in American discussions of Soviet dissent and of Soviet political life. To base United States policy on the explicit or implicit expectation that the U.S.S.R. will change its political system invites very dangerous misunderstanding. Courageous as Alexander Solzhenitsyn and Andrei Sakharov are, their often horrible experiences at the hands of Soviet authorities have taken them away from the mainstream of Soviet life. It may be humanitarian, or consistent with American values, to make an issue of the plight of individual dissidents in the Soviet Union, but it is foolish to base American policy on the hope that liberal, democratic, Hebraic, or Christian values will somehow supplant the Muscovite or Marxist-Leninist orientations of the Soviet system.

This illusion is often intertwined with another. The debate over the Jackson Amendment in 1973 and 1974 carried the often explicit notion that the Soviet economy required the importation of Western techniques to survive. This assumption made plausible the diplomatic linkage between trade and Jewish emigration, and a powerful political alliance developed in Washington. Possibly the objective merited the attempt, but it created for Soviet leaders a strong interest in breaking the linkage, which they did in January 1975. The fact was, and is, that the Soviet economy, for all its deficiencies, not only can survive without American

34

or even Western technology, but is capable of impressive achievements even within an autarkic framework. To suppose otherwise is to perpetuate a self-serving myth and to create conditions within the American political system that will complicate future foreign policy decisions.

These fantasies simply cannot be sustained. Their existence is dangerous for American welfare. The Soviet Union is a global military superpower. Its economy is strong enough to maintain overall military parity with the United States. It probably can achieve that apparent objective while still providing a steady, if unspectacular, improvement in the standard of living enjoyed by the Soviet people. The illusions that the United States can attain superiority in the military relationship and that the Soviet system will somehow disintegrate or evolve into a pluralistic, democratic, and capitalist one create dangers within American domestic politics. To achieve military superiority, or even to attempt it, would require defense expenditures on a scale that would threaten the entire fabric of American democracy. Talk about "superiority" or military power "second to none" may also create expectations that will make other security objectives more difficult to achieve in Congress. Ultimately these lines of argument in American national life will open old wounds and create political divisions that will prove counter to the interests of national security.

The facts of Soviet power, however, should not obscure the opportunities for modifying the United States–Soviet relationship or for securing American interests by a proper management of it. On the contrary, the 1980s hold difficult decisions for Soviet policy makers. Even the composition of the Soviet leadership will be affected by the nature of these decisions.

It is the contention of this study that several lines of Soviet political and economic development may intersect in the early to mid-1980s to produce an important policy crunch. First, there are some indications that rates of economic growth may decline throughout the next decade. Second, the strategic military competition with the United States will almost certainly force difficult decisions about expensive weapons systems during a period of increasing competition for total resources within the Soviet political process. The intersection of these economic and military lines will force long-standing policy differences to the surface. Issues of trade, of consumer interests versus heavy industry, of high-technology and scientific inquiry will all persist and may become sources of sharper disagreement. Third, much of this policy debate will take place along the division between the modernist and orthodox elements in the Communist Party of the Soviet Union (CPSU) that has persisted since Stalin's death. Vital American interests are affected by the outcome of this debate, and they will probably be better served by the design of a foreign policy that encourages the modernist impulse in Soviet political life. This argument does not imply that the United States can, or should, intervene in the resolution of policy disputes in the Kremlin. However, it may be possible to exercise some influence on Soviet policy making by the establishment of foreign and security policies that promote cooperative interaction and, thereby, may bolster political forces in Moscow that favor cooperation as a framework for solving the difficult policy choices they face.

TWO

Elements of Soviet Power in the 1980s

Power is an elusive concept. Everyone recognizes it as the currency of politics, but there is little agreement on what it is. For the United States and the U.S.S.R., power is both a primary cause of their competition and a measure of their capacity to conduct that competition successfully. Competitive interests would clearly exist between the world's two most powerful nations even if their political cultures and ideological values were less divergent. Power is also an elusive measure of their relationship, one that is complex and often subtle in its calculation. For example, military strength between the two countries has not always, or even normally, been strictly "balanced." Yet the notion of the military relationship as being stable, of providing a reliable basis for deterring either party from aggressive actions against the other's vital interests, has proven amazingly persistent. Thus the relationship between them has generally been accepted as being characterized by a "balance of power."

Clearly many factors determine the quality of the Soviet-American balance of power—military capabilities, economic performance, character of the political culture, quality and will of leadership, preoccupations and priorities of policy. The capacity of the Soviet Union to act in international affairs combines all of these and many other factors as well. It is the combination of these which somehow determines a nation's power. Yet no mechanical calculation of them gives a reliable index of the power relationship between the superpowers. It would be a very great mistake—one made by Napoleon with respect to Russia, by Hitler with respect to both Britain and the Soviet Union, and by the United States with respect to North Vietnam—simply to calculate the relative strengths of the Soviet Union and the United States according to only a few parameters of national power.

These calculations can, however, tell us other useful things in anticipating the Soviet-American relationship of the 1980s. Economic projections will provide some indication of the preoccupations of political leaders in the future. Military programs require long lead times, and Soviet and American strategic and conventional programs for 1985 are already being funded. These programs define to a large extent the future military relationship. With the knowledge that we can provide only the broad contours of the future policy environment and keeping in mind that projections may be affected by decisions in the intervening years, we can examine some possible developments in Soviet national power during the 1980s.

American attitudes about world economic power have clearly, and justifiably, changed since the early 1970s. In fact, one popular intellectual fashion now seems as single-mindedly to suppose that the reorientation of the world economic order is an accomplished fact as another intellectual fashion of 15 years ago seemed to suppose that United States dominance would never lessen. Both fashions only demonstrate people's capacity and desire to create visions of inevitable and unalterable reality. The tendency to behave as if the reordering of the international economic order had already been accomplished no doubt reflects broader reactions in Western societies to the shock of the OPEC embargo. But we need to be reminded of some basic economic realities. As Figure 1 makes clear, the United States and the Soviet Union are still the world's largest economic powers. All comparative economic data for gross national products are only approximate. There are obvious discrepancies in the sophistication of collecting and reporting data, and substantial problems arise from currency conversion and from pricing in very different economic systems. These data, however, do suggest something of the gross comparative strengths of world economies. The United States is by far the largest economy, and the Soviet Union is by far the

FIGURE 1

World Gross National Product, 1978 (in percentages)

Total: 9,660 Billion 1978 U.S. $

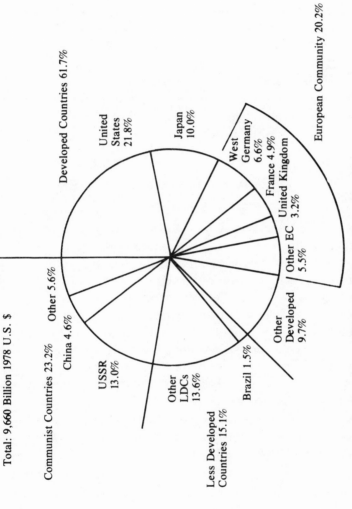

Communist Countries 23.2%   Other 5.6%

China 4.6%

USSR 13.0%

Other LDCs 13.6%

Less Developed Countries 15.1%

Brazil 1.5%

Other Developed 9.7%

Other EC 5.5%

United Kingdom 3.2%

France 4.9%

West Germany 6.6%

European Community 20.2%

Japan 10.0%

United States 21.8%

Developed Countries 61.7%

SOURCE: Central Intelligence Agency, Research Aid, *Handbook of Economic Statistics*, 1979 Washington, D.C., August 1979, p. 1.

second largest. The developed capitalist and democratic states of North America, Japan, and Western Europe generate far more than half of the global product. The socialist countries generate nearly 25 percent of the world's GNP.

Figures 2(a)–2(d) compare the relative strengths of Japan and the European Community, the United States, the Soviet Union, the People's Republic of China, and Eastern Europe for the years 1960–1978 in terms of selected criteria. These simple trend lines suggest that, while there may be some alteration of relative positions and some variations in production, the United States and the Soviet Union will continue to be significant and possibly dominant economic powers for many years to come.

SOVIET ECONOMIC POWER

Not only is the Soviet Union the second largest economic power in the world, its economy has generated steady growth and has gradually reduced the relative if not the absolute difference between its GNP and that of the United States. If performance has not quite been up to the enthusiastic predictions of First Secretary Nikita Khrushchev during the late 1950s, it has been impressive nonetheless. The absolute size of the Soviet economy and its steady progress constitute hard facts on which American policy toward the Soviet Union in the 1980s must be based. The partially ideological tendency to denigrate Soviet economic achievement reflects an illusion whose tenacity does a disservice to sound foreign policy analysis of Soviet-American relations. Figure 3, by isolating the relative performances of Soviet and American GNPs, underlines this point.

Declining Growth

Even though impressive output and steady growth are the basic characteristics of Soviet economic power, it is also true that the growth of GNP has declined. Of course, slower growth comes

FIGURE 2(a)

**Growth in Gross National Product, 1960–1978
(Billions of 1978 U.S. $)**

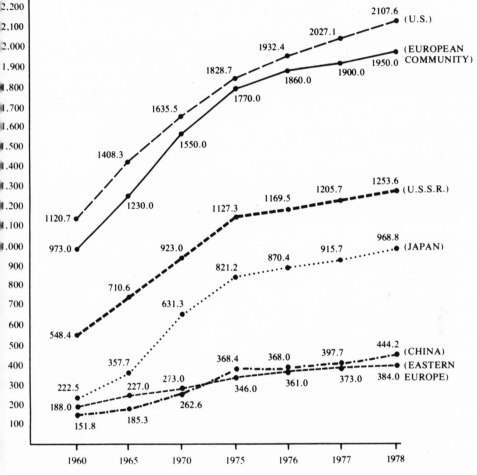

SOURCE: Central Intelligence Agency, Research Aid, *Handbook of Economic Statistics, 1979*, Washington, D.C., August 1979, pp. 22–23.

FIGURE 2(b)
Grain Production, 1960–1978
(Million metric tons)

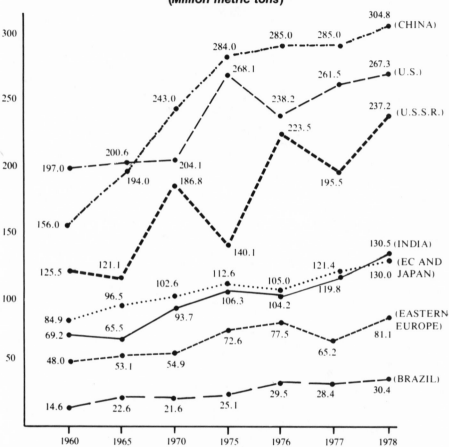

SOURCE: Central Intelligency Agency, Research Aid, *Handbook of Economic Statistics, 1977*, and *Handbook of Economic Statistics, 1977–1979* editions, Washington, D. C., September 1977, October 1978, and August 1979. These data have been checked wherever possible with the United Nations, *Monthly Bulletin of Economic Statistics*, and the U.S. Department of State, *Economic Trends and Their Implications for the United States*. Data for 1978 *only* were taken from the 1979 *Handbook of Economic Statistics*, even though that source revised some estimates for earlier years.

FIGURE 2(c)

Crude Steel Production, 1960–1978
(Million metric tons)

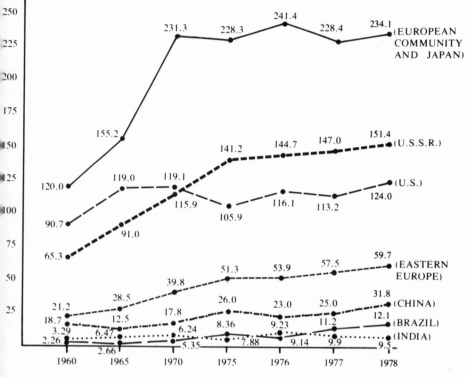

SOURCE: (See Figure 2(b).

FIGURE 2(d)
Gross National Product, 1978
(Billions of 1978 U.S. $)

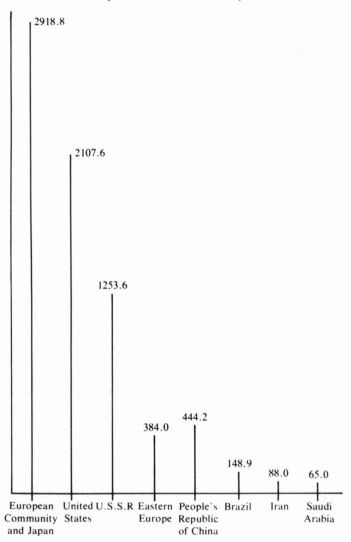

SOURCE: Central Intelligence Agency, Research Aid, *Handbook of Economic Statistics, 1979* Washington, D.C., August 1979. These data have been checked wherever possible with the United Nations *Monthly Bulletin of Statistics,* and the U.S. Department of State, *Foreign Economic Trends and Their Implications for the United States.*

FIGURE 3

Estimated Gross National Product at Market Prices (1978)
(U.S.S.R. Estimates Use United States Purchasing Power Equivalents)
(Billion of U.S. $)

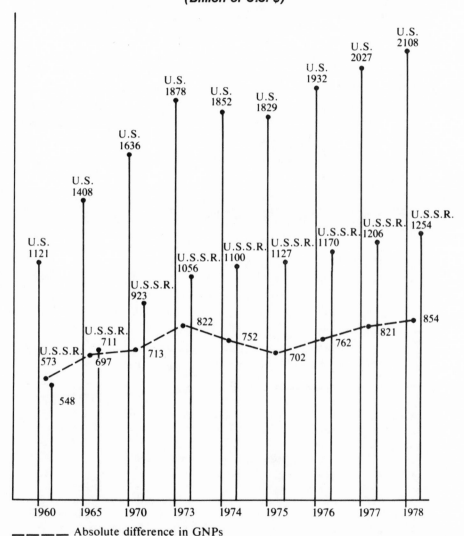

—————— Absolute difference in GNPs

SOURCE: Central Intelligence Agency, *Handbook of Economic Statistics, 1979,* Washington, D.C., August 1979; see also U.S. Department of Commerce, *Selected Trade and Economic Data of Centrally Planned Economies,* Washington, D.C., January 1978.

in part from the success of the past.[1] The sheer size and complexity of the Soviet economy make almost inevitable the same kind of decelerating growth already experienced by other developed countries. One cause of this phenomenon is clearly the shift of emphasis from high-growth sectors, such as steel and energy, to more technologically complicated sectors that require coordinated development in many separate industries. For example, the computer and chemical industries depend on technological development across a broad spectrum of supporting goods and services, and the Soviet need for growth in these industries requires capital investment in a range of economic enterprises previously slighted in favor of concentrated growth in other selected industries. This requirement of future growth has combined with demographic reductions in the labor pool and shortages of critical factor inputs like energy to lead most forecasters of Soviet economic development to predict declining rates of growth for the 1980s.

The Soviet Union's GNP grew, on the average, 5.5 percent from 1966 to 1970 and 3.8 percent from 1971 to 1975. This latter figure fell well below the planned growth of 5.8 percent, although it was considerably better than that of the Western economies for the same period.[2] The current Soviet Five-Year Plan for 1976–1980 anticipates a slightly reduced rate of growth (5 percent) and, if performance is again below what was planned, the actual slowing of growth will, of course, be greater.[3]

[1]Among a number of good general discussions of Soviet economic growth, two series published regularly by the Joint Economic Committee of Congress are helpful: *Allocation of Resources in the Soviet Union and China,* Hearings before a Subcommittee of the Joint Economic Committee, 95th Congress, 1st Session, June and July 1977, is the most recent; but see also *Soviet Economy in a New Perspective,* compendia of papers submitted to the Joint Economic Committee: 94th Congress, 2nd Sess. Oct. 1976, and 96th Congress, 1st Sess. Oct. 1979.

[2]The CIA's projections have thus far dominated discussion in the United States: Central Intelligence Agency, *The Soviet Economy: Performance in 1975 and Prospects for 1976,* May 1976; *Soviet Economic Problems and Prospects,* Joint Economic Committee, 95th Congress, 1st Session, August 8, 1977; Central Intelligence Agency, *The Soviet Economy in 1976–77 and Outlook for 1978,* August 1978.

[3]The basic guidelines of the Tenth Five-Year Plan were carried in *Pravda,* March 7, 1976; these were revised slightly by a report of N. K. Baibakov to

The CIA's Office of Economic Research touched off a national debate in the spring and summer of 1977 by releasing two studies that predicted substantially reduced Soviet oil production by the mid-1980s and consequent depression of growth rates for the GNP.[4] While some analysts disagree on particulars of the CIA's predictions, most agree that the Soviet Union will have real difficulties in meeting its domestic petroleum requirements and its foreign commitments to deliver oil by the middle of the next decade.[5] The challenges to the CIA analysis have not yet been persuasive, and the impact on Soviet economic policy and on Soviet-American relations could be profound.

The CIA study predicted that Soviet oil production will peak around 1980 at 11–12 million barrels per day (mbd) (the total was 10.4 mbd in 1976), but that Soviet production will not be adequate to meet domestic requirements by 1985. The study went on to observe that the traditionally close correlation between rates of growth in energy consumption and in GNP means that these energy projections will induce a corresponding decline in the growth of the GNP.

The reasons are complicated, and the assumptions on which the projections are based might prove softer than they seem in 1979, when a great deal of analytical attention has just recently been devoted to the issue. Two basic problems face the Soviet Union's petroleum industry.[6] First, geography complicates, and

---

the Central Committee on October 25, 1976, *Izvestia,* October 28, 1976; they are also reported on annually at the December meeting of the Supreme Soviet. See, for example, N. K. Baibakov's report in *Izvestia,* December 15, 1977. Most of these major documents of the Soviet government and the Communist Party are translated at least in part by the *Current Digest of the Soviet Press.*

[4]Central Intelligence Agency, *Prospects for Soviet Oil Production,* April 1977 and *Prospects for Soviet Oil Production: A Supplemental Analysis,* July 1977.

[5]See Leslie Dienes, "The Soviet Union: An Energy Crunch Ahead?," *Problems of Communism,* September-October 1977, pp. 41–60; Emily E. Jack, et al., "Outlook for Soviet Energy," in U.S. Congress, Joint Economic Committee, *Soviet Economy in a New Perspective,* Washington, D.C., pp. 460–478.

[6]Soviet discussion of difficulties in the energy industries, especially in transport, has been rather candid in recent years. See, for example, R. I. Kuzavatkin's article in *Ekonomika i organizatsia promyshlennovo proizvodstva,* No. 6, November-December 1976; Yu. Kazmin's article in *Pravda,* April 1, 1977; Ye. T. Mitrin in *Ekonomicheskaya gazeta,* No. 43, October 1977; N. Konaryov,

will probably depress, output. Soviet oil production has focused since World War II in the region west of the Volga River and in the Caucasus Republics. Reserves are greater in Siberia, but to shift production eastward is costly—population and equipment must be transported to the fields, often under difficult climatic and topographical conditions, and the oil, once located and produced, must be transported back to the west, where consumers are located. The operations in both directions are capital intensive. In a sense, this geographical problem surrounding discovery and exploitation of new resources reinforces a second problem, depletion. Wells in the western and southern parts of the Soviet Union can be dug deeper and exploited further. But these wells are steadily less efficient—that is, the water content of fluid lifted from them increases as production continues. Therefore, existing wells compete with new oil fields for drilling and pumping equipment. Moreover, an increasing percentage of new capacity has been required simply to offset the depleted existing sources of oil. Figure 4 makes clear that rates of depletion have placed new Soviet production under severe pressure. The Soviets have had to run steadily faster just to keep pace, and their impressive increases in production of oil achieve only modest increases in overall output because the depletion of existing oil fields has been accelerating.

Soviet options for dealing with these problems are not attractive. First, they can shift exploration eastward to the west Siberian fields in Tyumen Oblast, especially on the Ob River. These fields may continue to expand their output, but it is unlikely that growth there alone will compensate for declining production in the west and south, and it is possible that even these fields will peak by the 1980s and begin to decline thereafter because of continued water encroachment. New production in Siberia, especially along its perimeter in the Arctic or Sakhalin regions, requires large capital outlays for exploration, production, and transportation. Large-diameter pipe has long been a basic item in the Soviet import bill, and it is doubtful that the Soviets can

---

Deputy Minister of Railroads, in *Izvestia,* October 12, 1977; S. Vtorushin and A. Murzin, *Pravda,* August 10, 1977.

FIGURE 4

Additions to Oil Producing Capacity, U.S.S.R.

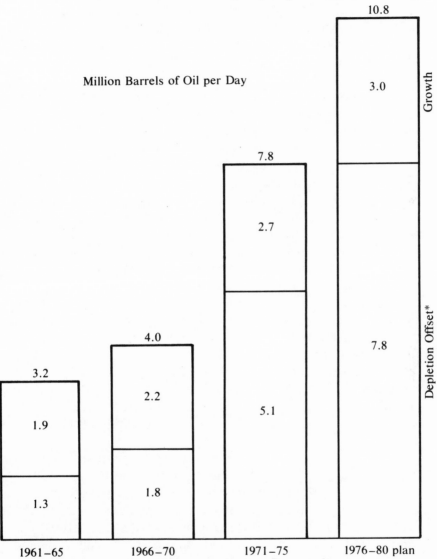

*Amount of new production that has to be brought on line to offset that which has been depleted.

SOURCE: CIA, *Prospects for Soviet Oil Production*, Washington, April 1977, p. 4.

acquire sufficient pipe and make it operational soon enough to compensate for declining production in established oil fields.

Second, the Soviet Union can import equipment and press exploration while trying to hold production in existing fields, but that will require foreign exchange, to which Soviet access is already under serious pressure, as is detailed in the next section of this chapter.

Third, conservation can be pressed, but it will require the reversal of habits that have developed throughout the past fifty years of forced-pace, quantity-over-quality economic growth based on cheap energy and labor and, therefore, will not be easy. Furthermore, changes in national habits of this magnitude will bring about head-rolling, especially along generational lines, as new planners and managers will replace those who acquired their responsibility in times when gross indicators made careers and when efficiency and cost-effectiveness were not rewarded. Almost certainly, these broader economic issues will continue to create divisions within the political leadership as they have in the late 1960s and throughout the 1970s.

Finally, declining oil production, or even steady production against increasing domestic requirements, will make Soviet export commitments to Western Europe and to its Comecon partners more difficult and further strain hard-currency earnings. This may well be the most immediate and most serious implication of the petroleum production crunch of the 1980s. While the oil sector had once been a source of hard currency, it will almost certainly become a drain on hard currency in the next decade.

Table 1 suggests some dimensions of the potential impact on Soviet trading policies of declining growth in the oil industry. From 1965 to 1975 petroleum production slightly more than doubled, as did total exports of oil. But supplies for the Soviet Union's East European allies very nearly tripled over those same years, reflecting economic growth among those countries and a substantial foreign policy effort by Moscow to encourage economic cooperation in the Council of Mutual Economic Assistance (CMEA). Reduced Soviet capacity to increase oil exports to CMEA will reduce economic growth in Eastern Europe and undermine Soviet political objectives there.

TABLE 1

Soviet Oil Statistics, 1965–1980

	1965	1970	1975	Plan 1976–80
Soviet Oil Production				
Millions of metric tons	242.90	353.00	491.00	620.00–640.00
Millions of barrels per day	4.60	7.06	9.82	10.80
Soviet Oil Requirements				
Millions of metric tons	180.40	261.80	368.00	470.00
Soviet Oil Exports				
(millions of metric tons)				
To Communist Countries	28.90	50.40	77.70	
(to Eastern Europe)	22.40	40.30	63.30	
To Noncommunist Countries	35.50	45.50	52.60	
(to Western Europe)	22.70	38.00	44.00	
Soviet Oil Imports				
(millions of metric tons)	1.90	4.60	7.60	

SOURCE: Based on Emily E. Jack, J. Richard Lee, and Harold H. Lent, "Outlook for Soviet Energy," in U.S. Congress, Joint Economic Committee, *Soviet Economy in a New Perspective,* Washington, D.C., 1976; and CIA, *Prospects for Soviet Oil Production: A Supplemental Analysis,* July 1977.

These data in Table 1, moreover, can be interpreted in a way even less advantageous to the Soviet Union. Oil production may actually fall due to the factors outlined above into the 8–10 mbd range by 1985, while domestic consumption will probably be in excess of 10 mbd, assuming current patterns of fuel use and continued economic growth. The implications for hard-currency trade of such projections are even more serious. Some such estimates project a need for the U.S.S.R. to import 2.7 mbd by 1985, assuming no radical alterations in conservation measures, no substantial substitution of other fuels, and continued commitment to export petroleum at least to its Eastern European clients. Thus, Soviet capacity to obtain hard-currency imports will possibly come under dual pressures: the need to increase importation of Western technology for the exploration, drilling, and transportation of oil, and the need to compete for petroleum on world markets.

The Trading Option

Soviet energy policy, then, will have a powerful and dual impact on Soviet trade and foreign policy by the mid-1980s. To maintain continued growth of domestic petroleum output will require substantial imports of foreign equipment, and to maintain export commitments to Europe will probably require increased imports of foreign oil to the Soviet Union. These anticipated demands for additional trade fit the general political and economic policy of the current Soviet leadership. The desire to increase trade has been a major influence on the détente policy of General Secretary Leonid Brezhnev, who has frequently made the case that the potential exists for substantially increased Soviet-American trade. For example, at the Twenty-Fifth Party Congress, he held out high hopes for increased foreign trade in the Tenth Five-Year Plan, especially in what the Soviets call "compensatory agreements," by which foreign investments in Soviet enterprises are repaid by export of the products thus financed. After the election in November 1976, William Simon, Treasury Secretary in the outgoing Ford administration, visited Moscow, and Brezhnev held out the prospects of a 500 percent increase in annual Soviet-American trade for the 1977–1981 period (to $10 billion) as a signal of cooperation to the newly elected Carter administration.

The Tenth Five-Year Plan anticipates that total foreign trade will increase between 30 percent and 35 percent between 1977 and 1981, but trade actually increased by 186 percent in the period of the Ninth Five-Year Plan (1972–1976), when only 35 percent had been anticipated, and it is probable that other targets in the Tenth Plan will require that it also exceed its foreign trade targets considerably.[7] Trade with Western, industrialized nations constitutes the most rapidly increasing sector of all Soviet trade, as Figure 5 demonstrates. Thus the prospects held out by Brezhnev to Secretary Simon for what were clearly political purposes may not exaggerate the potential greatly. In fact, the United

[7]Central Intelligence Agency, *Soviet Economic Plans for 1976–80: A First Look,* August 1976, p. 30. For some interesting specific case descriptions, see *Hearings Before the Senate Committee on Commerce: American Role in East-West Trade,* 94th Congress, 1st and 2nd Sessions, 1977.

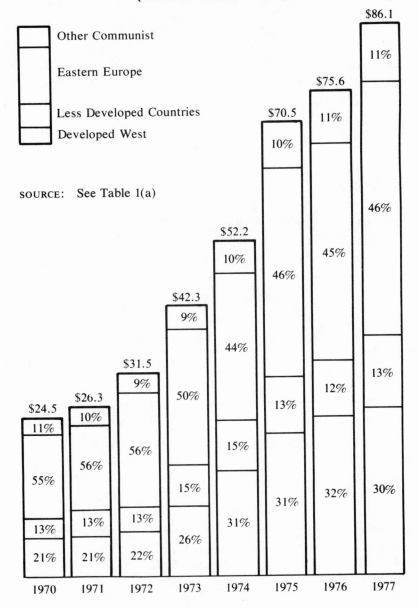

FIGURE 5

U.S.S.R.: Foreign Trade, by Major Area
(in billions of U.S. dollars)

SOURCE: See Table 1(a)

States has participated with Britain, France, Japan, and West Germany in negotiations on compensation agreements that would be undertaken between 1977 and 1980, amounting to more than $20 billion in offshore oil exploration and aluminum, copper, liquefied natural gas, and wood processing. These are agreements in which investing countries and businesses commit themselves in advance to purchase the output of enterprises they help to finance. If all of these projects, or even most of them—especially the large credits being sought by Moscow for the North Star and Yakutsk liquefied natural gas (LNG) plants—are undertaken, they will have a substantial impact on trade in the mid-to-late 1980s.

The attraction of compensation agreements to the Soviet leadership is clearly rooted in Moscow's hard-currency trade deficits, since these agreements obviate the Soviet Union's need to use its export earnings to service import debt. Debt service in the mid-1970s reached something on the order of 20 to 25 percent of export earnings, a figure which would place severe restrictions on Soviet trade by the 1980s if past trends were to continue.

TABLE 1(a)

U.S.S.R. Growth in Total Trade Turnover

	Percentage Increase from Previous Year	
	Volume	Dollar Value
1971	5	7
1972	10	20
1973	14	34
1974	17	24
1975	10–15	35
1976	——	7
1977	——	14

SOURCE: Central Intelligence Agency, *The Soviet Economy: Performance in 1975 and Prospects for 1976,* Washington, D.C., May 1976; CIA, *Handbook of Economic Statistics, 1977 and 1978,* Washington, D.C., September 1977 and October 1978; Department of Commerce, *Selected Trade and Economic Data of Centrally Planned Economies,* Washington, D.C., January 1978.

Soviet debt at the end of 1977 approached $16 billion, and the current leadership demonstrated a continued willingness to incur a hard-currency balance-of-trade deficit on the order of $2.4–$4.0 billion per year.[8] This deficit in the balance of trade has been financed out of gold sales ($1.2–$1.5 billion), arms sales ($1.5–$2.0 billion), tourism and transportation (just under $1 billion net), and borrowing on international capital markets ($3.5–$4.0 billion). Thus, the Soviet Union in the mid-1970s has had an actual inflow of hard currency. Some of the hard-currency surplus will undoubtedly be used as a hedge against less favorable international capital markets, against increased need to import grain in a bad harvest year, and to finance increased import orders, particularly for machinery and steel.

Under favorable conditions in international trade in the mid-1970s, then, the Soviet Union has demonstrated what its "best case" strategy for foreign trade may be. Trade is expanded as a feature of domestic economic planning, and imports from hard-currency countries are allowed to exceed exports. The resulting balance-of-trade deficit is financed by arranging credits, selling gold and arms, and pushing tourism and Soviet merchant marine transport. That the strategy is cautious is revealed by the accumulation of hard-currency surpluses, out of which successive increases in trade are financed. But the strategy is vulnerable to a downturn in any number of variables: reductions in credit availability; economic recession in the West, which would depress Soviet exports; weakened gold markets.

The Tenth Five-Year Plan stresses growth for the Soviet economy in areas that make imports from technologically advanced economies especially attractive. For example, the emphasis on increased productivity and quality of output makes products like Western computers and communication equipment desirable. In particular, agricultural output and related consumer standard-of-living goals make probable continued imports of feed grains, and the Soviet-American agreement by which the Soviets have agreed to import at least 6 million tons of grain from the United States represents a floor beneath imports that can be expected

[8]Central Intelligence Agency, *USSR: Hard Currency Trade and Payments, 1977–78*, March 1977.

to range from 6 million to 10 million tons in good harvest years to 20–30 million tons in poor harvest years.[9] The development of Soviet energy sources in Siberia will require continued imports of large-diameter steel pipe, and the perception among the Moscow leadership that the Soviet Union must rely on exports of raw materials has made attractive the complementary strategy of expanding the Soviet capacity to process raw materials at least to a semifinished state. This objective provides a large market for imported fabrication technology—pulp-processing plants, natural gas liquefaction plants, and petroleum chemical refinement processes.

Thus, there are solid Soviet motivations for continued increases in trade with the West, and the United States should be in a good position to expand its trade during the 1980s with the U.S.S.R. if negative political conditions do not intrude. Trade is, by itself, an incentive to maintain stable political relations with those economies that offer the technology required to meet domestic economic objectives. But the Soviet pattern of financing hard-currency imports provides an added incentive as well. Long-term credits would be especially vulnerable to a deterioration in political relations, and these have been necessary to finance past balance-of-trade deficits. Credits are even more important for the large capital investments implied in compensatory agreements for the development of Siberian resources. The sensitivity of Soviet exports to economic recession in the hard-currency economies—which was demonstrated in the mid-1970s—provides a solid and ironic Soviet interest in the prosperity of the West. While orthodox Marxist-Leninist economics predicts ever-deepening cycles of depression in capitalist economies, these would clearly prevent or slow down the achievement of Soviet economic goals. As the anticipated volume of Soviet trade increases, conflict may sharpen between those elements of the Soviet leadership favoring trade as a means to modernizing the

[9]For the text of the agreement, see *U.S. Department of State Bulletin,* November 10, 1975, pp. 663–664. That agreement permitted the Soviets to contract with private grain companies for 6 to 8 million metric tons of grain without United States government intervention. The ceiling which triggers government intervention was raised to 13 million metric tons in the fall of 1977.

economy and those with more traditional ideological reservations over the trading strategy. And it is of course possible that there will be a challenge to the foreign trade strategy during the 1980s.

Although there is general agreement, as seen within the official Soviet plan for the 1976–1980 period, that economic growth will slow, the rates of change depend heavily on the size of the labor force; labor productivity, especially the substitution of technology for labor; weather and agricultural output; the international climate and the prospects for trade; and domestic political stability. The rate at which growth decreases will have profound political implications. Growth rates at the upper level of projections—based largely on favorable assumptions for all the variables cited above—will probably permit the government to continue past practices and insulate it from the need to make radical changes. The lowest rates of growth, projections of which are based on unfavorable assumptions about several of the critical variables, would almost certainly produce major political changes. If, on the other hand, growth were to be reduced somewhere near the mid-range of projections (in the 3 percent per year range), the timing of economic difficulties and of the need to make decisions on foreign policy, defense, or domestic leadership will become far more critical. Subsequent chapters will analyze the possibility of a conjunction between a crisis in the economy and the need to make difficult political decisions.

It is not likely, however, that slowing rates of growth in Soviet GNP will have a great impact on Soviet military power.[10] In fact, available data suggest that the military sector will be isolated from whatever strains reduced growth might produce (see Table 2). Unfortunately, the Soviet budget does not reveal accurate figures for the defense sector, and "nonmilitary" categories such as machine building clearly carry a heavy component of defense-oriented production. These sectors have demonstrated relatively

[10]For two excellent technical discussions of the question, see Lars Calmfors and Jan Rylander, "Economic Restrictions on Soviet Defense Expenditure: A Model Approach," and Hans Bergendorff and Per Strangert, "Projections of Soviet Economic Growth and Defense Spending," in *Soviet Economy in a New Perspective;* see also Central Intelligence Agency, *Estimated Soviet Defense Spending in Rubles,* May 1976.

TABLE 2

Soviet GNP and Defense Expenditures, 1966–1977

	1966–70	1971	1972	1973	1974	1975	1976	1977
Growth of GNP (*percentage change*)	5.3	4.1	1.5	7.4	3.8	2.0	3.7	3.9
Growth of Defense Expenditure (*percentage change*)	2.5	3.5	5.2	4.3	5.7	(5.0)	(4.0)	(4.0)
Announced Soviet Budget for Defense* (*in billions of rubles*)	17.9	17.9	17.9	17.9	17.7	17.4	17.4	17.2

NOTES: ( ) Represents estimated increases which are especially tentative.

*The announced budget is reported annually at the winter meeting of the Supreme Soviet. See, for example, USSR Finance Minister V. F. Garbuzov's 1977 report in *Pravda,* December 15, 1977.

A controversy appeared during the 1976 United States defense budgetary process between Department of Defense and CIA over estimates of Soviet defense spending. These data reflect a general consensus which appeared in the U.S. at that time that Soviet defense spending had been understated in the past. These estimates are highly charged politically and at this time it is difficult to be certain of the accuracy of the data.

SOURCE: Central Intelligence Agency, *A Dollar Comparison of Soviet and U.S. Defense Expenditures, 1965–75;* CIA, *Handbook of Economic Statistics, 1977;* Harold Brown, *Department of Defense Annual Report, Fiscal Year 1979,* Washington, February 2, 1978; CIA, *The Soviet Economy in 1976–77 and Outlook for 1978,* Washington, August 1978, p. 10; see also Secretary Rumsfeld's testimony in U.S. Congress, Subcommittee on the Department of Defense, Committee on Appropriations, *Hearings,* Department of Defense Appropriations for 1977, Part I, Washington, 1976, pp. 685–686.

good performances in the past and are planned to sustain their growth during the 1976–1980 Five-Year Plan. Most evidence suggests that the relative improvement of the Soviet position in the military balance during the past ten years has been financed largely out of growth in GNP. Although our data are particularly unsatisfactory for Soviet defense expenditures, the total defense share of the Soviet GNP has probably not increased.

For now, however, one conclusion is suggested by the present data that has significance for our projections into the 1980s. It is probable that the Soviet leadership has been able to fund its impressive improvements in military capabilities—four or five new strategic missile programs, a major ship-building program, and rapid improvements in conventional armaments like tanks and aircraft—from growth in the GNP, and has been able simultaneously to finance unquestionable improvements in the standard of living from those same increments in the GNP. It so far has also avoided substantial clashes over economic priorities, at least since 1969. The absence of overt evidence of policy disagreement undoubtedly depends in part on the Soviet obsession for secrecy on these matters. In none of the recent removals from and promotions to the Politburo has there been any persuasive evidence of disagreement on economic policies, and there has been no evidence concerning disagreement over defense spending. The demotions of Voronov, Shelest, Shelepin, Podgorny, and Mazurov cannot be related to any defense issues, and the promotions of Grechko, Gromyko, and Andropov in April 1973, and of Ustinov at the Twenty-Fifth Party Congress in 1976 appear primarily to reflect a consensus that the Ministries of Defense, Foreign Affairs, and State Security deserve institutional representation on the Politburo. But those promotions do not suggest more with respect to defense policy than that these members concur with the general policy lines followed by General Secretary Brezhnev. The promotion of Chernenko in November 1978 was even more strongly reflective of his generalized support for Brezhnev, on whose staff he had served, rather than identification with any policy position. Finally, Romanov, also promoted at the Twenty-Fifth Congress, has a power base traditionally represented in the Politburo—First Secretary of the Leningrad party apparat.

Those cases where disagreement did surface in the leadership over different issues reinforce the conclusion that, had there been any substantial disagreement on the defense-spending issue, some evidence would have come into the open. The impression is supported by the one case in which there was evidence of substantial disagreement in the leadership over economic issues—the December 1969 Central Committee Plenum.[11] Again defense was not the issue. The resolution of this controversy coincided with the adoption of a foreign policy of détente and created the broad consensus with which the leadership has been characterized during succeeding years.

Therefore, it seems safer to assume that defense spending has not been an issue of significant disagreement within the Politburo led by Brezhnev. There has been essential consensus on improving military capabilities and at the same time pursuing a foreign policy of détente and improving living standards for the Soviet people. This has been the political and economic program of the experienced and increasingly aged Kremlin leadership. The program has depended on the performance of the Soviet economy, and specifically on net increments to the GNP. In the 1980s this consensus could disintegrate if a leadership crisis occurs and Brezhnev does not manage the succession competently, or if economic growth slows decisively.

Foreign constraints on the development of Soviet military power, then, will have to be transmitted through political choices and will depend, finally, on Soviet perceptions of its overall security relationships with the United States, Western Europe, China, and Japan. Trade provides one example of a constraint. Clearly the trading goals of the Five-Year Plan cannot be met without maintaining good relationships with more than one of the advanced industrial nations. In this sense, the Soviet economy does impose limits on the range of political options available to the leadership. The perceived need to trade conditions the environment in which other political choices must be made.

[11]See Brezhnev's speech in *Ob osnovnykh voprosakh ekonomicheskoy politiki KPSS na sovremennom etape* (On Basic Questions of Economic Policy of the CPSU at the Contemporary Stage), Moscow, 1975, vol. 1, pp. 414–429, translated in *Translations on USSR Political and Sociological Affairs,* No. 703, Joint Publications Research Service, November 26, 1975, pp. 26–39.

Similarly, declining rates of growth in GNP will help create the decision-making environment of the 1980s. The record of economic growth in the past enabled the Soviets to sustain and increase levels of military expenditures, but lower rates of growth will place the leadership under pressure to make choices and to weigh opportunity costs. This economic environment may present opportunities to manage the military relationship between the superpowers. If the United States were to present a new Kremlin leadership with aggressive foreign and defense policies, political elements in Moscow favoring tough responses would be presented with reinforcing arguments. Conversely, an American policy combining active arms control and clear restraint in defense might create incentives for moderate Kremlin policies stressing domestic priorities.

SOVIET MILITARY POWER

The performance of the Soviet economy alone in the 1980s will probably not increase incentives for the Soviet leadership to control military costs or arms competition with the United States. The size of Soviet military forces will be a function of the general political environment—relations with industrialized nations and China, and the prospects for revolutionary advance in the Third World. The configuration of these complex relations in world politics is not likely to become so unambiguously favorable in the perception of the Soviet leadership that it will reduce Soviet arms unless a conscious and persistent effort is made by the United States to achieve that end. This objective may be worthwhile, but it will require a far more sophisticated program of incentives and disincentives than anything Washington has yet attempted. Short of a sudden crystallization of a new national consensus on arms control in the United States, it is probable that the 1980s will be colored no less than the 1940s, 1950s, 1960s, and 1970s by Soviet military power and by Soviet-American competition in arms.

The dimensions of Soviet power are impressive. Yet, for a subject on which nearly all informed observers agree on the basic data, the implications of Soviet military power for United States

61

national security and for the international system remain one of the most controversial issues in American political life.

One view, for example the one associated with "Team B," holds that Soviet military doctrine and capabilities point unambiguously toward its desire to achieve superiority, hence gravely threatening the United States.[12] This analysis was prepared before President Carter took office by a team of defense analysts led by Russian historian Richard Pipes of Harvard. Its views were echoed by former President Ford and former Secretary of Defense Rumsfeld just prior to their leaving office.[13] An alternative assessment of the Soviet-American balance was prepared by analysts at top levels of the government after Carter took office. This study, described publicly as Presidential Review Memorandum-10 (PRM-10), asserts that the United States and the U.S.S.R. have achieved a rough strategic balance.[14]

My own judgment parallels that of PRM-10. The view that the strategic and overall military balances between the two powers approximate parity does not mean that forces are exactly equal, nor does it mean that improvements might not need to be made in the forces of *either* side to maintain stability. It does mean that the scale of military power possessed by both the Soviet Union and the United States is so great that asymmetries inevitably develop and that these might be worrisome if allowed to persist over time; that the strategic and military balances are not vulnerable to sudden breakthroughs by either superpower; and that no single advantage can reasonably be thought to constitute a threat to the essential parity of the relationship.

The balance in strategic weapons themselves has probably been overstressed in comparisons between the two powers. But it underlines their power relative to each other and to "secondary" nuclear powers (see Table 3).

[12]For a summary of the "Team B" argument, see Richard Pipe's "The Soviet Strategy for Nuclear Victory," *The Washington Post,* July 3, 1977. See also Drew Middleton, "Report on Soviet Nuclear Strategy Says Moscow Emphasizes Victory," *New York Times,* June 25, 1977, p. 7.

[13]Donald Rumsfeld, *Annual Defense Department Report, FY 1978,* January 17, 1977; President Ford's interview in the *New York Times,* January 12, 1977.

[14]See Hedrick Smith, "Carter Study Takes More Hopeful View of Strategy of U.S.," *New York Times,* July 8, 1977, pp. 1, 4.

TABLE 3

Strategic Forces of Six Selected Countries, 1979

	ICBMs	SLBMs	Long-range Aircraft	Deliverable Warheads
United States	1,054	656	574	11,330
Soviet Union	1,398	950	156	4,500
Great Britain	(1)	64	50(2)	NA
France	(1)	64	None(2)	NA
China	(1)	None	90	NA
India	None	None	50	NA

NOTES: (1) Britain, France, and China have MRBMs and IRBMs, but none has as many of these weapons as does the U.S.S.R. Since they are omitted from the Soviet totals they are not included here for the others as well.

(2) France's Mirage IVA, Britain's Buccaneer and Jaguar are not included, nor are China's TU-16s because these might be considered theater weapons and parallel forces have been excluded from the Soviet and American totals. These planes, of course, might have a strategic role in some scenarios, and, in any case, are more effective in many roles than the Canberras counted for India because their range approximates that of the newer and more capable British Vulcans which are counted here.

SOURCE: International Institute for Strategic Studies, *The Military Balance 1979–1980*, London, 1979; and Harold Brown, *Department of Defense Annual Report, Fiscal Year, 1979*, Washington, February 2, 1978; and Memorandum published in *Salt II Agreement*, U.S. Dept. of State, Selected Documents, No. 12A, Washington, 1979, p. 49.

A number of more comprehensive indices can be devised to stress the relative military power of the United States and the Soviet Union. For example, although conversion problems are especially acute for defense budgets, and data especially unreliable, it seems quite safe to estimate that the U.S.S.R. and the United States both have defense budgets in excess of $110 billion and that no other country has a budget 20 percent as great. In 1976, the Soviet Union had 3.6 million men under arms, the United States 2.1 million. With the exceptions of China (3.5 million) and India (1.1 million), no other country maintained military forces equal to 25 percent of the United States figure.

It is obvious that the United States and the Soviet Union are in a class of military power by themselves. But such gross comparisons of military power have limited value and probably *understate* the degree to which Soviet and American forces outclass those of other countries. The technology their forces employ provides the best measure of their status as superpowers. In particular, the regular appearance of new military hardware also constitutes the most impressive and, to some, threatening aspect of American and Soviet military power.

New Soviet weapons have always caused a stir among the small fraternity of Western intelligence analysts and defense specialists. They have also formed the most effective arguments used by the Pentagon to obtain larger defense budgets on Capitol Hill. Perhaps the regularity with which American defense interests have trotted by the congressional budgetary review process each year—sounding the alarm over the most exotic new Soviet weapons—and the habitual portrayal of Soviet power as overwhelming, have contributed to a certain indifference in the general American public. But Soviet military power is real. It constitutes a central fact with which American thinking about the international system of the 1980s must come to grips. It is not only the sheer size of Soviet power that matters. The Russians have demonstrated something of a peasant-like, hoarding propensity with respect to military equipment. As they bring new systems into their inventory, they do not retire older ones. Hence, quantitative indicators of military power are somewhat misleading. Not all aircraft, or tanks, or artillery in Soviet inventories constitute equal, or even comparable, threats to NATO or the United States. Weapons innovation, however, does provide a kind of qualitative index of military power, and it is in this respect that Soviet military achievements have been especially impressive under the Brezhnev leadership. Even a partial list of new systems that have come into the inventory since 1969 provides some indication of the Soviet commitment to modernization. They have tested four new ICBMs (SS-16, 17, 18, and 19); a new SLBM of intercontinental range (SS-N-8); four to seven new attack aircraft (MiG 21J, MiG 23B, MiG 27D, Su-17, Su-19, and the Backfire, which can have intercontinental capability); they may be testing still two more multi-purpose aircraft; two new tracked armored personnel carriers (BMD and M-1970); at least one new heavy tank (T-72); and three new aircraft carriers with helicopters and short-takeoff planes. The list could easily be augmented but should make obvious the point that the Brezhnev leadership has devoted a great deal of energy to modernizing the U.S.S.R.'s military forces while conducting a foreign policy of détente. In nearly every category of weapons, the Soviet Union has produced and deployed technology in many ways comparable to that of NATO and the United States.

The vigor of the Soviet program during the period of détente must be evaluated for its implications for the 1980s. The Soviet leadership has said explicitly in the SALT I and II contexts that its weapons development programs are geared to achieve what it regards as parity, and that it would not negotiate agreements to close down production programs already under way.[15] The unstated implication has been that current programs would be closed down once they completed their production runs. Moscow's line of argument, of course, is the antithesis of strategic negotiations. The United States could not accept a SALT environment in which the Soviet Union proceeded independently with its weapons production, did not communicate the levels of deployment actually contemplated, and set its own perception of parity as the limit to which it deployed. That is the stuff of which the arms race is made. These same recent Soviet production programs have led to the development of new American systems—the SS-9 promoted MIRV, and the SS-16-20s increased incentives for the Mark 12A and cruise missiles. Both sides must understand that the ambiguities of intention inferred from weapons deployment breeds competition in arms.

Given the assumption that the military share of the Soviet GNP

[15]This line was generally taken by the Soviet leadership in response to American perceptions of the SS-16/17/18/19 series after the Vladivostok meeting between Brezhnev and Ford in November 1974. Soviet comments opposed the American alarm at the pace of their missile programs as attempts to obtain "one-sided advantages." For an excellent and thoughtful defense of the Soviet view, see G. Arbatov, *Pravda,* February 5, 1977, and his assessment of the Carter administration in ibid., August 3, 1977; see also an authoritative "Commentator" article, ibid., January 1, 1976, and the *Pravda* editorial summarizing Soviet reactions to the Vance mission to Moscow in March 1977 in ibid., April 14, 1977.

will not increase dramatically, rather that increases in the defense budget will continue to be drawn from increases in the GNP, declining rates of growth may put pressure on the leadership to control military costs in the 1980s. A particularly interesting scenario might develop if growth were to decline, especially as a result of a confluence of negative turns in a number of economic variables within a relatively compressed time period, e.g., agricultural production, hard-currency shortages, and a series of disappointments in exploration for new sources of petroleum. Two or three years of economic difficulties in the early 1980s would probably create hard choices for the Soviet leadership about the funding of military research and production. Such predictions are, of course, especially vulnerable to intervening events. However, without the dramatic intervention of a domestic or foreign crisis, those responsible for the Soviet military budget will soon face decisions regarding particularly costly hardware.

There is some evidence that Soviet procurement of military systems has been cyclical. Strategic rocket forces and air forces have been funded in cycles that have fluctuated inversely.[16] Similarly, naval procurement in the late 1960s seemed especially active and air force production remained constant or declined slightly. By the mid-1970s these two cycles had reversed. Thus increases in the overall defense budget have been absorbed by different components according to a generally cyclical pattern. The evidence is only suggestive. It reinforces the commonsense impression that the Soviets cannot do everything at once, but must face economic choices even within their relatively favored defense industries.

Some emerging technological developments will cause Soviet defense planners clear difficulties. In the strategic field, the United States Mark 12A warhead was deployed in the fall of

[16]See the formal statement of the chairman of the Joint Chiefs of Staff, *Department of Defense Appropriations for 1977*, 94th Congress, 2nd Session, Part 1, pp. 735, 767; and the Secretary of Defense, *Department of Defense Appropriations for 1976*, 94th Congress, 1st Session, Part 1, p. 20; *A Dollar Comparison of Soviet and U.S. Defense Activities, 1965–1975*, p. 4.

1977. It promises to improve significantly the accuracy of American Minuteman ICBMs. Cruise missiles place Soviet forces under the same kind of pressure. The Soviet Union may rely only on its present systems and on its research and development to compete in terms of accuracy. But it would not be atypical of the Soviet Union also to produce new systems whose purpose would be to cope with perceived American "advantages." There is some evidence that the Soviets have already tested new systems which will compete for defense rubles in the 1980s.[17]

SALT II and III can affect the pace and direction of this competition, but negotiations are unlikely to eliminate it. Moreover, our thesis is that the *timing* of the Soviet response to their perceived vulnerability is critical. If a combination of American deployments and a SALT environment enable the Soviet leadership to defer some of the decisions it will probably have to make on weapons systems until 1980 or 1981, or even to 1985, the relationship of these strategic decisions to the performance of the Soviet economy may be profoundly different.

The strategic decisions are likely to be paralleled by others in conventional arms. Leaders in the Soviet Union and Warsaw Pact may perceive the need for deployments to offset the acquisition of F-14s, 15s, and 16s by the United States and NATO. Cruise missiles in particular will have a dramatic effect on PVO (Soviet air defense) forces, and their claim for rubles will certainly grow stronger.

The pattern with respect to ground forces is less easy to predict. At least one expensive piece of hardware is likely to continue to be added to inventories during the next few years—the T-72 main battle tank. Its production has been underway since 1976.[18] Its performance characteristics in comparison with the prospective U.S. XM-1 and NATO's main battle tank are not yet clear, but if Soviet military commanders should determine that they require still another Soviet tank or significant retooling of the

[17]Harold Brown, *Department of Defense Annual Report, Fiscal Year 1979* and *Fiscal Year 1980*, Febraury 2, 1978, p. 50 and Jan. 25, 1979, p. 72, respectively.

[18]*Department of Defense Appropriations for 1977*, p. 740.

T-72, they can be expected to compete for funds in the 1980-1982 time frame. In any case, adjustments in Soviet doctrine regarding armored combat suggest added production costs for tanks. PGMs (precision-guided munitions) generally, and antitank guided weapons in particular, might be thought by analogy with the Western experience to make possible less costly alternatives to armor.[19] Although Moscow is clearly interested in the American and NATO efforts with antitank weapons (TOWs and Dragons), there is no evidence to suggest that the Soviet Union will alter its dependence on tanks. On the contrary, it seems likely that, between 1979 and 1985, Soviet armor will actually require increased resources by virtue of the need to survive in the ATGW (antitank guided weapons) environment and to compete with the XM-1 or other NATO tank.

Thus, there is some military evidence to suggest that the early 1980s could be a period of very vigorous demands on economic resources by military programs—strategic, ground, and air. While the past pattern of arranging acquisition according to compensating cycles may continue, these separate demands may converge in a rather compressed period in the early 1980s. This time frame could be drawn out if political tensions continue to abate, enabling the Kremlin to buy its tanks, missiles, and aircraft across time or on separate cycles of accelerated production. But should political tensions between the United States and the U.S.S.R. intrude, or domestic organizational struggles require a number of decisions to be made within a short period of time, then the cycles of military development and procurement might create political instabilities.

Even without an external or internal political crisis, the conjunction of declining growth rates and the perceived need to make substantial investments in new military hardware is quite possible. It is only prudent that American policy anticipate this possibility, and it would be shortsighted not to consider the timing of reciprocal military developments. Whether United States interests will best be served by uncontrolled arms competition, a

[19]See, for example, Phillip A. Karber, "The Soviet Anti-Tank Debate," *Survival,* May/June, 1976, pp. 105–111.

loose system of constraints, or a vigorous program of arms control will find no unanimous agreement in Washington and depends on conditions we cannot predict with accuracy. But if in the 1980s the Soviet leadership experiences difficulties with economic growth and must also face difficult choices about defense posture, the political and economic consensus they have demonstrated during the past decade would be severely tested.

The picture drawn here takes on additional importance for the development of military power because all of the new weapons systems require high technology. The Soviet Union, and Russia before it, has always perceived itself to be lagging behind the West in this category of economic development.

SCIENCE AND TECHNOLOGY

Probably no single factor has contributed so decisively to the pressures in Moscow for détente and cooperation with the major industrialized capitalist states as the Soviet perception that it must improve its capacity to exploit what it has termed the "scientific-technical revolution." Elements in the Soviet leadership with economic responsibility have consistently supported the Brezhnev policy of relaxing tensions and have sought to import technology as a solution to Soviet economic problems. These pressures to maintain the lines for technology transfer will continue and may even increase in the 1980s. Both the Five-Year Plan and the foregoing assessment that the Soviet leadership will perceive a need for increased investment in military technology suggest that some elements of the leadership will continue to press for a vigorous policy of trade with technologically advanced economies. It is also possible that Moscow's perception of the technological lag will continue, but that it will attempt an autarkic solution to the problem. On the other hand, this perception of technological lag might be reduced by Soviet achievements, and the resultant increased confidence could either encourage or discourage trade.

In any case, the trade decision is crucial. Both an autarkic reaction to the perception of technological inferiority or the decision to reduce trade as that perception ameliorates would have profound consequences for Soviet-American relations. This would be especially true if the possible scenarios developed in the previous section should materialize and the Soviet leadership should be faced with a series of major decisions on military programs in a relatively short time. In this context, the sacrifice of the option of trading for technology is very likely to be accompanied by a general deterioration in cooperative relations.

In summary, we can establish some basic elements of Soviet power in the 1980s.

- The United States and the Soviet Union are the first and second largest economies in the world. While the international economy is far from bipolar, American influence will remain great, and Soviet potential for increasing its international economic influence is substantial. Even issues which seem to stress the limits of American and Soviet economic power, such as those of the "new economic order," will prove more manageable and less disruptive if the Soviet Union and the United States cooperate.

- American and Soviet military power will remain in a class by itself. The absolute difference between their military capability and that of even secondary and significant powers is not likely to be eroded. Some countries, particularly oil-rich ones, may improve their relative position on the scale of world military power, but it is not probable that any will overtake such significant powers as Germany, Britain, France, and China. Therefore, the absolute difference between the superpowers and other significant military powers seems likely to hold for the 1980s. Military power will remain bipolar in important dimensions.

- The Soviet economy, despite its weaknesses, has made impressive achievements. It would be a mistake to underestimate the resources, skills, capacity, and dynamism of the Soviet economic system. Even in sectors of supposed weakness—agriculture, for example—it has enormous productive capacity and relies very little on imports.

- Despite this basic strength, it is possible that rates of economic growth will decline during the 1980s. That development, should it occur, would be the product of economic constraints imposed by several critical inputs, such as labor supply, technical education, and high technology.

- Declining growth rates could subject the political consensus of the past 15 years to considerable stress. The Brezhnev leadership has been able to expand arms production and personal consumption through net gains in the GNP, but if growth falls to the middle or lower ranges predicted by American analysts, competition for resources will clearly increase.

- Soviet military power is formidable, but it is the pace at which Soviet strategic and conventional weapons have been modernized in the period since 1969 that has been most impressive and that has created the most controversy within the United States concerning Soviet intentions. Even taking into account these achievements in the recent past, it is probable that Soviet defense authorities will perceive the need for further deployments of current systems and further research and development on new systems in the 1980s. This observation draws attention to current American systems that are likely to be perceived in Moscow to require a "response"—the Mark 12A neutron warheads; the Trident, cruise, and MX missiles; the XM tank; and F14/15/16/18 tactical aircraft.

- Although a thoughtful and carefully coordinated arms control and weapons deployment policy by the United States might affect the timing of future Soviet responses to current developments in the military balance, it is sensible to anticipate that declining growth rates and the resultant increase in competition for economic resources might actually coincide with stiff pressure from Soviet officers and the Ministry of Defense for costly new weapons development and deployment.

THREE

Soviet Policy Making in the 1980s

United States influence over Soviet behavior depends on two kinds of reciprocal effects. First, internal Soviet developments and Soviet behavior in international affairs clearly interact symbiotically. Second, superpower relations equally clearly affect Soviet domestic and foreign policies and are, in turn, affected by them. American influence, then, both depends on and inevitably achieves access to Soviet policy making. Conversely, Soviet behavior also influences the development of American foreign and domestic policies. These relationships are complicated, and our understanding of them is imperfect.

How Soviet politics will evolve in the 1980s, who will exercise power, and what influences will prove decisive are all questions critical to the formation of United States policy, but the answers must be highly tentative. Two levels of analysis may prove helpful. First, the Soviet political system might experience one of at least three variants of change: radical transformation, including the remote possibility of an abandonment of the Communist Party dictatorship; adaptation of the system to changing requirements; and bureaucratic entropy. Although the first of these possibilities should not be utterly discounted for the 1980s, it is improbable. The real question is whether the system will adapt or stagnate. Again, there will be reciprocal effects. Bureaucratic stagnation will produce a strong bias toward ideologically orthodox solutions to questions of economic priorities, military expenditures, trade, and the scientific-technical revolution. Decisions to modernize sectors of the economy, to maintain high levels of economic growth, to alter budgetary priorities for defense, to trade with capitalist states, and to advance Soviet science and technology in phase with those of other industrialized nations will require institutional adaptation.

A second kind of analysis is more particular. The age pattern of the central leadership in the U.S.S.R. and the Communist party make it probable that significant changes will take place before the mid-1980s. Several scenarios for replacement of the membership of the Politburo and Central Committee deserve examination. The failure of the leadership to co-opt significant numbers of new personalities at the Twenty-Fifth Party Congress in February 1976 suggested a delicate balance of power in the Kremlin and may have been influenced by instability in the United States leadership and difficulties in the Soviet-American relationship. It is, therefore, highly probable that the present leadership will be carried intact well into 1980–1981, and it may be difficult to rebuild the Politburo and Central Committee significantly prior to the Twenty-Sixth Congress, probably in 1981, unless death should intervene. But the ages of the present Politburo members make it improbable that it can survive unchanged, or little changed, even until 1985. (See Appendix Two.) Undoubtedly the key to the pace and scope of Politburo changes is the role of General Secretary Brezhnev. If his health holds, he may manage the transition or at least delay it.

Nonetheless, this age pattern suggests that large-scale replacement will occur within the Politburo during the next five years. As will be detailed below, replacement can happen in one or a combination of three ways—by increments (appointments made *seriatim* to replace members who die or are incapacitated, as in the case of the vacancy left by the death of General Grechko in April 1976 and his replacement by Dmitriy Ustinov); by a sizable intrusion of new personalities in a short period of time; or by a disruptive exodus and influx after a major policy confrontation.

The unusually large number of new faces that will appear in the Politburo during the next five to ten years will have two important effects. First, individual personalities will have a less secure grasp on their claims to leadership. Even if Brezhnev is successful in bringing new leaders into the Politburo incrementally—and it should be stressed that his success in doing so depends partly on fate, on the timing of death or incapacitation among current members—a Politburo that contains five or six new members and is led by people with limited experience in national leadership will be vulnerable to challenge by other members of the Communist party hierarchy who do not hold Politburo portfolios.

The second effect of the necessity to rejuvenate the Politburo is that the policy consensus may also be vulnerable to challenge. In 1953–1957, following Stalin's death, and in 1964–1966, after the ouster of Khrushchev, basic policy questions concerning relations with capitalist countries, economic priorities, and even the treatment of intellectuals came under intense discussion within the leadership. As will be argued below, all of these questions affect Soviet-American relations profoundly, and a disruptive intrusion of new leadership would probably produce another period of sorting out policy preferences. Should that happen, it will produce a unique opportunity for adjusting the Soviet-American relationship, although the outcome need not be favorable to United States interests. For even if Brezhnev is successful in bringing new leaders into the Politburo incrementally, that may only defer confrontation over policy, as rivalries emerge in the new leadership.

Thus it is not impossible that three important lines of Soviet development will coincide in the 1980s. As this study argued in Chapter 2, GNP growth rates could decline to somewhere under 3 percent, possibly as low as 1 or 2 percent, for some years. Should this happen at a time when new leaders face a series of fundamental policy choices, including the need to decide on costly new weapons, a critical period could emerge in Soviet-American relations.

PROBLEMS OF ADAPTATION IN SOVIET POLITICAL INSTITUTIONS

Two developments, then, make it probable that the 1980s will be a period during which new demands are placed on the Soviet political system: the prospective alteration in the top political and economic elite will afford opportunities for policy change, and declining economic growth will increase competition for resources. Conflicting influences will determine how the Soviet system responds to these pressures for change.

The principal means by which demands are processed in the Soviet political system are by elite anticipation of those demands and by the elite's representation of defined interests. Both are conservative means for adapting to demands for change because they insulate the system from new political forces, and, in the absence of new structures for meeting demands, these processes will probably incline the system toward unimaginative and conservative responses. If the pressures for change mount, and new means are not found to satisfy demands, the possibility increases for disruption of political processes.

Some new groups may need to articulate their interests within the Soviet political system in the future: managerial elites, agricultural interests, national minorities, scientific elites, and sections of the intelligentsia. But attempts by these underrepresented elements in Soviet society to press their demands have not been strong or persistent. The Communist party has varying sensitivities to these diverse interests and will probably be able to control successfully the timing of its responses to their demands. Whether any of the demands will become effective in the 1980s is uncertain, and they certainly will carry different political weights. But it should be noted that sensitivity to technological lag and the probable need for new military systems in the 1980s will increase the dependence of the system upon scientific elites, whose views tend to stress the need for access to Western techniques. Similarly, declining economic performance will surely increase friction between industrial managers and party bureaucrats over control of the economy. Neither set of pressures may force adaptation of the political system, but they will surely pose the issue anew in the 1980s.

Potentially the most significant pressure for adaptation of the political system will come from a kind of demonstration effect about industrial organization. Eurocommunism in particular holds the risk that *socialist* forms may differentiate in the future. Irrespective of that possibility, sensitivity by the Soviet leadership to the need for increased labor productivity and the perceived Soviet lag in acquiring the benefits of the scientific-technical revolution is likely to rise.[1] Difficult problems, like agriculture and the pricing of factor inputs for production, will make attractive the import of techniques. Many of these may be unsuited to the kind of central direction and ideological emphasis by political authorities to which the present leadership has been devoted. Even in the military, there have been periodic disagreements between elements whose emphasis has been on "professional" (technical) as opposed to "political" training. These debates have reflected military resistance to political interference in day-to-day operations.[2]

Nevertheless, the Communist party continues to command the political and economic system, and adaptation or entropy will begin there. Within the Communist Party of the Soviet Union (CPSU), the relative positions of the Politburo, Central Committee, Party Secretariat, and office of the General Secretary provide the key to the exercise of power. The debate of the 1966–1968 period over "collective leadership" versus "one-man authority" will possibly be revived and bring the relative strengths of these party organs under discussion once again as

[1]The evidence that the Brezhnev leadership has emphasized the need for increased productivity traces back to the December 1969 Central Committee Plenum, a date which corresponds with its commitment to détente. See his speech on that occasion, in *Ob osnovnykh voprosakh ekonomicheskoy politiki KPSS na sovremennom etape* (On Basic Questions of Economic Policy of the CPSU at the Contemporary Stage), Moscow, 1975, vol. I, pp. 414–429; see also the *Pravda* editorial, January 13, 1970. He has repeated that theme in every major address concerning domestic policy since. See, for example, his address to the Twenty-Fifth Party Congress, *Pravda*, February 24, 1976.

[2]The work of Thomas W. Wolfe has long set the standard in assessing these questions; see his *Soviet Strategy at the Crossroads*, Harvard University Press, Cambridge, Mass., 1964, pp. 91–109. Raymond Carthoff's description of Soviet behavior in SALT I contains some suggestive evidence in support of the Wolfe thesis; see "Salt and the Soviet Military," *Problems of Communism*, January-February, 1975, pp. 21–37. William E. Odom has mounted strong arguments in partial criticism of this thesis; see "The Party Connection," ibid., September-October, 1973, pp. 12–26. See especially, Christopher D. Jones, "The Revolution in Military Affairs and Party-Military Relations, 1965–1970," *Survey*, Winter, 1974, pp. 84–100.

leadership replacement occurs.[3] Two conflicting kinds of institutional arrangements would be engaged by such debates: intraparty political struggle may make it difficult for decisive leadership to emerge, at least in the early 1980s, as interests vie for influence and political position. This tendency would drive the Central Committee, its Secretariat, and possibly the Party Congress itself into institutional prominence as forums for brokering differences. A need for decisive policy actions may be raised by the international environment or by economic difficulties, and that need will drive the system toward decisive leadership. This line of development would make likely an increase in the importance of the Politburo and office of the General Secretary.

There may also be renewed pressure for devolution of decision making away from the central governmental bureaucracy toward the economic enterprises or to the regions.[4] Continued tension within the government between centralizers and localists could lead to the reappearance of the same conflict between the government and the party that surfaced in the late 1960s. In that case, the government developed some interest in economic devolution, which the party resisted because it would have undercut the latter's authority at the center.

[3]See, for example, Myron Rush, "Brezhnev and the Succession Issue," *Problems of Communism,* July-August, 1971, pp. 9–15; Michel Tatu has analyzed the early part of this period, *Power in the Kremlin from Khrushchev to Kosygin,* Viking, New York, 1969, pp. 516–522. After 1966, the work of Christian Duevel at Radio Liberty is the best source, and the author is grateful to him for making his files available during a visit to Munich in late 1972. This debate became less intense after the emergence of Brezhnev as *primus inter pares* in 1969 and in the Twenty-Fourth Party Congress (March 1971), but still emerges from time to time. See V. Zasorin, *Partiinaya zhizn,* February 1969, pp. 10–18; Yu. G. Turishchev, *Voprosy istorii KPSS,* December 1969, p. 11; and V. Zagladin, *Kommunist,* September 1972, p. 26.

[4]Jerry F. Hough, "The Brezhnev Era," *Problems of Communism*, March-April 1976, pp. 11, 13–16; Gregory Grossman, "An Economy at Middle Age," ibid., pp. 31–33; Leon Smolinski, "Towards a Socialist Corporation: Soviet Industrial Reorganization of 1973," *Survey*, Winter, 1974, pp. 24–35; for an intriguing discusson of the "second economy," which might be thought an ad hoc demand for decentralization, see Grossman, "The 'Second Economy' of the USSR," *Problems of Communism*, September-October 1977, pp. 25–40.

Finally, new institutions may rise in importance. For example, there has been an occasional and quiet effort to increase the functions of the Supreme Soviet, especially its standing committees, and the possibility cannot be excluded that adaptation might take place by the further development of this or other currently ceremonial institutions.[5] But these possibilities are not great and the impact of such adaptation would probably not be felt significantly in the time frame of this study.

All of these questions concerning the economic and political development of the U.S.S.R. during the 1980s suggest a debate that has characterized the society at least since the late 1960s and possibly since 1953: the debate between the orthodox and modernist persuasions of Soviet leadership. The differences are complex and profound. Individuals often favor a modern approach—adaptation—on some issues but not on others; these categories, therefore, do not describe anything approaching political factions. Still, the orthodox tendency in Soviet political life stresses ideology, centralized control, economic priority for traditional sectors of rapid growth (heavy industry), distrust of the capitalist world, and willingness to take relatively higher risks in advancing communist and anti-imperialist causes outside the U.S.S.R.[6] The modernist tendency, on the other hand, senses

[5]D. Richard Little, "Soviet Parliamentary Committees After Krushchev," *Soviet Studies,* July 1972, pp. 44–45; Darrell P. Hammer, *USSR: The Politics of Oligarchy,* The Dryden Press, Hinsdale, 1974, pp. 257–264; L. G. Churchward, "Soviet Local Government Today," in Richard Cornell, ed., *The Soviet Political System,* Prentice-Hall, Englewood Cliffs, N.J., 1970, pp. 271–286; Robert Sharlet, "The New Soviet Constitution," *Problems of Communism,* September-October 1977, pp. 1–24.

[6]The articulation of these views has become somewhat more circumspect since the Twenty-Fourth Party Congress adopted the "peace program" in 1971, but they do appear, usually in the context of particular issues. See, for example, M. A. Suslov's speech to the sixth All-Union Knowledge Society Congress, *Pravda,* June 21, 1972; Vladimir Shcherbitskiy's article in *Kommunist,* November 1974, pp. 14–25; Boris Ponomarev's important article in *Problemy mira i sotsializma,* no. 1, January 1975, pp.4–13; Konstantin Zarodov, "Leninism on Consolidating the Victory of the Revolution," *World Marxist Review,* April 1975, pp. 20–24; and for an "institutional" articulation of orthodox views, see Major-General D. Volkonogov's article in *Kommunist vooruzhennykh sil,* no. 3, February 1977, pp. 9–23.

the need to adapt the procedures if not the essence of the system, favors some devolution of economic power at home, favors pragmatic cooperation with other industrialized nations as a means of solving economic difficulties, and has therefore been inclined to reduce the risks of overt conflict in support of foreign communists and revolutionary groups, and has stressed "professional" or technical skills as a means to advance within Soviet society.[7] It is this outlook that underlies the above analysis that modernists will promote adaptation and that this persuasion in Soviet political and economic life will promote cooperation between the United States and the U.S.S.R. It therefore parallels more closely American objectives in the world than does the orthodox persuasion.

MODERNISM AND ORTHODOXY

The modernist impulse in Soviet political life tends to be optimistic and relatively less threatened in international politics. It holds that the international balance of power has shifted from capitalism to socialism, that "realistic" political leaders in the West recognize this fact and are, therefore, deterred from the most extreme temptations of "adventurism" against Soviet interests. This optimistic assessment of the international political system, of course, still depends on maintaining strong Soviet military forces, but it also implies a foreign policy designed to

[7]The fullest and most authoritative statements of these positions are found in Brezhnev's Central Committee Reports to the Twenty-Fourth and Twenty-Fifth Party Congresses, *Pravda,* March 30, 1971, and ibid., February 25, 1976; the foreign policy implications of this web of ideas are carefully articulated in A. Sovetov, "Peaceful Coexistence: A Real Factor in International Relations," *International Affairs,* Moscow, September 1972, pp. 11–13; G. Shakhnazarov's article in *Pravda,* December 27, 1975; Yu. V. Andropov's speech to the 1976 celebration of Lenin's birthday, *Pravda,* April 23, 1976; Leonid Brezhnev's speech to the CPSU Central Committee Plenum, *Pravda,* October 25, 1976. Since the advent of the Carter administration, modernist references have been more scarce. The author has discussed the evidence for the modernist/orthodox interpretation of Soviet politics in several places, including his analysis of the early SALT debate in the U.S.S.R. *Soviet Attitudes to SALT,* Adelphi Paper No. 75, Institute for Strategic Studies, London, 1971.

cooperate with the realists among the capitalists in achieving particular goals where Soviet interests and those of capitalist states coincide. Modernism thus advocates foreign trade and participation in such forums of arms negotiation as SALT and mutual force reductions.

In domestic policy, modernism has been associated in particular with exploitation of the "scientific-technical revolution." This is a complicated, but critical, connection. Again, relative optimism is the key. Perhaps because this impulse in Soviet politics is relatively less threatened from abroad, its adherents have also been more willing to criticize openly domestic economic performance. They have called for the importation of technology—hence the linkage between domestic and foreign policy. They have also stressed the need to improve productivity as a means of upgrading economic performance. Thus modernism's economic priorities have tended to be in high-technology areas where modernists perceive the U.S.S.R. to be at some disadvantage—chemicals, computers, precision machine building. There is little evidence that the modernist impulse also advocates a widespread liberalization of domestic life, such as extension of the rights of dissenters, although there is substantial evidence that people who take such a position also take a pragmatic approach to selective issues of "openness" in the political system. For example, the tendency accepts the need to promote scientific exchanges and to permit the operation of Western firms under relatively normal conditions in the U.S.S.R.

The orthodox impulse differs on each of these issues. While members of the Soviet elite taking this position normally make references to the imposing military capabilities of the Soviet Union and to a relative improvement in the position of the socialist states vis-à-vis the "imperialists," their emphasis is on the danger of "adventurism" from the other side and on the still-threatening capacity of American and German military power in particular.[8] This assessment of the international system pro-

[8]See, for example, the Soviet government statement carried in *Pravda,* April 10, 1969; in the Mutual Force Reduction negotiations after 1973, this Soviet tactic came to be centered in proposals designed to weaken the Bundeswehr and German-American military cooperation. See, for example,

vides the basis for a different set of domestic priorities as well. The sense of threat from the international environment seems to require particular ideological vigilance against penetration of the domestic system by capitalist ideology. Orthodoxy emphasizes the traditional bases of economic development—heavy "group A" industry—especially steel and investment in the means of production.

These two tendencies in Soviet political life are just that. They are not political interest groups in a sense we understand by analogy with pluralist systems. In many cases both tendencies exist in the minds of individual political leaders. The orthodox impulse is heavily socialized in the training of any communist, especially those who came into positions of national power in the more threatening days of the 1930s and 1940s. But these men and women have made progress, have achieved successes, and the modernist impulse is, in part, a pragmatic adjustment to altered international conditions and domestic needs. It is a human and natural condition of Soviet politics that past and present should war in this manner, that individuals with high-level political experience under conditions in which the modernist tendency became more feasible should also evidence characteristics of orthodoxy. In addition, however, to the division of individual minds between the two tendencies, there are times when political divisions take place along the lines of modernism and orthodoxy among members of the party. These divisions emerged early in the period of détente, under Brezhnev's leadership. The debates in the late 1960s over whether "material" or "moral" incentives would best improve economic productivity and over whether to join the United States in the SALT process displayed at least some of this division between the orthodox and modernist impulses.

Finally, the modernist/orthodox division occasionally emerges in patterns of bureaucratic politics that exhibit some deceptive similarities to those of pluralist political systems. For example, on questions of trade with the West, individuals with functional

K. Perevoshchikov and N. Polyanov's representative article in *Izvestia,* January 25, 1976.

responsibilities for economic planning and within the Council of Ministers have rather consistently taken public positions employing modernist arguments, while those who have ideological responsibility within the party have taken orthodox positions.[9]

ACCESS TO SOVIET POLITICAL INSTITUTIONS

To describe such differences between the modernist and the orthodox positions, of course, is not to address the partially separate question of American access to and influence over Soviet political processes. That question requires, in the first place, a distinction between two kinds of influence. *Systemic* influence is an inappropriate goal for American policy because efforts to achieve it are counterproductive. Efforts to change the nature of the Soviet political or economic system simply cannot be effective. Policies based on such expectations, therefore, are unrealistic. Furthermore, efforts to change the Soviet system force political divisions in this country to the surface and raise the chances of conflict with American allies. Still, one hears discussion in the American political debate that this country cannot or should not conduct business with the Soviet Union unless it becomes "democratic," or adopts individual "incentives," or permits open criticism. These arguments normally contrast the worst features of Soviet society with an idealized view of American society. That is not to deny very real differences between the two systems, but foreign policy must be based on less self-serving comparisons, and policies based on expectations for systemic changes in the Soviet Union are likely to prove self-defeating.

On the other hand, it is the appropriate, in fact inevitable, object of United States foreign policy to attempt to affect the selection of individual foreign and security policies in Moscow. It is plausible that a modest and consistent American national

[9]Contrast, for example, the speech by Mikhail Suslov to the celebration of the Fifty-Third Anniversary of the Revolution in the Kremlin, *Pravda*, November 6, 1970, and the article by Minister of Foreign Trade Nikolai Patolichev in *Izvestia*, December 11, 1969.

strategy for influencing the foreign and security policies of the Soviet Union may, across a considerable period of time, influence the evolution of the Soviet political and economic system.

Achievement of this latter and more modest objective, of course, requires use of a variety of points at which U.S. policy has access to the Soviet policy process: direct contacts between the President and General Secretary, between the Secretary of State and Foreign Minister, and between negotiating teams; the "back channel" between Presidents or Secretaries and the Kremlin elite; and personal contacts that circumvent established bureaucratic procedures. There are also less direct means like press releases, actions or comments of lower-level officials, and speeches by American leaders to other audiences that contain direct messages to the Soviet leadership. These means have long been employed and have achieved dramatic results, such as the resolution of the Cuban missile crisis in 1962, and, sometimes, less dramatic results, like the negotiation of the cultural exchange pacts.

The notion of political access carries ambiguous connotations. Considering the United States' recent experience with the Lockheed "bribery" cases and allegations of CIA penetration into the Christian Democratic Party in Italy, there is an appropriate hesitation about thinking in terms of "levers" that might influence the policy making of a foreign power. Moreover, Moscow has demonstrated throughout all phases of CSCE (Conference on Security and Cooperation in Europe) a deep concern for "ideological vigilance," bordering on paranoid fears that such NATO proposals in that conference as "freer movement of people and ideas" (Basket Three, as they have been called) would make socialist societies vulnerable to capitalist infiltration.[10]

Actually, the idea of access is less dramatic and controversial. The Soviet political elite has long differentiated between "progressive and realistic" and "reactionary" circles in capitalist countries. By these terms Soviet analysts demonstrate recog-

[10]See M. A. Suslov's speech to the sixth Congress of the All-Union Knowledge Society, *Pravda,* June 21, 1972; V. Zagladin and V. Shaposhnikov's article in *Kommunist,* No. 16, 1972, especially p. 92; Captain N. Shumikhin in *Krasnaya zvezda,* December 12, 1974.

nition that the outcomes of political debates in Washington, London, Bonn, Paris, Tokyo, Rome, and other capitalist states affect the interests of the U.S.S.R. *Pravda* carries warnings to the American political leadership during each spring's debates over the defense budget against permitting "reactionary, anti-Soviet" forces to dominate the budgetary process.[11] Moscow also times some actions in such a way that they will undercut or reinforce particular opponents or relatively more congenial elements in American or NATO politics. For example, exit permits for Russian Jews during the debate over the Trade Bill in 1973–1974 were clearly modulated to affect votes in the Senate and, then, to signal displeasure with political outcomes in the United States. While we cannot be certain, it is possible that the conduct of the May 1972 Summit between Brezhnev and Nixon, following the mining of Haiphong and the apparent revolt of some members within the Politburo, reflected Soviet conviction that a rebuff to Nixon at that time would have had at least unpredictable consequences and, possibly, very negative ones for the American presidential election.[12] The Soviet campaign against President Carter in the spring and summer of 1977 clearly sought to influence American allies in Europe and may have sought, in addition, to strengthen the hand of moderates and prodétente forces in the new administration.[13] These techniques are indirect and low pro-

[11]For an interesting discussion of this point, see V. M. Berezhkov's two-part article in *S. Sh. A.* (USA), February 1972, p. 10ff, and March 1972, p. 20ff; two articles by L. Tolkunov after his return from a visit to the United States with a Supreme Soviet delegation, *Izvestia,* June 18, 1974, and ibid., June 22, 1974; Georgy Arbatov, *Pravda,* February 5, 1977; the *Pravda* editorial, June 17, 1978.

[12]See Sergei Vishnevsky's article in *Pravda,* June 11, 1972; G. Arbatov, *Izvestia,* June 27, 1972.

[13]Even before the Vance mission to Moscow in late March, Brezhnev's speeches at Tula and to the Trade Unions Congress struck these themes. See *Pravda,* January 19, 1977, and ibid., March 22, 1977. But Soviet efforts to discredit the Carter administration's policies went to lengths never before witnessed in Soviet-American relations after the failure of that mission. See Foreign Minister Gromyko's news conference, ibid., April 1, 1977; the *Pravda* editorial, April 14, 1977. Brezhnev's visit to Paris, June 20–22, carried many indications of this Soviet policy. See especially the Russian version of this pretrip interview in *Le Monde* as carried in *Pravda,* June 16, 1977. In June,

file, but they imply a form of access and an expectation that influence can be generated. The habit of attempting to influence political outcomes in the other country, then, is clearly established by both countries.

American opportunities for influence within the Soviet political system, however, are certainly fewer than those available to the Kremlin for influencing American politics. But that is not to say there are none. Guarded as political disagreements are in Soviet political life, some evidence of them inevitably surfaces. The two tendencies described above as "orthodox" and "modernist" provide a useful framework within which to assess Soviet political differences.

The modernist/orthodox framework implies that an effort can be made to influence longer-term policy orientations or the development of political attitudes by persons further down in the political structure than the Politburo itself. This question of influence will be more difficult to deal with but more important in the 1980s. The circle of people in Moscow who have contact with visiting Americans is very tight, however. Georgy Arbatov, distinguished director of the USA Institute, and his deputy, Vitaly Zhurkin, are symbols of this difficulty. These men individually, and their institute, comprise a kind of organized access point for Americans and Europeans. They maintain contact with a wide variety of Americans—from senators, important businessmen, and "shadow cabinets" to lowly academics in a variety of different fields. It is traditional of the Soviet and Russian approach to foreigners to formalize contact in this manner. The tendency has its parallel in the elaborate "foreign communities" of Moscow in which most embassy officials spend their lives and from which most Soviets are carefully shielded, particularly officials of the party and government. Some progress has been made by Western journalists and embassy officials during the

---

especially following the Carter administration's decision not to foreclose the neutron bomb option, this campaign reached its height. See, for example, Gennady Vasilyev's article, ibid., June 29, 1977. These various difficulties led both Carter and Brezhnev to acknowledge in late June that relations had deteriorated visibly.

past five or six years of détente in getting outside the "protective" circle around their activities. But this progress still falls far short of what is desirable and absurdly short of what would be needed to achieve anything like the kind of access required for influencing political attitudes among future generations of Soviet leaders.

Nothing nefarious is implied by the effort to establish such influence and to obtain access to the Soviet system by which it might be effected. In fact, it might be argued that all the positive aspects of détente between the United States and the U.S.S.R. *require* that these points of access be increased. The kind of influence discussed here implies simple dialogue. So great is the Soviet resistance to these efforts that patience and firmness will be required. No American government action should be taken to achieve these ends, although it would be useful for a President or Secretary of State to support less formal efforts. What is required is that American and other Western organizations be firm in insisting that Soviet interaction with them be broadened and that strict reciprocity be observed when the West makes concessions to Soviet requests for privileges.

It would not be difficult to create a menu of institutions, even individuals—although that is more difficult—whom the United States should attempt to draw into dialogue, thereby extending the points of access between the two systems.

The National Political Elite

In the Soviet political system national power is concentrated and organized hierarchically. Therefore, to define the Soviet elite does not pose the kinds of problems raised in the more diffuse American political system. The possibility that a Jimmy Carter will appear in a remote republic or *oblast* and rise to challenge the Secretary General is dramatically less than in the United States, but possibly not much less than the chance for such a regional challenge to the center in more centralized but familiar systems like Great Britain or West Germany. And even if that happened in the U.S.S.R., this regional leader would have had years of experience in the national party apparatus.

Thus the current Communist Party of the Soviet Union (CPSU)

elite is relatively stable and narrow when compared to the national elites of the United States. This Soviet elite embraces the Politburo (13 full and 9 candidate members as of the November 1978 Plenum); the Central Committee (288 full and 132 candidate members) and especially the Central Committee Secretariat (a General Secretary—Brezhnev; 10 Secretaries; and 20 to 30 important departments). One might add the top party secretaries in the Union Republics (14) and officials in the most important *oblasts* and *kray* (regional divisions), *gorod* (city) party committees (possibly 50 out of more than 900), and in important urban or rural districts (or *rayons,* maybe 200 out of more than 3,200), although the most influential *oblast, kray, rayon,* and *gorod* officials are also included in the membership of the Central Committee. Thus the central CPSU political elite is composed of a definable group of between 500 and 700 individuals (see Appendix Two).

These positions constitute the primary pool from which the next generation of political leaders will be selected, assuming no radical disruption of the system. The more highly placed an individual is in the hierarchy, the earlier he might be expected to penetrate the top leadership (see Appendix One). Recruitment to the post of General Secretary, or First Secretary as the post was called during Khrushchev's tenure, has invariably come from the Politburo itself, and the Politburo has invariably been recruited from the Central Committee apparat, top economic management, or the Union Republic Party Central Committees. Thus, in the 1980s we can expect to find the political leadership drawn from the top of the present CPSU pyramid, and if the objective is to influence the political leadership that will succeed the present Politburo leaders, efforts can be confined to a narrow segment of the national leadership.

As noted earlier, the political elite of the CPSU in the 1980s might evolve according to one of three scenarios and possibly a combination of more than one of them. It is certain that replacement will occur not only in the Politburo but also in the other leading political institutions. In addition to the gerontocracy of the Politburo, evident from even a cursory examination of Appendix Two, the age and length of tenure in the national Party elite of the entire group—which has actually increased significantly during the years since Khrushchev was overthrown—has reached levels that cannot be sustained into the 1980s without large-scale replacement.

Incremental Replacement

The Politburo may simply continue the procedures it has followed since 1964, providing occasional demotions for reasons of policy or personality, but on the whole simply advancing individuals up the ladder as retirements and deaths leave vacancies. Such a procedure implies policy stability and may well support the interests of the present leadership, which hopes to preserve the delicate balance of disparate interests it has fashioned. In fact, that balance makes difficult the task of replacing the leadership *seriatim,* since new members must have preferences similar to those of the persons they replace or, at least, must be acceptable to the current balance of interests in the Politburo.

A Sizable Intrusion

This balance of interests will be easier to maintain if replacement takes place in stages involving several positions each time. This might be possible if several deaths or retirements were to occur simultaneously, or in sufficiently close proximity, so that several slots would open at a particular plenum of the Central Committee. Thus a new member was not added to the Politburo immediately on Grechko's death in April 1976, although in this case the Politburo may have been expanded by one at the Twenty-Fifth Party Congress in anticipation of a possible need to replace a member during the year, or in the case of Podgorny's removal in May 1977.[14] It is always possible that a policy crisis or palace revolt might replace several members in the ruling elite at any time, and the desire to maintain continuity will place an aging Politburo under pressure to bring new people into the elite or

[14]There was a net addition of one member in the Politburo at the Twenty-Fifth Congress, where Polyanskiy was dropped and Romanov and Ustinov added. *Pravda,* March 6, 1977. For the Podgorny removal, see ibid., May 25, 1977. For the Kuznetsov and Chernenko promotions, see ibid., October 4, 1977 and November 28, 1978.

risk a dramatic intrusion of new personalities forced on them by a faction of their own number or, less likely, by demand for change from the larger Central Committee.

A Sudden Disruption

Succession remains one of the most difficult questions for the Soviet political system. Lenin and Stalin died or were incapacitated in office, and Khrushchev suffered an ignominious and enforced retirement. Brezhnev has been persistent and resilient, and it is not inconceivable that he might rule until his eightieth year. But it is unlikely, and rumors that his health cannot hold out never drop far below the surface. The need for him to pass on the power of the General Secretary's office increases the probability that a sizable intrusion of new leaders or a sudden disruption of the present leadership will take place. There is such disproportionate power in his post within the Politburo that it is the one position which cannot be allowed to pass to someone whose policy preferences are very different from Brezhnev himself. Therefore, Brezhnev will either have to engineer a sizable intrusion of new leadership so that he can retain a balance of interests acceptable to him, or he will be prevented from transferring power by the same need to retain the present balance and thereby increase the chances of a sudden disruption in which he and several other members will be replaced simultaneously.

Although none of these scenarios can be predicted, the chances for either sizable intrusion or a sudden disruption might be thought somewhat greater at the Twenty-Sixth Party Congress in 1981, and the Twenty-Seventh—if complete replacement is not accomplished prior to then—in 1986. Whenever replacement does take place, the pool of individuals who will move forward is fairly clear. Appendix Two identifies those on the present Politburo who should survive by virtue of age—Andropov (64), Grishin (64), Gromyko (69), Kunayev (67), Romanov (56), Shcherbitskiy (61), and Chernenko (67). Although it is possible, especially in an incremental replacement, that a caretaker General Secretary might succeed Brezhnev, for example, Suslov or Kirilenko, neither is younger than Brezhnev and both could only be short-term solutions to the leadership problem. Figure 6 identifies Grishin, Shcherbitskiy, Romanov, and possibly Chernenko

FIGURE 6
Succession to General Secretary

Primary Candidates

V. V. Grishin
V. V. Shcherbitskiy
G. V. Romanov
K. U. Chernenko

Nationality Handicap*	Institutional Handicaps†	Government Elite in Exile
D. A. Kunayev	*Government Service:*	A. N. Shelepin
(G. A. Aliyev)	(M. C. Solomentsev)	D. S. Polyanskiy
(P. M. Masherov)	(P. N. Demichev)	K. T. Mazurov
(Sh. R. Rashidov)	(N. A. Tikhonov) §	
(E. A. Shevardnadze)		

Bureaucratic Base‡	Claims to Institutional Representation in Politburo
A. A. Gromyko §	Marshall of the Soviet
Yu. V. Andropov	Union V. G. Kulikov
D. F. Ustinov §	Marshall of the Soviet
B. N. Ponomarev	Union N. V. Ogarkov

( ) denotes candidates who are nonvoting members of the current Politburo, but who will presumably move to voting status in most replacement scenarios.

*These candidates presently hold the position of First Secretary in Union Republics identified with nationalities (e.g., Kazakhistan, Azerbaydzhan). These positions are not regarded as good power bases for immediate assumption of the top party posts.

†Careers made primarily in government management, as opposed to party affairs, do not establish strong support bases among *apparatchiki*.

‡These candidates, while possessing considerable national and international visibility, have strong bases in their bureaucracies (Foreign, Security, and Defense Ministries) but little experience in general party management.

§ Ustinov (71), Gromyko (70), Ponomarev (75),and Tikhonov (74) probably do not qualify as successors on the basis of age alone, just as Pel'she (81), Suslov (77), Kosygin (76), and Kirilenko (73) do not offer long-term prospects for succeeding Brezhnev (73).

91

as the "heirs" with fewest institutional shortcomings to their claims. Men like Andropov, Ustinov, and Gromyko might be thought too closely identified with the institutions they represent—the KGB, the Ministry of Defense, and the Foreign Ministry. Polyanskiy and Shelepin are past members of the Politburo who might, under some circumstances, stage a comeback. Solomentsev and Demichev have had experience too limited to the government hierarchy; Kunayev, Rashidov, Masherov, and Aliyev have had general party responsibilities, but are probably too far removed from the Moscow center to move into the General Secretary role in the near future. Shevardnadze is probably too recent an addition to the national elite to bid for succession to Brezhnev, and the Georgian Republic is not a strong base of party power.

These, then, are the probable CPSU leaders from whom the next General Secretary will be chosen, but American access to them is very limited. There is, however, another identifiable slice of the current leadership to whom access would be desirable. This is a broader segment of the national elite, those who will move up the leadership ladder, but of whom most will probably occupy positions below the Politburo itself in the 1980s.

First, "opinion leading" institutions clearly exist in the Soviet Union. Although these are under the direct supervision of the Central Committee Secretariat in most questions of policy, collectively they perform socialization and recruitment functions for the top elite. Within the apparat itself, the Departments of Administrative Affairs and Party Organizational Work, the Party Control Committee, and the General Department might be thought to exercise especially important functions in the supervision of party careers and of political training. In particular, the Higher Party School, the Institute of Marxism-Leninism, the Institute for Social Sciences, and some departments of Moscow State University have proven excellent vehicles to higher party power. These are institutions in which many university graduates will be found at some point during their rise within the CPSU.

Certain prestigious publications also exercise substantial influence by virtue of their informational function within the elite. Of course *Pravda* and *Izvestia,* the leading party and government papers, head the list. But there are a number of other influential journals, like *Kommunist Mirovaya Ekonomika i Mezhdunarodnye Otnoshenia,* and *Ekonomika Gazeta,* and party papers in major cities like Leningrad and Kiev that also enjoy a wide readership within segments of the elite.

Finally, the Central Committee and Academy of Sciences have established a number of prominent institutes that have attracted the sons and daughters of the top political leadership and a number of people who have been, or aspire to be, influential within the system. Americans have had considerable experience within the USA (G. A. Arbatov, director) and IMEMO (N. H. Inozemtsev, director) Institutes in Moscow, but the academy maintains a number of others on functional areas like economics and regional areas such as Africa and the Far East. The Ministry of Foreign Affairs also maintains three very prestigious institutes—the Higher Language (N. H. Lifanov, director) and Diplomatic (V. I. Popov, director) Schools and the Moscow State Institute of International Relations (headed by Nikolay I. Lebedev). Since many of these institutes maintain their own journals, they develop influence with the remainder of the elite by their publications and by their ability to attract individuals who already have access to the top Soviet party elite.

The National Economic Elite

The rigid division into government and party elites which one sometimes encounters in American commentary on the Soviet Union simply cannot survive close examination. Many top economic decision makers are included in the party hierarchy at the Central Committee level or higher. As Soviet decision making has, inevitably, had to rely increasingly on technical expertise, the number of technocrats (party officials with legitimate credentials in some technical field, in addition to having spent most of their careers in party posts) in the elite at the Central Committee level and higher has increased slightly. Furthermore, many members of the party elite have had economic responsibilities at some point in their careers, although more often in roles of party supervision than of direct economic management itself.

Nonetheless, a separate hierarchy of the Soviet economic elite can be identified. It starts with the Presidium of the U.S.S.R.

Council of Ministers (14 members) and includes the Union Republic Ministries and All Union Ministries (62) and State Committees (14). The distinction between All Union and Union Republic ministries is that while the former are simply ministries at the U.S.S.R. level, without subordinate units in the 15 republics, the latter have supervisory responsibilities over parallel organizations in the republics. There are a number of other organizations attached to the Council of Ministers which do not constitute ministries, and some of these have importance at least equivalent to the ministries themselves—for example, the Commission of the Presidium for Council of Mutual Economic Assistance Affairs (M. A. Lesechko), the Military-Industrial Commission (L. V. Smirnov), the Administration of Affairs (M. S. Smirtyukov), the All-Union Bank for Financing Capital Investments, the Main Administration for Safeguarding State Secrets in the Press, the Main Administration of State Material Reserves, and others.

Just below this national level, as in the party, the economic apparatus has duplicate republic Councils of Ministers and *oblast, gorod,* and *rayon* executive committees. These perform supervisory functions over many economic enterprises within their geographic jurisdictions, and also provide recruitment and training functions for personnel who will advance up the hierarchy.

Outside the ministerial framework there are, of course, some economic enterprises whose capacity and importance to the economy is so great that their managers can be thought more highly placed in the elite than ministerial personnel in whose geographic responsibility they may fall. In fact, it is probable, especially in defense-related industries, that enterprises are directly responsible to the All Union Ministers and not to regional economic functionaries.

Limitations on American Access

Analysis of the Soviet elite reveals two sharp limitations upon American access. Americans see only a narrow segment of the individuals at the top of the party and ministerial hierarchies, and have meaningful exchanges with a far smaller number of that total. And, there is substantial diffusion in those contacts Americans have. Many Americans obtain access to the limited circle of Soviets with policy roles that involve communication with foreigners. Naturally these contacts are made for a variety of reasons, and often diverse messages are conveyed by the persons involved. By the early 1970s the Soviets had become more sophisticated in their approach to Westerners and had deliberately sought out some groups that had been relatively less familiar with Soviet interests and positions, including conservatives and businessmen not involved in trading with the Soviet Union. As contacts expand some common themes might be amplified by these diverse groups having access to the Soviet system. For example, the bureaucratic complexity of doing business in Moscow, Leningrad, and other cities strains the patience of all Westerners. Such messages may get through slowly, but possibly in a way that will ameliorate conditions and change Soviet habits slightly. This is, of course, far from the kind of influence that might affect national security and foreign policy.

There are more important obstructions to the expansion of access to the Soviet elite and to the establishment of any influence over their thinking. One is the habit of "functional silence." Although we can identify the future generation of Soviet elites more reliably than anyone can predict future American decision makers, people who now hold positions in the party or economic elites below the Politburo, Central Committee, or Council of Ministers often speak out only on those issues for which they have functional responsibility.[15] It is a feature of the Soviet system that might be thought to magnify wildly the kind of "operationalism" Herbert Marcuse has found and criticized in capitalist society.[16] It is, of course, bureaucratically safer to speak out only on issues in which one has expertise. The chances

[15]The same can actually be said for most members of the Central Committee and Council of Ministers. Only Politburo members often discuss a wide range of policy issues, and even then members with primary responsibilities in Union Republics—like Shcherbitskiy in the Ukraine, Kunayev in Kazakhistan, and Aliyev in Azerbaidzhan—normally confine their public pronouncements to matters affecting their own political turf.

[16]Herbert Marcuse, *One-Dimensional Man*, Beacon Press, Boston, 1964, pp. 12–14.

for error are less and the chances of stepping on someone else's organizational toes reduced.

This functional silence creates substantial difficulties for influencing Soviet policy on a longer-term basis. We can predict with reasonable confidence that some individuals in the following group, or even all of them, will have more powerful positions in the 1980s: Yuriy Andropov, Viktor Grishin, Vladimir Shcherbitskiy, Grigoriy Romanov, Vladimir Dolgikh, Konstantin Katushev, Petr Masherov, and possibly even Mikhail Solomentsev, Dinmukhamed Kunayev, I. V. Kapitonov, Eduard Shevardnadze, Dmitriy Polyanskiy, Geydar Aliyev, K. V. Rusakov, M. V. Zimyanin, and Mikhail Gorbachev. But we cannot determine with any accuracy what their present attitudes are on most questions of interest to foreign policy formation in the United States. This problem is radically magnified as one moves down either the government or party hierarchy.

This limit on our information reduces our capacity to identify where we would need to establish access if we were to achieve influence. The problem is compounded by another obstruction to obtaining influence over the attitudes of the future Soviet leadership on important policy issues. The practice of maintaining generalist qualifications among the top party and economic elite is deeply engrained in Soviet life. Almost no one who rises to a top leadership position has had a career of specialization. Exceptions are evident in military and foreign affairs officials like Grechko, Ustinov, and Gromyko, but that same specialization probably means that they lack the necessary influence within the elite on questions outside their areas of expertise. Even among these exceptions, Ustinov, who became a civilian minister of defense in April 1976, more proves the rule of generalist background than he qualifies it. True, his career has consistently been made in economic management and particularly with oversight of the defense industry, but he apparently struggled long and hard under Kosygin's sponsorship to break into the top party elite (he became a candidate member of the Politburo in 1965), and his credentials may have improved when he was appointed head of the Supreme Council for the National Economy in March 1963, where his responsibilities certainly extended beyond the defense sector alone. Even he did not join the Politburo until he had established qualifications as a generalist in party/state management. This career pattern of moving among posts reinforces functional silence, making it very difficult to identify the policy orientations of people rising in the CPSU hierarchy.

The problem of American influence, therefore, is thorny. We can identify people who will have important responsibilities in the 1980s, but we have little access to them. Furthermore, we cannot be certain of their political views outside the areas for which they have already had functional responsibility. Thus, gaining influence will require approaches quite different and more indirect than those customarily used in Western politics. Personal friendships with the future leaders will be limited; these Soviets will continue to remain isolated from the international conference circuit; few will study or travel abroad or receive visiting foreigners; they will not chance participation in multilateral organizations or expose themselves in journals or debate. Our influence will have to be modest, indirect, and patient. It will be necessary to do many small things persistently and to expect that general Soviet policy orientations will adjust slowly.

The Modernist/Orthodox Lever

It should be possible, however, to affect the general orientations of Soviet policy over time by a judicious and persistent effort to restrain current Soviet foreign and defense policy actions and to encourage the entire Soviet elite to interpret its national interests so as to stress cooperation with the United States.

For this purpose the distinction between the modernist and orthodox orientations in Soviet policy will prove useful. The modernist orientation does provide concrete benefits to the United States. The viewpoint supports trade, and even in its current dimensions exports to the U.S.S.R. provide jobs for American workers and profits for American firms. Trade also creates interests in controlling levels of conflict between the two states. While those interests certainly are not powerful enough to override patriotic sympathies in a real conflict of vital interests, over time they affect decision making in a manner that promotes peaceful relations. This point is worth underlining. The Russians have a word that better describes the effect: *semyeistvennost* (or family-ness). It implies a patronage/client relationship in which parallel interests separate the family from other interests and induce cooperation. There has been an increase in the number of people who have had experience in dealing with the West and whose careers depend to some degree on the continuation of that cooperation, and even on its expansion. In Washington, the strange coalition of agricultural and large-business interests that joined with traditional liberals to support the Nixon-Ford-Kissinger policy of détente illustrates the effect. Such "families" of Soviets with personal interests in reducing conflict may develop the political clout across time to influence a variety of relevant issues.

The modernist orientation also underwrites arms control negotiations between the United States and the U.S.S.R. Of course the achievements to date have been modest. But they have also been real. The limits of the SALT Interim Agreement and the SALT II agreements may not have reduced arms programs greatly, but they have altered the nature of the internal debate in both countries. The U.S. was able in SALT II to make the point that complete military secrecy is not necessarily in Soviet interests, and the negotiations induced the Soviets to provide more military information than they had previously made public. And, although evidence of restraint on the Soviet side is not yet apparent, the arms control framework has enabled those with an interest in restraining arms developments in Washington to defer some programs and block others. To establish this pattern further, it will be necessary for evidence of restraint to emerge in Moscow as well. Even if one views the concrete hardware impact of the MFR and SALT frameworks as relatively insignificant, the discussions in Vienna and Geneva have unquestionably increased the sensitivity to the other side's perspective in both capitals. While this sensitivity may not prevent conflicts of interest, it certainly contributes to a calmer analysis of those conflicts.

Modernism, because it views the international balance of power as relatively favorable to socialism and because it holds the view that the international environment is less threatening, may have lengthened the time frame for the resolution of conflicts. For example, the modernist perspective has pressed for improvements in Soviet-Western relations during the period of détente, while tolerating substantial conflicts of interests in Vietnam and the Middle East.

It may be that no one on the political scene at responsible levels of decision making in the Soviet Union today has advocated purely modernist solutions to Soviet economic dilemmas. It is equally clear, however, that the prevailing orthodox preferences for heavy industry and moral incentives for the labor force will not improve the performance of the economy at critical bottlenecks. The modernist orientation at least has the virtue of advancing a program for breaking the bottlenecks in the short run—encouraging, for instance, imports of items in short supply—and of bringing in technology that may help overcome structural deficiencies in the long run. The question of whether the alleviation of deficiencies in the Soviet economy is in American, or Western, interests is another matter.

There may be some long-term effects of the modernist program which mitigate the most repressive features of the Soviet political system. There has long been a connection in Russian and Soviet history between a sense of backwardness vis-à-vis the West, and political repression. Peter the Great set the pattern by his forced-labor construction of his magnificent "Westernized" capital at Petrograd, now Leningrad. Alexander I squandered the early liberalizing promise of his regime following the Napoleonic Wars and the exposure of his armies to Western "decadence." Nicholas I launched the most thoroughgoing police state of his time following the abortive attempt by the Decembrists to modernize Russia along Western lines. Stalin magnified oppression in periods of threat—during the years just before the outbreak of World War II and in 1948–1953, as the cold war reached its apex.

The converse, of course, is not necessarily true: a reduced sense of backwardness need not induce an increased openness and amelioration of repression. However, there has been some—albeit contradictory—evidence that the Soviet leadership has been somewhat embarrassed by charges of repression and that it has adopted some moderating measures. The Jewish emigration and the release of Solzhenitsyn and other dissidents, of course, have the virtue of purging the Soviet population of persons the leadership may consider persistent embarrassments. It is appropriate, however, to observe that repression of dissent has continued throughout the period of détente. Possibly some of its features are the product of KGB independence, but on the whole it must be concluded that the current leadership does not find repression of a small, outspoken, dissident community inconsistent with a modernist foreign policy. If modernism is to improve internal conditions for intellectual activity, a new generation of leaders is presumably required. But even modest Soviet efforts to maintain the appearances of legality may, over time, provide for a substantive increase in liberalization.

Finally, the question of what will happen when the prospective new leadership assumes power greatly affects United States interests but cannot be answered with confidence. The new generation of leaders will have had very low-level responsibilities in the Second World War or none at all. They will have assumed their first national authority during the 1960s and 1970s, when Soviet power was on the rise. It may be that they will develop a heady sense of adventurism or will assert Soviet interests in conflicts with the United States more boldly. They may make demands for political gains that reflect the relative increase in Soviet military power vis-à-vis that of the United States. But the rise of the modernist syndrome in Soviet politics shows some hopeful signs that the emphasis will be on openness and cooperation. It is certainly no less probable that a new generation of leadership will prefer to increase cooperation with the West and to adapt Soviet institutions to the needs of further modernization than that it will retain orthodox preferences. In fact, incipient economic difficulties will make steady access to the technological and monetary markets of the industrialized nations attractive.

INFLUENCING SOVIET POLICY

Supposing that an effective political consensus can be built in the United States with respect to the desired pattern of conflict and cooperation in Soviet-American relations, the issue still remains of how to influence Soviet behavior in a manner that maximizes the possibilities for achieving the desired relationship. There are, inevitably, conflicting impulses within both the Soviet Union and the United States toward conflict and cooperation. Both societies are very complex, with high degrees of bureaucratic and organizational differentiation. Congressional perceptions have not been identical with those of the State or Defense Departments. Thus what seems to one individual or organization to constitute conflictive behavior may seem to another no more than an aberration in a generally cooperative framework. Similar conflicts of perception exist in the U.S.S.R., and increasingly a kind of implicit alliance has grown up between parallel interests in Moscow and Washington. To take a very simple example, positions taken by Pentagon spokesmen in the American debate over defense spending have been prominently represented by people in Moscow who favor higher military budgets as evidence in support of their claims.[17]

One source of misperception seems likely to become more important in Soviet-American relations. The two societies will certainly adapt to pressures for change from the international environment at variable rates. For example, the American political system has shown more concern for problems of population, food production, and pressure on global resources. As these issues command additional political attention in the United

[17]The role such statements play in the Soviet budgetary debate is a complex one, yet the degree of reference to American doctrinal and budgetary developments is striking. For example, during the American debate over the retargeting of some Minuteman forces in 1974–75, which produced what came to be called the "Schlesinger Doctrine," the Soviet military press was full of comment. L. Semeyko's article in *Krasnaya zvezda*, April 8, 1975 is representative but by no means extreme. A similar spate of articles appeared in early 1977, when Soviet civil defense became an issue in the American defense budget process. See, for example, General A. I. Radziyevsky's interview in *Literaturnaya gazeta*, January 19, 1977. A less spectacular, but possibly more troubling case, is posed by Soviet reactions to American and NATO decisions to increase defense budgets during 1978. See, for example, the analysis of *Pravda* in its weekly survey of international affairs, August 13, 1978; and its summary of Warsaw Pact meetings in the Crimea during August, ibid., August 27, 1978.

States, issues arising from this country's relationship with the U.S.S.R. may suffer from inattention, or there may develop some inclination for accommodation with the Soviet Union in order to focus more policy attention on the newer issues. Such developments, should the Soviet leadership be relatively insulated from pressures to shift its own policy attention, may tempt it to underestimate the determination of the United States to protect its national interests.

The rate at which these countries adapt to pressures from the external environment for changes in policy priorities constitutes one potential source of increased misperception between them in the 1980s. The fact that different elements within each country will be more sensitive to the needs for change than others raises parallel but not identical opportunities for misperception. Sharp domestic struggles will inevitably result from the attempt to alter priorities, and factions will be tempted to manipulate the image of Soviet-American relations in order to serve bureaucratic purposes at home. For example, those in the U.S.S.R. favoring a shift of resources to the development of Siberia or to new technology may be more inclined to perceive that Soviet interests lie in cooperation than will those who resist such a shift.

The influence the United States might exercise over the Soviet leadership, therefore, depends to some degree on differentiating between Soviet interests for cooperation or conflict. But even the selection of a desirable pattern for the relationship from the American point of view and identification of those interests in Moscow that might be appealed to in coaxing Soviet policy in a direction which promotes that kind of relationship will be insufficient if American policy makers do not stick to trying to shape Soviet foreign policy choices and refrain from trying to change the domestic political structure. Similarly, it will be inappropriate for the Soviet Union to attempt to alter the nature of the American political system—by direct actions or by the support of "radical" political groups within it.

The Soviet Domestic Arena

The issue cannot be flinched away. Through the long history of the cold war, American foreign policy toward the U.S.S.R. has had a dual purpose. In addition to promoting a satisfactory relationship between the two states, policy has, for many Americans, carried the burden of encouraging change within the Soviet political system and within the socialist bloc. The eloquent call by Nobel Prize winner Alexander Solzhenitsyn in his AFL-CIO speech of June 1975 for American interference within Soviet domestic politics picked up a thread of United States policy that had woven itself into several years of congressional debate on trade with the Soviet Union, into the negotiations over "freer movement of people and ideas" in the Conference on Security and Cooperation in Europe (CSCE), and, eventually, would wind itself into President Carter's "human rights" campaign.[18]

That impulse is strong in American politics, but its strength does not make it wise. The position given such persuasive articulation by Solzhenitsyn holds that whatever differences might be detected between orthodox and modernist orientations in Soviet political life are quite small, that these differences do not apply to the most reprehensible characteristics of state police control on which the entire elite apparently agrees, and that the West risks its own moral health by lowering its guard against the threat of determined Marxists. On the other hand, these arguments also contain the judgment that change within the Soviet system, if it is to come at all, must come quickly and by radical means. Therefore, the argument carries the implication that an American and Western refusal to cooperate with the regime will force it to rely entirely on its own devices, which, in turn, will be proven inadequate, thus forcing the Soviet system to change dramatically in order to survive. This impulse in American political life to interfere in Soviet domestic politics limits the range of options available to American policy in managing the external relationship between the two countries. In a sense, these policy objectives may be competitive.

Three arguments suggest that attempts to alter the internal Soviet regime are inappropriate objectives for American policy. First, the United States' capacity to affect either the nature of the Soviet political system or the composition of the socialist interstate system is quite limited. The Soviets are not dependent

[18]*The Washington Post,* July 6, 1975, pp. C1–C2.

on most kinds of American cooperation any more than the United States is dependent on most kinds of Soviet cooperation.

Trade is normally advanced as the most effective lever, whose denial will change Kremlin policies. But the example of the 1974 Trade Bill is instructive. The quantitative lever of American and Western trade simply is not adequate to the task. Total Soviet trade turnover (imports + exports) exceeded $86 billion in 1977, of which $25 billion (about 29%) came from or went to the industrialized nations. But trade with the United States amounted to only $1.85 billion for 1977 and $2.76 billion for 1978, of which grain deliveries from the United States amounted to $810 million. To put these figures in perspective, although the dollar value of Soviet trade has increased impressively during the period of détente, the total turnover with the West amounted to less than 3 percent of the Soviet Union's $1,047 billion GNP, and the American slice of this Western trade was considerably less than 10 percent. While selective economic requirements seem to constitute adequate incentives to trade, the existence of alternative sources for Soviet imports, the small dimensions of Soviet-American trade, and Soviet interest in avoiding dependency or the appearance of dependency mean that the denial of trade cannot achieve dramatic Soviet concessions.

Second, pressure by the United States on Soviet domestic policies or Soviet relations with the socialist states, while it has achieved some short-term concessions in the past, has often provided those in the Soviet leadership who have the most orthodox ideological concept of Soviet-American relations with material for making their case that the aims of United States policy are ideological and require an ideological response. Thus one consequence of such pressure is often the strengthening of those impulses in the U.S.S.R. most reprehensible to the very public in the United States that advocated putting pressure on the Soviet Union.

Finally, Roy Medvedev, the dissident Soviet historian, has made a third argument for not attempting to effect changes in the Soviet political system by means of outside pressure: even if those changes are deemed desirable and an appropriate end of policy, they will more likely be achieved by emphasizing cooperation in the United States–U.S.S.R. relationship than by attempting to exact concessions in some areas as a price for cooperation elsewhere.[19] To attempt linkage by threatening to forego some cooperative effort (e.g., SALT) in an attempt to get the other side to modify its position on a question of conflicting interests (e.g., Jewish emigration) supposes that the latter issue is more important than the former in any case. But Medvedev's point is more profound. He has argued that reform of Soviet political life will have to come from internal sources and not external ones, that external pressure will only strengthen those elements of Soviet society most resistant to reform. He has argued that the surest method to change Soviet social structure is by creating a prolonged era of cooperation, of integrating the Soviet Union as fully into the international order as possible. Peaceful relations will promote the interests of individuals with the greatest stake in cooperation, and will weaken the position of those who argue that the external threat to communism is the justification for repression at home.

Those who, like Solzhenitsyn, attempt to make transformation of the Soviet political system a goal of American policy argue that the issue of interference by the United States in Soviet internal or socialist bloc affairs is a moral one. It does, of course, involve hard choices among moral values. On the one hand, it is contended that cooperation to reduce the risk of war is itself a moral value, and it is hoped that by stressing cooperation in the Soviet-American relationship the evolution of the Soviet political system might blunt its most repressive features. In opposition stands the contention that amelioration of restrictions on the right of national and democratic minorities to emigrate, a reduction of arbitrary police rule, and assertion of rule by law are moral prerequisites for meaningful cooperation, and their achievement should constitute primary objectives of United States policy. But as Secretary of State Kissinger has argued,

[19]To the knowledge of the author, this excellent and important statement is available only in a translation by Radio Liberty: R. A. Medvedev, "The Problem of Democratization and the Problem of Détente," Radio Liberty, November 19, 1973. An article based on the piece was written by Hedrick Smith in the *New York Times,* November 8, 1973.

the issue is purely a moral one—a choice between different moral values and not a choice between moral values on one side and political values on the other.[20]

It is possible, then, to urge a policy that avoids explicit efforts to influence the nature of the Soviet domestic regime, even while recognizing that the Soviet leadership itself has a general, long-range commitment to altering the internal system of the United States. By the mid-1970s, American vision on these ideological questions had become badly out of focus. The foreign policy of Presidents Nixon and Ford and Secretary of State Kissinger toward the Soviet Union has been represented as overly rational, based on "realpolitik," Machiavellian, divorced from the "heart" of the American people on the one hand, and "soft" toward the Russians on the other.

These criticisms of past administrations do not concern the current argument. It is not an unusual fate for losers in politics. But it is more serious if the détente policy toward the Soviet Union has suffered from American disillusionment with wiretapping at home, with CIA and FBI excesses, with Watergate, and a president's resignation in disgrace.

The process by which the détente policy has come under attack since 1974 has been complicated. The decline in Soviet-American relations can be explained partly by the initiative of the right in American politics, which has seized upon the general public's disillusionment with the Nixon years to alter the national mood. Even the China opening has been turned into an anti-Soviet policy. For their part, the Soviet leadership has been extraordinarily insensitive to the impact on this shifting American mood of their continued military build-up, their intervention in Africa, and their ongoing repression of dissent at home. Still, the American domestic political tragedy has blurred the nation's vision of the Soviet-American relationship. The years 1969–1974 were ones of solid achievement in that relationship. While it was natural for American politics to reach back toward its simpler, pop-

[20]Mr. Kissinger said this in a statement to the Senate Foreign Relations Committee, September 19, 1974, Department of State, *Special Report*, Washington, D.C., 1974.

ulist roots after things had so obviously gone wrong in the Vietnam and Nixon years, it would be a serious mistake to adopt either the isolationism or the moral crusading that characterized American foreign policy in those possibly easier years before the achievement of world power and responsibility.

It may be desirable to infuse American political life with a higher moral content, to draw attention to the values on which a system of law, of human rights, or representative government is based. But to take the further step of drawing self-serving comparisons between the United States and the Soviet Union is likely to exaggerate the virtues of the former and the evils of the latter. To move in Soviet-American relations toward renewed emphasis on the "moral good" of democracy and capitalism and the "evil" of communism is to take a long stride backward toward the cold war and a more dangerous world.

The position of Roy Medvedev seems wiser to this author than the one advanced by Alexander Solzhenitsyn. American policy should concentrate on the management of conflict and extension of cooperation in its relationship with the Soviet Union. For the 1980s that objective will be sufficiently taxing. It may be that changes within either country will come partially as a result of emphasizing cooperative interests across time, but it is inappropriate to base the relationship on explicit demands that changes be made in the domestic system of the adversary.

Soviet Foreign Policy

The proposition that the United States should eschew making the alteration of the internal political system of the Soviet Union a foreign policy goal can hardly be considered exceptional. America's capacity for inducing change in Soviet society is slight in any case, and the expectation that countries must conduct their domestic affairs in a manner worthy of American approbation has been grafted onto the foreign policy of the United States largely in the years since 1945. Furthermore, that expectation has been applied in the most inconsistent manner, and its projection into the conduct of American foreign policy will inevitably create unnecessary divisiveness at home. It is far more

107

appropriate, then, to reduce the question of influence to an examination of the kinds of Soviet behavior in world politics that might be considered desirable during the 1980s from the perspective of American interests and from the perspective of a stable international order.

Even with respect to Soviet foreign and defense policies, the issue of American influence involves several kinds of difficulties. First, it may be that the United States cannot affect some kinds of Soviet foreign and security policies nor modify the actions of the U.S.S.R. in international affairs without achieving a broad consensus among its various foreign policy constituencies about what constitutes intolerable and acceptable Soviet behavior. For example, policy that attempts to moderate Soviet support for national liberation in Africa, Asia, and Latin America is likely to be particularly divisive in the United States, especially if the spectre of Vietnam is raised. There is no reason to suppose that it will be any easier to achieve consensus on such issues in the 1980s than it was in the 1960s or 1970s, unless one assumes a substantial deterioration of Soviet-American relations, which might induce the kind of broad consensus associated with the most threatening days of the cold war. Second, even if the difficulties of consensus can be overcome in the United States, the closed nature of the Soviet system makes it very difficult to identify which points within the system would be appropriate to influence. And, even if it were possible to identify factions or individuals whom American policy should attempt to influence, access by the United States or by any external influences is severely limited and jealously resisted by the entire Soviet elite.

In the long run, each society may gamble that peaceful competition will modify the domestic system of the other in ways more satisfactory to its own values. In fact, it is possible that history will be enriched by this mutual gamble. The problems of the last quarter of the twentieth century and the twenty-first century seem certain to confound the stereotypes of eighteenth- and nineteenth-century political philosophy. Marxism, Leninism, capitalism, liberalism, positivism—none of these is likely to chart the way through the twenty-first century. It is just possible that a persistent effort by both American and Soviet societies to meet the emerging challenges, combined with the efforts of other societies organized by quite divergent patterns of political and economic experiment, will provide the creative solutions that will be required. It may be in the interests of each country that the other is working at these problems with very different assumptions and forms of political, economic, and social organization.

This vision, however, projects further into an uncertain future than does the focus of the present study. Our concern is with the far more concrete mid-range problems of getting from the present to the twenty-first century in one piece. In the 1980s the principal concern of decision makers must continue to be the *means* applied by both the Soviet Union and the United States to achieve their short-range policy objectives. The concern of this study, then, is squarely on foreign policy—on what these two nations *do* in the international system.

CONCLUSION

It might be argued that there is little concrete evidence that the "younger generation" of CPSU leaders, which will become increasingly important in the 1980s, supports modernism. The absence of such evidence, however, reflects what was described above as the Soviet tendency toward "functional silence." It should not be interpreted as evidence of the contrary proposition, that younger party leaders have orthodox preferences and will return to a foreign policy of confrontation. On the contrary, the experience of the post-Stalin years may repeat itself: after a period in which the leadership sorts itself out, years of silent dissent will give way to the sudden assertion (as at the Twentieth Party Congress in 1956) of a reformist program. Although that possibility cannot be predicted with any certainty, and although we should remember that Khrushchev's reformist domestic policies were accompanied by a more vigorous, if blustery, assertion of Soviet interests in Berlin, the Middle East, and the Formosan Straits, cautious and firm American policies stressing mutual interests seem more likely to encourage modernist impulses among any new generation of leadership. It is certainly more likely that the new leadership will evolve policies in support of cooperation if it is not faced with a number of critical defense decisions at the same time it faces tough decisions forced by declining rates of growth in GNP. Thus the benefits of opening an arms control alternative to new defense programs and of offering trade as a means of economic revitalization would seem to be particularly desirable in a time when a new leadership is settling into its pattern of decisions. It should be expected, of course, that no new leadership will choose to appear ''soft'' on capitalism or imperialism, but a mature American and Western leadership should be able to weather demonstrations of Marxist and Soviet toughness and still nurse the relationship in a cooperative direction.

FOUR

Strategies of Economic Interaction

An unfortunate cast has developed to much of the discussion in the United States about economic relations with the Soviet Union. It is difficult for the nonideological observer to avoid some sympathy with the Soviet analyst who concluded that many Americans believe that the

Soviet Union is a "colossus with feet of clay," that it is more interested in détente and in economic ties with the West than the West with it, and that this makes it possible to "squeeze" more unilateral concessions from the U.S.S.R.[1]

The habits of the cold war die slowly. Trade has more often been discussed as a "lever," as a tool to some other policy end, rather than as a legitimate goal of its own. The debates surrounding the Jackson Amendment, in fact the whole discussion of most favored nation (MFN) treatment for the Soviet Union, have often had the ring of the cold war. The notion has developed a wide following that the carrot of American trade might be used to pry concessions out of the Soviet Union—the emigration of Jews or enforcement of Basket Three provisions of the Final Act of the Conference on Security and Cooperation in Europe (CSCE). Moreover, the entire notion of "linkages," made popular in other contexts by Secretary of State Henry Kissinger and reintroduced by the Carter administration in the context of the

[1]G. Arbatov, *Pravda,* August 3, 1977.

Ethiopian-Somali conflict, contains similar assumptions about the Soviet Union's "feet of clay." The notion that the United States could withhold agreement on SALT II to obtain Soviet endorsement of American-sponsored terms in the Middle East and in the Horn of Africa, or the notion that force reductions in Europe and collateral restraints on military activity by the Warsaw Pact could be sacrificed to elicit agreement on measures for the "freer movement of people and ideas" in the CSCE negotiations—all of these kinds of linkage imply that the Soviet Union has a greater interest in trade, or in arms control, than does the United States or NATO. While these may constitute examples of astute diplomatic bargaining, in which context Soviet efforts to break the linkage also constitute the legitimate exercise of their diplomacy, they do reveal a common assumption about Soviet power. The assumption, and therefore the wisdom of linking one interest to the other, can be effectively challenged.

There is a fine, but meaningful, distinction between using trade as a lever to force Soviet concessions on tangential issues and encouraging trade because it makes good economic sense and because it constitutes part of the internal program of modernist or reformist members in the CPSU. Chapter 3 contended that the modernist orientation in Soviet politics advocates foreign trade with capitalist states, partly as a means of acquiring the benefits of the scientific-technical revolution. Trade, then, may have the incidental political benefit of encouraging modernist policy preferences in the Kremlin, and the long-range effect of such a policy by the United States might be to encourage adaptation within the U.S.S.R. and a more cooperative foreign policy. But the time frame is longer than that implied in the strategy of withholding MFN to achieve immediate policy goals—like emigration—or of denying individual economic agreements—like Control Data's Cyber 76—in part as a signal of commitment to "human rights" or of displeasure with the state of the overall relationship.

It was argued in Chapter 3 that the level of American trade with the Soviet Union is so small a portion of total Soviet trade, and trade so small a feature in Soviet GNP, that leverage is not great in any case. But in looking to the 1980s the question of strategy becomes far more important. If Soviet-American trade is to develop as its partisans on both sides believe it can, the volume may become far more impressive, and it may become even more tempting to create linkages between immediate economic benefits and political objectives. What faces the United States, and increasingly perhaps also the Soviet Union, is a choice between two strategies.

On the one hand, either leadership may choose the strategy of the Trojan Horse. In this conception, economic relations are conceived as a means of getting inside the walls of the adversary's system. As the quantity of trade increases, or as it develops in certain areas critical to the other side, it is seen as a lever to exact concessions in the broader negotiating framework between the two superpowers. Elements of cooperative behavior are conceived as bargaining chips to be used in managing conflictive behavior between the players. This strategy is shortsighted and self-defeating.

Even if the United States might seem to have the stronger hand in the current economic relationship with the Soviet Union, any Soviet leadership will have a strong political interest in breaking linkages between trade and political concessions. Thus the bargaining chips, if they exist at all, can hardly be played often. More importantly, such a strategy almost inevitably places severe limits on the quantity of trade. After the experience of the 1970s— with large American deficits in the balance of payments and the uncertainty of future oil supplies—it is arguable that increased trade with the Soviet Union is at least as much in American interests as long as the Kremlin is willing to run trade deficits and has the convertible hard currency to pay for them. If Siberian energy resources are considered in these calculations, OECD's energy-consuming nations actually have larger interests in high levels of trade organized by stable, businesslike ground rules. It is possible that the United States will actually participate in developing and buying Siberia-based raw materials, in which case the temptation to use trade as a political lever might be reversed. Even if the United States declines such partnership, some or all of its pluralist-capitalist competitors will probably expand the levels of their economic activity with the Soviet Union and its socialist partners. In either case, Western economic activity in the Soviet Union is likely to increase in the 1980s, and the utility of American trade as a political lever will decline.

Trade conceived as a Trojan Horse will certainly be erratic. In years of Soviet vulnerability, especially of bad weather and poor harvests, trade might be large and leverage might be effective. But the Soviet interest in breaking these linkages would inevitably mean that in years of relative strength the Kremlin would reduce trade with the United States as far as possible. This pattern of large orders in some years and small ones in other years can almost certainly be far more easily sustained by a state trading organization faced with numerous capitalist sellers than by a pluralist and democratic system open to the pressures of trade unions and business. In fact, it is arguable that even the question of overall trade levels, as distinguished from the issue of fluctuating levels, places the state trader at an advantage. To the degree that the political linkage strategy depresses the volume of trade turnover, it probably places the United States government in conflict with its own commercial and labor interests.

An alternative strategy exists: the strategy of the Yankee Trader. This supposes that American businessmen have long been perfectly capable of deciding when trade is in their commercial interests. This strategy does not advocate totally a laissez faire approach to trade. On the contrary, while sharp disagreements have arisen on specific items—like the Cyber 76—there has been amazingly general agreement among business, national defense, and foreign policy groups that some controls must be exercised over technological transfers to the Soviet Union on the grounds of national security. With this exception, the Yankee Trader strategy assumes that political considerations intrude as little as possible on economic ones. The strategy does not need to be politically naive. It holds that trade does have political effects, but its time horizon is longer than that of the Trojan Horse strategy. Trade by itself opens the Soviet system. Moreover, it encourages the modest, incremental, political adaptation promised by the modernist persuasion in Soviet political life. The Yankee Trader strategy, then, offers higher levels of trade turnover, a more stable climate of economic relations, and the prospect that by bringing the Soviet Union into a long-term

114

economic relationship with other industrialized nations Soviet interest in a cooperative international system is increased. Furthermore, the effect of these international interests, over decades or even generations, may well be to modify the harshest aspects of Soviet political life at home.

Particular Soviet economic difficulties discussed in Chapter 2 contain serious implications for Soviet international behavior and therefore for Soviet-American relations. The current Soviet leadership's emphasis on increasing productivity and efficiency, and the argument in Chapter 2 that the rate of growth of Soviet GNP will decline in the 1980s, suggest a coming crunch in several key factor inputs to the Soviet economy. For example, increments to the labor force will fall precipitously during the late 1970s and early 1980s.[2] Although they will increase slightly after 1986, additions to the working-age population will remain below levels enjoyed in the 1950s and 1960s. Another example of declining factor inputs for economic growth was provided by the speculation that petroleum output would drop below consumption. While natural gas production and, possibly to a lesser degree, coal production will continue to increase, these increases are not likely to offset declining petroleum output. It seems almost certain that annual net increases in energy output will fall at least during the first half of the 1980s. High rates of growth for the Soviet GNP have traditionally reflected comparable or higher rates of growth in energy output and have relied on a large and expanding labor force. Another declining factor input, which the current Five-Year Plan anticipates cutting by more than half, is new fixed investment, substituted by renovation of older enterprises. Furthermore, a shift in emphasis away from new plant construction toward renovation and modernization of fixed capital assets increases the incentive to import technology. The Soviet construction industry is largely autarkic, and technological modernization of equipment is relatively dependent on foreign markets.

The combination of these factors provides strong incentives

[2]Central Intelligence Agency, *USSR: Some Implications of Demographic Trends for Economic Policies,* January 1977; also Central Intelligence Agency, *The Soviet Economy in 1976–77 and Outlook for 1978,* p. 8.

for trade. Imports of these kinds of technology, however, will compete with the Soviet need to import energy. If the economic leadership does not find means to alter petroleum production and consumption patterns, the U.S.S.R. might have to purchase oil for domestic consumption on the world market by 1985. The most immediate consequence of such a development would be a reduction of Soviet supplies of oil to its CMEA partners. Moscow increased the prices of its raw material supplies to its East European partners following the worldwide increase in oil prices during 1973–74.[3] None of its options in the event its own oil production falls below its consumption requirements is likely to be attractive, and all would have serious consequences for the international system.

If the Soviet Union reduces supplies to its CMEA partners or refuses to make them at all, East European governments will be forced into the world market, thereby reducing Soviet influence and CMEA's much-advertised solidarity under the Comprehensive Plan of 1971. The CMEA could enter world petroleum markets as a unit, which would at least preserve the appearance of unity. But either case would place added inflationary pressures on oil and alternative energy sources, and increased energy costs will put additional downward pressure on economic growth in socialist states.

It is, moreover, utterly without peacetime precedent that the Soviet Union should find itself dependent on external sources of any commodity as basic as oil, and the strong autarkic biases of Soviet planning would certainly be put under considerable strain. East European leaders would be subjected to even greater strains, especially in Poland, Hungary, and Czechoslovakia, where consumerism has gained considerable influence already. These governments will also be relatively more exposed to developments in Western European communism, and the combi-

---

[3]CMEA sources are very reluctant to discuss pricing publicly, but there have been rather explicit references in Soviet sources to price increases for raw materials exported to CMEA partners. See the article by N. Mitrofanov, *Planovoye khozyaistvo,* no. 4, April 1974, pp. 41–49; by A. I. Zubkov, *Istoria SSSR,* no. 1, January-February, 1976, pp. 52–70; and by V. Rybalkin, *Planovoye khozyaistvo,* no. 6, June 1976, pp. 47–53.

nation of pressure on economic growth and a probable continued demonstration of ideological dynamism in Eurocommunism may create irresistible pressures for reform. Both the need of the Soviet Union and CMEA for guaranteed external sources of oil supply and the possibility of political instability in the Eastern European states may tempt the Kremlin leadership to experiment with military solutions. It is not conceivable that these kinds of pressures could be tolerated without at least some exercise of Soviet power.

To some extent the labor-power problem cuts in the opposite direction. As the labor supply continues to contract, and if major improvements in productivity are not forthcoming, some pressures may develop to reduce military manpower and costs. As Chapter 2 suggested, however, this is not likely. Military demands on the economy have had first priority, and that pattern is deeply ingrained in Soviet and Russian culture.

Projections for the Soviet economy, then, create a two-edged sword, cutting both in the direction of cooperation and conflict. Current and probable future plans make increased levels of trade attractive to the Soviet leadership. In particular, Soviet requirements for long-term credits on a continuing basis make stable and cooperative relations necessary. On the other hand, declining production of oil will almost certainly foster greater competition between the Soviet Union and its socialist allies, and other industrialized nations. The Soviet Union's shift toward foreign markets to meet some of its primary energy needs may increase political competition, especially in the Middle East, and may induce strain in Soviet relations with its Warsaw Pact partners.

This fundamental ambiguity between the attractions of cooperation with the United States and the possible temptation to employ Soviet power in resolving the inevitable problems of economic adjustment is likely to persist throughout the 1980s. It will certainly once again bring to the fore the issues of modernism versus orthodoxy in debates within the Soviet leadership. Soviet responses to the new economic environment will most likely fluctuate, and different leaders will probably emerge at different times as the post-Brezhnev leadership wrestles with these difficult choices. But the interest in cooperation, especially with respect to the importation of technology, is very strong. By making trade with the United States possible for the Soviet Union and by adopting the Yankee Trader strategy for Soviet-American relations, the United States can support the modernist impulse in Soviet politics and economics.

FIVE

Stability in the Strategic Relationship

The Soviet-American relationship rests firmly on the bedrock of its capacity to sustain stability in strategic weapons. And that stability depends, in turn, on mutual deterrence: on the mutually held perception that the costs to either power of a nuclear conflict between them are absolutely unacceptable. In fact, it is mutually understood that those costs are so high that the direct inhibition against nuclear conflict extends constraints to other conflicts in which the risks of escalation to nuclear conflict are uncertain. Furthermore, this stability in the Soviet-American strategic relationship depends on the fact that each power has nuclear weapons in such numbers that it enjoys reasonable confidence that no sudden development in the capability of the other can disarm the credibility of its own deterrent.

This understanding of the strategic relationship can be, and should be, elaborated. It implies an irreducible, countervalue nuclear strategy: that whatever happens in the strategic balance between the United States and the U.S.S.R. will happen slowly and, at least in the short run, that no technological development or clandestine alteration of defense posture could deny either power's capacity to destroy both an intolerable number of its adversary's cities and its economic infrastructure. This "mutually assured destruction" (MAD) is the foundation of the confidence that each power is deterred from choosing war with the other as a rational policy. But obviously it is not the end of strategy for either side. MAD simply constitutes the "bottom line" of deterrence. Many strategists, including former Secretary of Defense James Schlesinger, contended that MAD was not stable and that stability could be increased by retargeting even American second-strike forces away from a countercity to a counterforce mode.[1] He argued that no American president, having experienced a disarming first strike against American land-based ICBMs and the Strategic Air Command, should be left only with the option of retaliating against an enemy's cities alone when to do so would invite the certain destruction of American cities as well. While the retargeting of second-strike forces provoked controversy, most analysts agree that a first-strike force that possesses only countervalue capabilities is destabilizing and has limited deterrent value, especially if it is opposed by counterforce capabilities.

The proposition that at rock bottom the Soviet-American strategic relationship rests on confident second-strike and countervalue capacity is not meant to deny the possible desirability of retaining or developing other strategic options which may upgrade deterrence, hence stability. Rather, the strategic relationship is assumed, ultimately, to be endowed with substantial stability because the minimum deterrence of a countervalue second strike cannot easily or quickly be denied by *any* foreseeable strategic development between the superpowers.

This condition of minimum deterrence, however, is not one which occupies many military strategists or arms control planners in Moscow or Washington. Their workdays, and possibly their nightmares, are occupied by far more complicated issues. Nonetheless, minimum deterrence and the fundamental stability it implies for Soviet-American strategic relations may help explain the demonstrated intolerance of the general public and even the Congress for the analytical refinements of professionals who follow these issues. This basic condition—that neither side can deny the other its capacity for a second strike capable of inflicting

[1]The best statements are contained in his reports to Congress in 1974 and 1975. James R. Schlesinger, *Annual Defense Department Report,* FY 1975, Washington, D.C., March 4, 1974, pp. 32–45; and *Annual Defense Department Report,* FY 1976 and FY 1977, February 5, 1975, pp. II-1 to II-11.

unacceptable damage—defines the need for cooperation and prescribes boundaries for conflict between the superpowers.

Neither the United States nor the Soviet Union has ever limited its expectations for strategic weapons simply to minimum deterrence. Each has made explicit or implicit threats to employ strategic nuclear weapons in securing or protecting its political interests. This diplomatic behavior imparts far more exacting standards to the credibility of deterrence. "Deterrence" implies forestalling war, but diplomatic use of strategic threats requires credible war-fighting capability, including usable nuclear arsenals. This condition represents a fundamental dilemma for strategic thinking and for international politics.

The conflictive side of Soviet-American relations has meant that both Washington and Moscow have perceived that military capabilities are required to secure national interests. At one level, that perception has provided each with the incentive to maintain impressive conventional, war-fighting capabilities. But at another level, strategic forces must also be usable. That is, to be credible in extending deterrence to the protection of political interests, strategic nuclear forces must be capable of graduated response. Minimum deterrence implies that strategic weapons be used in only one scenario: a single, second-strike, countervalue salvo. But the political requirement for strategic forces implies more complicated scenarios. Strategic weapons must be scaled to a variety of uses.

The dilemma is this: credible deterrence in many scenarios requires that strategic forces be usable, but usability may erode the deterrence of Armageddon itself. This is one fundamental way in which the political demands made on the Soviet-American strategic relationship have strained its stability.

Political demands have threatened the management of the strategic relationship in other ways. On both sides demands have been made for military forces whose ultimate logic is clearly based on the hope for superiority. However, the size of defense efforts on both sides, and the capacity of each economy to sustain those efforts, means that superiority is a mirage. The size, variety, and technological competition of those same defense efforts also mean that ambiguities will persist in the military balance between them. That ambiguity ensures that the military balance will be a political issue in both capitals.

In the 1970s especially, the strategic relationship and arms control negotiations designed to manage it have been made to carry the weight of quite separate political issues, especially on the American side. This, again, is the notion of linkages discussed in the preceding chapter. The Strategic Arms Limitation Talks (SALT) have come to symbolize the broader détente relationship, and successive American leaderships have threatened to sacrifice cooperation with the Soviet Union in the SALT process when confronted with evidence of conflict with the Soviet Union on other issues. Such attempts were made in the Angolan, Middle Eastern, and Ethiopian-Somali conflicts.[2] At a time when technological developments in strategic weaponry are themselves placing the process under considerable strain, it can be argued that SALT cannot sustain responsibility for solving other issues by this process of linkage.

Finally, SALT has clearly been affected by conflicting bureaucratic politics in both Washington and Moscow. Especially between January and November 1975, the SALT II process came to be focused primarily along the Potomac, as various bureaucratic and political interests bargained over the B-1 bomber, cruise missiles, the MX, and the meaning of Soviet strategic programs. The Vladivostok guidelines went aground for many months primarily on the rocks of Washington's bureaucratic process and of technological developments.[3]

It may be that in the 1980s the strategic relationship and the consequent system of constraints against the use of military power will experience further erosion. In fact, *the* central issue

[2]See Secretary Kissinger's December 23, 1975 news conference on Angola, *New York Times,* December 24, 1975; on Ethiopia and Somalia, see President Carter's speech at Wake Forest University, ibid., March 18, 1978, and an interview by Terrence Smith with Zbigniew Brzezinski, ibid., March 20, 1978.

[3]This story became public during the summer, after the Soviets began to insist on including cruise missiles in SALT II. See John W. Finney's article, "New U.S. Missile Snags Arms Talks," *New York Times,* June 16, 1975, pp. 1, 16; and coverage of the Ford/Brezhnev meeting in Helsinki, ibid., August 3, 1975.

of Soviet-American relations may be whether the political will can be found to resist the erosion of deterrence. In a sense, we have learned in the tortuous negotiations over SALT II that expectations for arms control have placed too large a political burden on the process. The United States and the Soviet Union face a fundamental choice about the purposes of managing the strategic relationship. Given military parity between them, strategic arms limitations will be successful if the agreements advance three simple goals: reducing the risks of nuclear war by channeling arms competition into the least unpredictable and least destabilizing systems; reducing the damage of war should it occur by building a structure of doctrinal understanding and habits of communication; and increasing confidence of allies and other actors in the international system that the superpowers have the will and wisdom to control their military relationship. If these goals are pursued patiently and with determination and if both sides resist the temptation to encumber the negotiating process with impossible demands that tangential issues be solved and that absolute margins of security be retained or achieved in particular features of the arms competition, then political confidence will grow and the stability of the relationship will be shored up.

The strategic relationship, however, is threatened along a technological axis in addition to the political one. The strategic military balance could be threatened across time either by excessive political expectations about the processes by which we manage it or by technological developments which seem to proceed in many ways independent of those processes. It is improbable that a single technological development would hold such promise of strategic advantage that either leadership would choose to forfeit political cooperation as a result. The military advantages to be achieved are marginal and the political risks of pursuing them substantial. However, the symbiosis of placing unrealistic and extensive political demands on bilateral strategic arms control and the uncertainties of technology might well undermine the determination of either or both sides to manage their strategic relationship. The strategic balance and the perception of stability may be more fragile than we have assumed during much of the

1970s, and prudence in planning for the 1980s requires that we anticipate the directions of technological uncertainty.

STRATEGIC WEAPONS

It cannot be altogether discounted, although it may be improbable, that a single technological development or a combination of several in the next ten years might destroy confidence in minimum deterrence. General Secretary Brezhnev, at the Twenty-Fifth Party Congress in February 1976, repeated a vague reference heard before from Soviet leaders to "new types and systems of weapons of mass destruction."[4] Although that reference was in one place (but not in another) linked to the American Trident submarine and B-1 bomber systems, in the previous year the reference had occasionally been to "new categories of mass destruction weapons," those "more terrible than the nuclear weapon."

Such references have always been made in the context of statements supporting arms control agreements to assure the banning of such weapons systems, but also suggest that the present Kremlin leadership is cognizant that deterioration of the strategic relationship might come from technological developments. The most probable technological threats to the strategic balance, however, would seem to be not the evolution of new weapons of mass destruction, as Brezhnev has worried publicly, but the development of new "supporting technology" for current forms of thermonuclear power. For example, laser technology may open the way to defense systems that would erode the assuredness of an effective second strike; antisatellite technology may disrupt command, control, and communications and, hence, either side's confidence in verification of arms control agreements and its ability to exercise restraint in crises; or technological advances in antisubmarine warfare (ASW) and satellite surveillance may reduce the invulnerability of mobile weapons systems

---

[4]*Pravda*, February 25, 1976. He had made the same point in a speech to his constituents six months earlier, ibid., June 14, 1975.

on which the current stability of assured second-strike capability depends.

Strategic stability, then, is assumed to require at least an invulnerable second-strike capability on both sides of the American-Soviet balance. More weapons, larger warheads, more powerful delivery vehicles, more accurate targeting, even arms control measures that reduce the numbers of weapons—all of these developments may or may not promote stability. The strategic effect of any of these technological developments depends on how it affects survival and deliverability of sufficient retaliatory weapons following the absorption of a first strike to make a credible and unacceptable second strike against the attacker. Retention of such a second-strike capability is assumed to deter any rational employment of a first strike and, hence, to promote international stability and to reduce the chances of war between the Soviet Union and the United States.

Assuming, then, no radical technological breakthroughs will threaten the viability of American-Soviet second-strike capabilities in the 1980s and that threats to that stability are more likely to take place by incremental developments in current ICBM/SLBM technologies and in defenses against them, several directions of potential technological development can be discerned by which the strategic balance might be eroded.

Quantitative Increases

The most remarkable feature of the strategic balance during the past decade has been the quantitative increase in deliverable nuclear warheads. In 1966, the United States had 904 ICBMs and 592 SLBMs, each with a single warhead. Only the 630 B-52s carried more than one nuclear weapon each. The total deliverable United States warheads, counting only the Hound Dog air-to-surface missiles (ASMs) aboard the B-52s and not their payloads in more conventional bombing missions, was on the order of 2,700. The figure for the U.S.S.R. was, making parallel assumptions about bombers, certainly no more than 600. In 1979 the figures for the United States are at least 11,000 deliverable warheads and for the U.S.S.R. not more than 5,000 using the SALT II method of counting all missiles as having the maximum number of MIRV warheads with which they have been tested. Assuming that SALT II rules continue in force to 1985 (an aggregate ceiling of 2250 delivery vehicles (DVs), an aggregate ceiling of 1320 MIRVs, and subceilings for MIRVs of 1200 on SLBMs, 1CBMs and ASBMs of which only 820 may be placed on ICBMs) and assuming that each side will maximize the number of warheads but will retain roughly the current ICBM/SLBM mix of weapons, the United States will have something under 10,000 re-entry vehicles (RVs) and the Soviet Union approximately 7,000 in the mid-1980s.[5]

This quantitative increase in deliverable warheads is not automatically destabilizing. In fact, increases in the ratio between RVs and DVs can be argued to be stabilizing. As the destructive capacity of each DV increases, deterrence improves because a second strike of unacceptable risk to any potential attacker is guaranteed by the survival of a smaller number of missiles, each carrying more RVs. Thus, MIRV might have been seen historically as a stabilizing development. But, in fact, it is hard to argue at the turn of the 1980s that MIRV has done anything but complicate the strategic balance between the superpowers.

MIRV has been the central strategic development of the 1970s, and the United States deployed this decisive new technology with what seems in retrospect appallingly little national debate. The problem with the argument that increases in RV:DV ratios are stabilizing is the familiar one of perception colored by national bias. When the Soviets began to test, then deploy, their series of new MIRVed missiles (the SS-17s, 18s, and 19s) in the mid-1970s, the perception in Washington changed and gave rise to the Schlesinger Doctrine. Especially the large SS-18 worried Ameri-

[5]This assumes for the Soviet side 300 SS-18s with ten warheads, 520 SS-17s and 19s averaging 5 warheads, 500 SS-N-6s and SS-N17s and 18s averaging 3 warheads, 930 SLBMs and ICBMs with single warheads; for the American side 550 Minuteman IIIs with 3 warheads, 192 SLBMs in 12 Poseidon boats backfitted with Trident I missiles with 7 warheads, 7 Trident submarines carrying 24 missiles each with 7 warheads, 304 Poseidon missiles with 14 warheads, and 450 Minuteman II missiles with single warheads. Note that these projections upgrade Soviet deployment rates on several weapons systems.

can strategists. In that system, very high RV:DV ratios seemed possible, and the possibility that the Soviets might undertake a pre-emptive strike against American land-based Minuteman ICBMs and bombers loomed ominously. Higher RV:DV ratios coupled with hard-site accuracy of the kind the Soviets were projected to achieve in the early 1980s now seemed destabilizing. The nightmare was this: the Soviets might launch a first strike against the 1,000 American Minutemen with only a very small portion of their ICBM force (say, 300 SS-18s each armed with 10 RVs). An American President might, then, face the decision of attacking Soviet cities with his remaining nuclear forces (principally SLBMs) while the Soviet Union still retained the largest portion of its own ICBM fleet to hold American cities hostage against that threat.

The dilemma is fundamental, and inescapable. On the one hand, quantitative increases in RVs coupled with improved accuracies have made fixed-site, land-based DVs vulnerable to counter-force attack. Thus the possibility that either side's forces might be used in a pre-emptive first strike has become technically more feasible. On the other hand, each missile which survives a first strike carries more RVs, thusly making a second strike more devastating and thereby increasing deterrence. Whether highly accurate MIRVs are stabilizing second-strike weapons or destabilizing first-strike ones depends on the mind set and bias of the analyst. But it clearly takes an incredible and naive act of national faith to see "ours" as stabilizing and "theirs" as destabilizing.

The SALT II agreements are helpful—whether they are ratified by each side or remain in force by tacit agreement. They limit each side to a single, new, "light" ICBM. They establish aggregate ceilings on numbers of DVs, and they limit the number of RVs that can be deployed on each. Combined, these ceilings reduce the uncertainties of the strategic environment. It was, after all, uncertainty over the pace and number of new Soviet programs in the 1970s which contributed significantly to the alteration of mood in Washington regarding the overall superpower relationship.

However, rapid changes in the RV:DV ratio may be possible during the 1980s in the absence of SALT II and of continued political determination to extend the framework of strategic arms limitations. Even with SALT II, the Soviets will certainly develop their SLBM MIRV technology and will probably deploy a new ICBM as well. The United States will deploy the TRIDENT SLBM force and may deploy the expensive new MX ICBM. Cruise missiles are certain to complicate the strategic and tactical nuclear balances, and the impact of all these developments threatens to alter the calculation of deterrence on which stability depends.

In fact, even the kind of ceilings contained in the SALT II accords may be destabilizing. Assuming that each side has 1,320 MIRVed DVs and something on the order of 7,000–10,000 RVs with CEPS (a circular error probable measure of accuracy) under 0.25 miles, it is theoretically possible that either side could achieve a preemptive strike against the other's land-based force by employing something on the order of 20 to 30 percent of its own RVs. In such an environment, pressures to adopt launch-on-warning strategies will increase, and crisis stability will be severely reduced.

This problem has led in Washington to pressure for a mobile ICBM system, including various versions of MX missile deployment. While there will certainly be considerable controversy surrounding that weapon system, the threat that the quantitative balance in RVs poses to land-based strategic systems certainly implies additional superpower competition in the early 1980s. The scenarios described in Chapters 2 and 3 for Soviet economic difficulties and for replacement of the Soviet leadership suggest that particularly expensive strategic options will be under discussion in the Kremlin at a time when political instability may be inevitable and when the economic opportunity costs of these systems will be dramatic. Moreover, even if these quantitative problems prove manageable in the SALT II environment and if the Soviet-American commitment to strategic dialog enables the Kremlin to weather its leadership and economic difficulties without making strategic choices which contribute to domestic turmoil, a variety of qualitative issues will complicate the strategic relationship during the 1980s.

Qualitative Competition

The discussion of the quantitative feature of Soviet-American strategic competition has already suggested that the most destabilizing elements of it are produced by coupling increases in numbers of warheads per missile with improvements in on-board technology that miniaturize payloads and increase RV accuracy. On the American side, technological advance seems quite "promising" in the areas of command and control and of further improvement in missile technology. For example, the Command Data Buffer System and cold-launch techniques both suggest stabilizing lines of technological developments by providing the national command structure with more time in which to evaluate a threat and more certainty that options for response will be retained in a second-strike environment. Other technologies probably cut in the opposite direction and tend to be destabilizing. Most American advances in accuracy have grown out of the Advanced Ballistic Reentry Systems (ABRES) program, and the maneuverable re-entry vehicle (MaRV), including a terminally guided version (MaRV I), promises to be the next major American advance. This technology and the NAVSTAR global positioning system both promise to maintain the United States "lead" in accuracy, and suggest that the next cycle in Soviet-American strategic competition will be characterized by continued Soviet perception of technological inferiority and by the perceived need to offset that inferiority. These developments can either contribute to stability or reduce it. It is possible that accuracy of land-based ICBMs will move below 0.25 nautical miles on the Soviet side and 0.10 on the American side in the 1980s, but there is also a widespread assumption that these differences will *eventually* be eliminated, although probably not during the 1980s, and that their importance diminishes as accuracy increases under 0.25 in any case. The purpose of this technological development is to give RVs a credible counterforce capability, and that development is unavoidably ambiguous. On the one hand it makes a first strike more nearly possible. On the other hand, it renders a second strike more credible by opening counterforce options and slowing the resort to countercity attacks by each side.

It is, however, difficult to avoid the conclusion that SLBMs will remain the least vulnerable, hence the most stable, systems available to either superpower in the 1980s, but even at sea, qualitative advances in the United States Trident program may be perceived in Moscow as suggesting an increased danger of a first strike. One possible result of SALT II will be to "drive the Soviets to sea" with an increased percentage of its own MIRV force. The SALT II ceiling of 1,320 MIRVs and subceiling of 800 land-based MIRVs will increase Soviet incentives to deploy up to 500 MIRVs at sea. Initially, at least, this shift to sea of the Soviet force will emphasize technology in which the American advantages are substantial. The effect, once again, will be to increase qualitative competition between the superpowers.

Qualitative competition cannot be monitored as closely as quantitative, but within the kinds of quantitative limits SALT II establishes, the risks of these various qualitative developments will probably be acceptable to both sides throughout the 1980s. In fact, future strategic arms agreements may need to be negotiated on precisely this basis—to define the quantitative limits within which qualitative competition will proceed.

Verification

These qualitative dimensions of American-Soviet competition in strategic weapons suggest a further difficulty for maintaining stability in the 1980s. Verification of any arms control agreement by "national technical means" will become more complicated and less effective. There is no reason to suppose that political relations between the United States and the U.S.S.R. will advance to the point where inhibitions against on-site inspection will be significantly ameliorated, and in the absence of such inspection it will be impossible to monitor compliance with arms control agreements on many kinds of strategic developments that will affect the central balance. The difficulty is, of course, that arms competition in the 1980s will increasingly stress qualitative technological development. The MX is designed to conceal its location, Trident II will retrofit Trident I tubes, Trident I the Poseidon tubes. More importantly, in the competition over accuracy in RVs, even on-site inspection of missile components—while highly improbable for political and national security reasons—would not be very helpful for reducing uncertainties, and will be less helpful as CEPs move downward. Thus, the competition for accuracy is not a useful candidate for arms control, and on-site inspection remains a bogus issue.

Possibly the most obvious case of complication in verifying SALT II and agreements beyond is raised by the cruise missile. Physical size will be less reliable as an indicator of such basic performance characteristics as range. A missile might be tested within a range permitted by agreement—say 600 kilometers as set for GLCMs and SLCMs in SALT II—and deployed with a longer range by adjusting its instrumentation package and fitting it with engines tested in static conditions. Furthermore, the numbers of these missiles cannot be verified because they do not rely on fixed-site launchings. Thus, cruise missiles constitute a destabilizing development from the perspective of both qualitative and quantitative arms control.

There are other examples of the greater difficulties posed for verification by the emerging profile of qualitative capabilities in Soviet-American arms competition—NAVSTAR and other command and control innovations, shelter systems and other land-mobile ICBM techniques—but all point toward the conclusion that future agreements will be less verifiable than present ones. Of course, surveillance technology will also improve, but that prospect seems unlikely to match the difficulties raised by qualitative competition and is severely qualified by the prospects of a race in antisatellite weapons (ASAT). Security, if it is to be affected at all by arms control, will probably increasingly depend on acceptance of the notion that the quantitative weapons balance is sufficient to make qualitative cheating on agreements of no practical value. The point is familiar in our present environment, and is not unlike the case of a happily married spouse who contemplates infidelity. Either side could "cheat" on the SALT

II limits, but the marginal advantage to be achieved in this manner makes little difference to the overall balance and risks upsetting the whole fabric of trust on which the mutual interests embodied in the treaty depend: the costs of discovery far outweigh any conceivable advantage to be achieved while cheating goes undetected.

This condition, however, points to the importance of the political relationship. In a relationship characterized by high levels of conflict on other issues, it is improbable that the uncertainties likely to be generated by the strategic environment can be made to fit into a structure of arms control agreements. Of course, both the Soviet Union and United States could tolerate a relationship that would be essentially "managed animosity," and would survive the continued arms competition implied for the 1980s in that relationship. While the risks of miscalculation and war in such an environment might be greater, the general inhibition against nuclear war might well induce great caution in their bilateral relations. Neither side would, of course, permit quantitative constraints to hold in the long run if it felt the qualitative competition were endangering its vital security interests. But to hold any significant variables constant will promote stability by permitting both sides to react to potentially destabilizing technological developments with more calm in the short run. In this case, short-run calm is greatly to be desired and stability may depend on avoiding precipitous reactions to new developments which unleash the interactive competitive spiral.

The essential case for stressing arms control as a feature of a general strategy for cooperative relations seems to this author to derive from the coincidence of two sets of circumstances in the early 1980s. It may well be a period when political and economic priorities in the Soviet Union will once again be in exceptional flux. It will almost certainly also be a period when the focus of strategic competition will increasingly be on its qualitative dimensions. This competition will exacerbate uncertainty in the short run, but need not damage the overall United States–U.S.S.R. relationship or upset the strategic balance between them. The conjunction of these two sets of circumstances constitutes the central drive of the argument for an American foreign policy stressing cooperation with the Soviet Union in the 1980s.

The strategic uncertainties seem inevitable. They will almost certainly be more manageable for a relatively inexperienced Soviet leadership if the United States persists in holding out the possibility of a Soviet-American relationship which stresses cooperation to control conflicting interests. Conversely, a new leadership confronted by a high-conflict relationship will almost certainly be tempted to make orthodox policy choices. Although American leverage on those choices is not great, it will be easier to encourage modernist choices early during a new leadership's tenure in the Kremlin than it will be to reverse orthodox choices after they have been made.

One underappreciated feature of the SALT process and the Vienna SALT II agreements reflects diplomatic efforts by the Nixon, Ford, and Carter administrations to achieve the kind of modest, long-range goals for the Soviet-American relationship which Chapters 3 and 4 argued constitute the proper focus of United States policy. For the first time, the Soviets named their own strategic systems and identified the number of RVs on each in Article III of the treaty. In the Memorandum of Understanding, they provided aggregate data on their weapons systems: ICBM launchers, SLBM launchers, heavy bombers and MIRVs. These are not spectacular achievements, but neither are they insignificant. They represent a marked reduction in Moscow's obsession for secrecy in all military affairs. It may well be that the most important effect of the SALT process is not between the superpowers, but within them. New habits of dialog between Soviet military and civilian authorities and increased confidence that Soviet security is not compromised by public knowledge of some military data—these are small steps for a safer superpower relationship. Across time they may prove the most significant results of the SALT process to date.

SIX

Geopolitical Competition

The dynamics of Soviet-American competition and cooperation interact symbiotically with other bilateral and multilateral
relations between the superpowers and many other parties
around the globe. The fundamental fact of international politics
in the last quarter of the twentieth century has been that the
Soviet Union and the United States are both global superpowers
at a historical moment that has witnessed a geographic diffusion
of salient issues in world affairs and, possibly, to some degree,
a shift in the very definition of power. Thus, as the Soviet Union
and the United States have begun to compete for the first time
as genuinely global military powers, the focus of international
politics has been drawn away from the familiar East-West axis
to newer, less well-defined arenas. The superpowers have com-
peted globally since 1945, but it was only in the 1970s that the
Soviet Union actually acquired the means to project military
power at long distance outside its own periphery. The globality
of their power fuels competition, but may also create shared
interests in defining the limits of that competition and stabilizing
political and economic relations in some regions where interests
are in potential conflict.

This superpower, geopolitical conflict is particularly, but not
solely, the product of the ideological dimension in their relations,
and it constitutes the essence of the Soviet insistence in CSCE—
the Conference on Security and Cooperation in Europe—and
elsewhere that peaceful coexistence cannot mean the abandonment of ideological struggle between socialism and capitalism.

Throughout the period of improved American-Soviet relations, the notion has persisted in Soviet pronouncements that the U.S.S.R. must be unhindered in its support of "progressive and peace-loving forces" in the world. That formula has long meant three kinds of political efforts: support for communist parties in their efforts to achieve political power; support for "anti-imperialist" (often anti-American) states, principally in the Third World; and support for leftist political elements whose views are relatively favorable to Soviet purposes, in cases where actual exercise of power by communists is impractical. Support of candidates for political power within the third-party states and of client states in international affairs is not peculiar to communist ideology. It does, no doubt, form part of the foreign policy of any major power. These features of American-Soviet competition are not only ideological.

For American foreign policy this competitive Soviet behavior in world affairs poses especially difficult questions. The fundamental issues are whether American-Soviet rivalry need be treated as a zero-sum game, in which "their" gain is "our" loss, and whether the United States has the capacity to engage the U.S.S.R. at every point where the latter might assert its interests. The political base may no longer exist in the United States for this zero-sum competitive attitude toward the Soviet Union, and almost certainly the "policy" will become more difficult to sustain as the political influence of Americans who have matured in the fifteen years between John Kennedy's election and the final collapse in Vietnam is extended.

Among the questions which need to be asked, and positions which need to be debated thoughtfully, are these:

- Is it counter to American interests to have communist governments in power anywhere in the world, or might some communist-led states be preferable to certain kinds of noncommunist ones?

- In regions of established priority for United States foreign policy, such as Latin America and Europe, do communist governments pose sharper dangers than in Asia and Africa? Or has the emergence of the energy and raw material issues made the existence of communist governments in other regions of equal concern?

- Does participation in political power by communists pose the same kind of threat to United States interests as the exercise of power by them as a single-party dictatorship? Or, should American policy differentiate among communist parties operating in multiparty states according to their parliamentary tactics? Is a communist government that seeks power by legal means preferable to one that seizes power?

- Does Soviet support for any political faction in a third-party struggle for power preclude the possibility of American support for that same faction or does it require that the United States support opposing factions? (An especially sharp issue in the failure of American policy is Angola!)

- Should a Soviet-sponsored alliance, or the possibility of one, between communist and other leftist parties in third-country political struggles require American support for centrist and rightist claimants for power?

- Do American interests require opposition to states that espouse a highly verbal policy of anti-imperialism and which have received Soviet backing? Or is it the nature of Soviet aid to such countries, their geographic location, or even their actual behavior, that should determine support or opposition by the United States?

- Do active Soviet clients in disputes require the offsetting presence of American clients?

- In cases where American interests require opposition to a faction struggling for internal power, should that opposition be made by covert United States activity, direct United States participation, or through allies in the region of the dispute?

Of course, many of these questions cannot be decided in general, but deserve consideration within the individual context. They do suggest, however, the nature of American-Soviet competition for influence on a global scale, and they suggest the need to work for the establishment of rules by which that competition might be regulated and the dangers for war reduced.

In the 1960s, Soviet analysts, no doubt heavily influenced by American involvement in Vietnam, began to use the concept of "globalism" to define United States foreign policy.[1] This development, paralleled by the partially derivative evolution of Soviet strategic and naval power, has produced a condition in which the two powers anticipate global competition in the 1980s and beyond. The development of the means to project power globally by the U.S.S.R. is the reason that the Diego Garcia, Angolan, and Somalian issues surfaced as important ones during 1975 and 1976, and why negotiations over the Indian Ocean were undertaken. The concern expressed by some participants in the American debate—for example, by the "Sonnenfeldt Doctrine" and by "Team B" during the transition between the Ford and Carter presidencies—was that the Soviet Union now had the means to realize its alleged expansionist ambitions.[2]

However one judges the validity of this concern, it will clearly be a costly and dangerous enterprise for the superpowers to expand their direct rivalry into new geographic regions. What is needed instead is a whole new form of dialogue that recognizes the legitimacy of some Soviet claims to global parity and defuses the risk of direct conflict between the two major powers. To expect regional and global power relationships to remain unchanged is unrealistic, given the basic conflict of Soviet and American interests and the recent change in the power relationship between them. Such expectations would condemn United States policy to worldwide rearguard action that would result in many defeats, would risk global war, and would, in any case, be inconsistent with the mood of the country in the 1970s. However, there is no reason to believe that the U.S.S.R. is in a good position to influence the emerging international issues any more decisively than the United States. In many cases it is decidedly less well prepared to do so.

[1]While there has been much serious Soviet analysis of "globalism," perhaps the two most extensive were: Yu. P. Davidov, et al., *Doktrina Niksona* (The Nixon Doctrine), Moscow, 1972; and V. M. Kulish, et al., *Voennaya sila i mezhdunarodnye otnosheniya, voennye aspekty vneznepoliticheshikh konseptsi S. Sh. A.*, (Military Force and International Relations, Military Aspects of U.S. Foreign Policy Concepts), Moscow, 1972, especially pp. 10–19 and 57–60.

[2]See Drew Middleton's summary, *New York Times*, June 25, 1977, pp. 1, 4.

In most kinds of third-party disputes, differences of opinion probably exist within the Soviet leadership. Thus, the United States has some leverage in its bilateral relations with Moscow to affect Soviet perceptions of their interests. It has two general means of affecting Soviet behavior. The United States can bargain directly with Moscow not to employ unacceptable means of influencing third-party disputes and not to press advantages for their client factions and states to the point where rival factions and states with United States backing are eliminated. It can also maneuver in support of clients to block the success of Soviet-supported factions and states. The second of the two techniques appears likely to be increasingly constrained by domestic resistance in American politics, especially, for example, because of the reduced support for the CIA that has attended recent investigations. As a result, it is desirable to broaden cooperation with the Soviet Union in defining tolerable means of influence and acceptable outcomes for third-party disputes. On the other hand, the Soviet Union has a serious interest in not provoking crises around which American political consensus might reemerge along cold war lines—a risk the Brezhnev leadership has not adequately appreciated in Africa since 1975.

Some simple rules might constitute the base of consensus on which an effective political coalition could probably be constructed in the United States and which would also be consistent with the interests of those elements in the Soviet leadership favoring cooperation and modernist policies. At a minimum, both sides must recognize that their actions in international politics induce reciprocal domestic political effects.

Modernist forces in Moscow find that their cause suffers by aggressive assertions of American power because such actions fit the perceptual framework of the most ideological and orthodox members of the Soviet elite and because actions to counter such assertions of United States power are a part of the orthodox Marxist-Leninist-Stalinist political program. Probably less well-recognized in Moscow, however, is that the modernist policy program also suffers when there is a successful assertion of Soviet power. Such actions, although they may have broad appeal within the Soviet elite, induce a reaction in Washington that makes cooperative relations less tenable.

This reaction to a successful assertion of new Soviet interests was illustrated by the consequences of Soviet policy in Angola in late 1975. In that instance, the mood in Washington became very unfavorable toward cooperative Soviet-American relations, and moderate, prodétente forces found themselves on the defensive for many months. Similarly, the aggressive use of United States power in Vietnam from 1965 onward strengthened the hand of elements in the CPSU least congenial to economic and political reform. A more subtle case is the Nixon trip to China in 1972 which may have strained Brezhnev's policy of détente. Thus, on both sides superpower behavior is complicated by the effect that an exercise of influence by one can have on the internal political forces operating within the other.

Therefore, the risks of global competition between the Soviet Union and the United States might be ameliorated by paying attention to some general guidelines such as the following:

1. The perception of a mutual interest in cooperation is probably spread widely enough in both capitals to create a tolerance for modest assertions of influence by the other side. Of course, particular caution is required when important interests of the other power are at issue. And clearly direct applications of military power are risky, since such actions would likely strengthen antagonistic elements in the opposing superpower.

2. It may be considered mutually unacceptable and too destabilizing for either power to be left without an effective client in any regional balance of power, or to be driven from any region where the other power is perceived to be hegemonic. This would almost certainly produce severe stress on political forces favoring cooperation.

3. Since the competition for resources will almost certainly increase in the future, denying access to them would undermine the political support for moderate policies in either capital. In addition, adjustments in the international economic order will strain political and economic institutions in both superpowers, and each will need to forego temporary economic advantages that are likely to undercut the consensus for cooperation in the other's leadership.

4. Current developments in military technology probably increase the viability of the defender at low levels of military force. Since it will take relatively greater force to dislodge small units of defenders equipped with modern weapons, the relative advantage of establishing political bases will increase. Thus, competition for clients by political, economic, and covert means may increase. And the requirement that political leaders retain direct control over CIA and KGB operations will become more critical.

5. Advances in communications technology, with their implications for command and control of military forces, may be useful in extending direct political control over bureaucracies operating overseas. But these technological changes, by making it more feasible to control the projection of power abroad, also facilitate interference in local affairs and in regional political balances, thereby requiring greater caution regarding the limits of competition between the superpowers.

6. Because the absolute military power of both superpowers has grown, the capacity of each to intervene abroad has actually improved in recent years. This fact may make it important to extend the framework of arms control to embrace agreements of regional abstention.

Thus the rules of superpower behavior will need to be modified in the era of their global competition. The challenge of sustaining a cooperative relationship will become more complicated—and more vital—in the 1980s. The increasing complexity of international affairs will require imaginative responses. The challenge can be better illustrated by particular reference to geographic regions—Europe, the Far East, the Middle East, Africa, and other selected areas of potential conflict.

EUROPE

Nowhere has the Soviet-American relationship been subjected to the tension between the revolutionary and pragmatic impulses of Soviet foreign policy in quite so pure a form as in the confrontation since World War II across divided Europe. In Europe the pragmatic concerns of the Soviets have always been most prominent, because there they have always lived in closest proximity with powerful capitalist and democratic adversaries. Consequently, in recent years the U.S.S.R. has stationed large military forces in Europe to protect its national interests and has sought to maintain a relationship with NATO powers that has embodied the very definition of peaceful coexistence. Revolution could be promoted in the Third World, but in Europe the prospects were too slight and the risks for Soviet security too great. There, stability has been the objective of Soviet foreign policy. Even Soviet actions which seemed to the outside world to involve high risks—Hungary in 1956, Berlin in 1961, and Czechoslovakia in 1968—undoubtedly were taken in part because they seemed necessary to maintain politically reliable and stable regimes along Russia's western border.

Still, the revolutionary element in Soviet policy has not disappeared from Europe. Rather it has become submerged in the question of Eurocommunism. On the one hand, those sizable risks Moscow took in 1956, 1961, and 1968 were justified by the Soviet leadership's need to enforce its conception of revolutionary ideology on the socialist states of Eastern Europe. On the other hand the Communist Party of the Soviet Union has fought a long and wearying rearguard action against the more "liberal" communist parties of Yugoslavia, Italy, and, more recently, France. The rise of the Italian and French communist parties and the bid for power by the Portuguese communists in the mid-1970s serve as reminders that revolutionary expectations still influence Soviet policy even in the arena where its actions have been most conservative and most like those of other nation-states. Thus, American-Soviet European relations in the 1980s will probably continue to mix traditional superpower interests with the unique problems of ideological struggle.

The Pragmatic Syndrome

During most of the postwar period Soviet policy toward Europe has maintained a two-tiered set of priorities. At the base were two unalterable political realities, and on these were constructed

142

a series of specific policy objectives. As has also been the case, since the end of World War II, for the Western powers, Soviet foreign policy has demonstrated a firm sense of the need to avoid military conflict in Europe between the two major blocs. This need to preserve the peace no doubt reinforced the general tendency toward détente, but it also created risks for Soviet policy within its Warsaw Pact alliance. It was by no means coincidental that as détente in Europe gained momentum the Soviet Union promoted an extensive campaign to "intensify" coordination and institutional cooperation within the Council for Mutual Economic Assistance (CMEA) and the Warsaw Treaty Organization (WTO). This campaign was partly motivated by the desire to contain the risks of détente. The challenge to Soviet leadership in the socialist bloc by China, the radical deterioration of Moscow-Peking relations during 1969, and the disruptive effects of the Czechoslovakian intervention combined with the perception in the Kremlin that détente carried dangers of reducing bloc cohesion to make appealing the campaign to intensify alliance integration. These two considerations—to avoid military conflict and to promote tighter alliance cohesion—formed the foundation on which specific policy objectives seemed to rest.

The collective leadership, in response to a changing international environment and in attempts to affect that environment, has modified priorities among the specific objectives it builds on this foundation. For example, the decision in late 1969 to opt for a period of emphasis on bilateral negotiations was in response to the change in the European political environment created by initiatives from the new Social Democratic government of Willy Brandt. The appearance of the Brandt coalition in Bonn made it possible for Brezhnev to pursue his foreign policy objectives by direct negotiation with the Federal Republic of Germany.

Soviet policies toward Europe during the period from 1969 to 1972 combined two long-standing objectives and a more recent one. First, since World War II, the policy has had as its principal objective the acquisition of international recognition of the postwar political and territorial status quo in Eastern Europe. Second, the policy had also been designed during the cold war to achieve a reduction of American influence in Western Europe. However, a third objective had begun to take on added importance for the post-Khrushchev, collective leadership, although it surely ranked considerably below the other two in priority: the Soviets attempted to acquire access to markets in Western Europe for modern technology.

In 1972, with the conclusion of the Moscow-Bonn Treaty, the Warsaw-Bonn Treaty, and the signing and ratification of a new Four-Power Agreement on Berlin, a new set of priorities began to take shape among these objectives.[3] First, the desire for access to Western markets assumed greater significance and had perhaps even become the primary objective of Soviet policies toward Europe. Second, accelerated development of the European Economic Community, and the nervous perception that this threatened major Soviet interests, made Moscow especially anxious to find some way of influencing Western European policies. Third, America's preoccupation with Vietnam and the demonstrated weakness of the United States trade position in Europe must have begun to raise the question in Moscow of whether the traditional opposition to American influence in Europe was really so important. It almost seemed that Moscow sensed that both it and Washington might have lost whatever ability they once possessed to shape economic and political developments in Western Europe. Finally, the Soviet Union no doubt still valued a multilateral recognition of the gains it had made during the period of bilateralism, but that objective seemed likely to be secured by pursuing other objectives, and the sense of urgency was significantly blunted.

Soviet policy toward Europe during the early 1970s was quite successful and contains suggestive lessons for the 1980s. The policy reflected a growing confidence in Moscow that developments in Europe were distinctly favorable to Soviet purposes. In part, this confidence grew out of a profound sense of relief, one little commented upon in the West. The Brezhnev leadership has been entirely composed of men who made important personal advances in the party apparat during World War II. They also

[3]See, for example, G. Arbatov, *Izvestia,* June 27, 1972; and the *Pravda* editorial, June 8, 1972.

share their countrymen's deep and merited sense of achievement in the war. They persisted for 25 years to obtain Western recognition of what they always thought were the deserved fruits of their national sacrifice between 1941 and 1945. Thus, Soviet rhetoric on the successful conclusion of CSCE probably had more substance than was apparent from the perspective of Western analysis.

The success of Soviet policy was thought in Moscow to be based on four elements: (1) the need to avoid war was recognized by socialists and imperialists alike; (2) acceptance of this situation by imperialists was based on a fundamental shift in the balance of forces between the two blocs; (3) the shift depended on the growing unity of the socialist bloc, often expressed in terms of functional and institutional cooperation; and (4) it depended also on a number of favorable trends within the capitalist camp.[4]

In the 1980s it is likely that Soviet policy toward Europe will continue to be pragmatic, adaptive, and based on the same fundamental assessment of the historical balance of forces. The ideology is flexible enough and the politics of Europe varied enough that Soviet leaders should be able to find "positive developments" adequate to justify their claims that the tide of Europe is running toward socialism. However, several political developments could disrupt this favorable assessment and this pragmatic Soviet policy toward Europe.

First, Germany is the unparalleled focus of Soviet security policy in Europe. A return to power by the Christian Democrats in Germany might be an important negative event from the Soviet perspective. A significant downturn in West German economic performance that increased the popularity of the right in German politics—for example, along the lines represented by Strauss and his Bavarian-based Christian-Socialist Union or exacerbated by the kind of instability threatened by terrorists of the left during the 1960s and 1970s—would produce a harsher Soviet policy toward Germany and possibly a retreat from détente policies in Europe generally. Even then, however, current levels of Soviet

[4]See Brezhnev's speech to the World Peace Congress on October 26, 1973, *Pravda,* October 27, 1973; and Foreign Minister Gromyko's speech to the 57th Anniversary Celebration of the Revolution, ibid., November 7, 1974.

military forces would probably be considered adequate to secure Soviet interests, and policy alterations would be most likely verbal or produce low-level confrontation politics in Berlin. Certainly any West German government which abrogated the *Ostpolitik* treaties of the early 1970s could trigger a more violent reaction from Moscow, but Soviet policy toward Europe would most likely continue its cooperative line with other Western European states even if relations worsened with the Federal Republic of Germany, provided that East Germany remained unquestionably loyal, that the Kremlin leadership retained cooperative options in France, Britain, and Italy, and that American policy did not seem to be moving in the direction of a "Little Atlantic Alliance" (i.e., a Bonn-Washington axis within NATO, which has long been most threatening to the Soviets).

A second source of disruption to the pragmatism in Soviet policy toward Europe might develop in Eastern Europe. Because Warsaw Pact/Comecon cohesion has represented the Soviet hedge against the negative effects of détente and against the kinds of disaffection that were threatened by Czechoslovakia in 1968, any dramatic threat to the appearance or substance of that tighter alliance might well cause substantial reassessment of the Soviet Union's overall policy toward Europe. It has strong ideological and national security interests in retaining a loyal socialist alliance in Eastern Europe, and the Soviet Union may find itself caught in dilemmas partly of its own making during the 1980s.

On the one hand, it has tied Eastern European economies to its own. It has already begun raising raw material prices in this highly "protected" market and has served notice that, especially with respect to energy, the 1980s will bring further changes. Ironically from the Soviet perspective, these economic changes will increase the incentive of even loyal communist regimes to diversify their sources of raw material supply and, thereby, to reduce Soviet leverage in the Eastern European market.

On the other hand, the Soviet Union will undoubtedly encourage the growth of Western European communism, but should that movement continue to exhibit the vitality and independence it had promised in the mid-1970s, a demonstration effect could result which would profoundly alter the character of Eastern European communism. Communists, including Marx and Lenin, have always been more threatened by political forces on the left, which are ideologically closer to them, than by their overt opponents on the right. Thus, a prosperous and politically dynamic Italy, France, or Spain—in the governing of which the communist parties participate, but which did not experience the kinds of repression that have accompanied one-party rule in Eastern Europe—would imply substantial risks of undercutting the political authority of regimes in socialist Eastern Europe and, possibly, even in Moscow itself. The current restrictions on travel to "capitalist" Europe would be harder to justify, for example. Already the communist newspapers of Western Europe—especially *L'Humanité* and *L'Unità*—are sources of occasional agitation among the intelligentsia of the socialist states. Should these papers continue to reveal the independence and success of these parties, their greater availability in Moscow, Budapest, Warsaw, etc., would seem to threaten contagion by revisionist ideas and introduce strain into East-West political relationships.

For reasons that are partly ideological and partly the product of the way post–World War II immigration from Eastern Europe has colored American perceptions, it has seemed particularly difficult for political commentary in the United States to acknowledge the incremental transformation of Soviet relations with its Eastern European allies since 1968. This transformation has been partly a product of forces external to Eastern Europe. Exacerbated Sino-Soviet difficulties in 1969 and the vitality of Western European communist parties have encouraged the Soviet Union to adapt its policies toward Eastern Europe in an effort to reinforce its leadership of the international communist movement. Developments in Eastern Europe itself—especially the continued independence of Ceaucescu in Romania, the major challenge to the Polish leadership in 1971, the sustained reformation of Hungary's domestic policy under Kadar's leadership, and the political and economic changes in Yugoslavia as preparations are made for the post-Tito period—have encouraged the Soviet Union to exercise patience and to tolerate more independent national policies among the socialist states and their communist parties. Gradually a framework has been created in which

147

the Soviet Union has permitted some devolution of power and shared responsibility for decision making. While falling far short of the pluralism taken for granted in the European Community and Atlantic frameworks, both the Warsaw Pact and Comecon have developed habits of consultation and institutional diversification since the March 1969 meeting of the former's Political Consultative Committee and the latter's adoption in July 1971 of the Comprehensive Program of Further Co-operation and Integration.[5]

Some of the Soviet motivations for this controlled devolution of power in Eastern Europe are clear—as responses to détente (especially the CSCE negotiations) and to the Sino-Soviet dispute, as a palliative for higher prices of Soviet raw materials, and as a hedge to the demonstration effect of European Community integration by providing at least the appearance of parallel development in CMEA. Nonetheless, these apparent motives may not be sufficient to explain the intensified consultation among Eastern European communists.

Perhaps there is an ideological motivation to create a "mature" set of political and economic institutions reflective of the increased confidence and stability in the region. Both the Warsaw Pact and CMEA will probably continue to evolve cooperative frameworks for shared decision making in the 1980s. It is possible that they will become frameworks for expressing national grievances with Soviet domination. In fact, to the degree that integrative efforts in the 1970s were responsive to the Soviet perception of a need to promote cooperation and reduce coercion in bloc relations, nationalist leverage will continue to grow. It is difficult to imagine how the Soviet Union can manage the various forces which have encouraged the limited diversification of the 1970s without more concessions. This matrix of issues contains volatile potential for disruption of the pragmatism in Soviet foreign policy.

Political developments in the West constitute a third source of possible disruption of pragmatic Soviet policies. On the one hand, weakness in the West may undermine Soviet incentives

[5]*Pravda*, March 18, 1969, and ibid., July 30, 1971.

to deal pragmatically with Western states. Rapid deterioration of Western European economies or dramatic political instability tempt ideological reactions from the Soviet Union. By its own folly, the West can present political and economic "targets of opportunity" that reinforce orthodox and ideological responses from the Soviet Union. On the other hand, Western strength also heightens a sense of insecurity in Moscow and Eastern Europe and places pragmatic policies under other kinds of strain. For example, overt pressure by pluralist governments for Soviet concessions of the kind implicit in Basket Three of the CSCE negotiations, the Jackson Amendment's attempt to use MFN to obtain political concessions, and President Carter's human rights policies all increase the probability of orthodox Soviet responses and blunt the pragmatic thrust of Soviet policy. The reason is partly bureaucratic. This kind of aggressive behavior by the West fits the explanations offered by orthodox Marxists-Leninists and strengthens their position within the Kremlin political struggle. Dramatic increases in NATO's military posture undoubtedly also strengthen the hands of those who advocate orthodox and ideological policies in Moscow, while solid economic performance in the European Community probably increases incentives to trade.

The line between policies that encourage the pragmatic syndrome in Soviet policy and those that will stimulate ideological responses is a delicate one. This does not imply that Western policies have a determining effect on policy making in Moscow, or that affecting Soviet policy constitutes a high priority of Western European and American policy. However, it would be myopic to ignore the possibility that developments in the West contain not insignificant potential for the disruption, or the encouragement, of the pragmatic syndrome in Soviet foreign and security policies.

Finally, the stability of the pragmatic syndrome in Soviet policy toward Europe depends in the first instance on the East-West consensus that war in Europe would be absolutely intolerable. It was argued earlier that this inhibition may be especially poignant to the leadership that has dominated the Soviet politics since 1953, almost all of whom were profoundly influenced by their own experience in World War II. The leadership of the 1980s will increasingly have had different experiences in the Great Fatherland War, and it remains to be seen if the inhibition will thereby be diminished. A leadership that first achieved political positions of significant national responsibility during the 1960s, as the relative power of the U.S.S.R. and the United States was undergoing dramatic transformation, may be more inclined to seek political and economic payoffs for the improved Soviet power positions.

Much attention in the United States and NATO throughout the 1970s, as earlier, has been focused on the Soviet "build-up" of its conventional forces in Europe. While Soviet determination to retain powerful military forces in Eastern Europe can hardly be questioned, the issue has been exaggerated in the West. The Soviet Union increased its forces stationed in Czechoslovakia by five armored divisions following the 1968 invasion, and troop levels remained approximately the same during the following decade. The Warsaw Treaty Organization (WTO) has modernized its forces, especially Soviet armored and air units, but these programs have been a constant feature of the Soviet commitment to its Warsaw Pact strategy. Occasionally, political elements in NATO will point to these ongoing WTO programs with alarm, usually in efforts to convince their parliaments to vote higher defense funds. Improvements in NATO force posture have undoubtedly been required and some have been made, but the political tactics of exaggerating the Warsaw Pact threat were discredited in the 1960s and 1970s. Soviet forces in Eastern Europe represent a formidable military adversary, but the effect of claims like those that they can drive to the Channel in forty hours is to reduce incentives for NATO governments to make marginal improvements in their own commitments to the joint military effort. The facts indicate substantial Soviet and Warsaw Pact advantages, also some significant NATO advantages, but claims of overwhelming WTO superiority depend on worst-case assumptions for both military and political variables.

With respect to the 1980s, major issues of political and military strategy face NATO and the United States. The debate over the neutron bomb, or rather the surprising lack of meaningful public

TABLE 4

NATO/Warsaw Pact Military Balance, 1978

	Total NATO	Total Warsaw Pact
Combat Manpower		
Northern and Central Europe	626,000	943,000
Southern Europe	550,000	388,000
Tanks		
Northern and Central Europe	7,000	21,000
Southern Europe	4,300	6,800
Tactical Aircraft		
Northern and Central Europe	2,375	4,055
Southern Europe	938	1,645

SOURCE: International Institute for Strategic Studies, *Military Balance, 1979–1980,* London, 1979.

discussion, is suggestive. This development and others, like the shift in Soviet airpower from a largely air defense role to ground-attack and interdiction, suggest that war may actually be more feasible in Europe during the coming decade. That possibility needs dispassionate and thoughtful public discussion. Furthermore, it is increasingly apparent that the mutual force reduction (MFR) talks which have gone on between NATO and the Warsaw Pact in Vienna since October of 1973 have been misshaped. The Soviet development of the Backfire bomber and the SS-20 mobile intermediate-range missile points to the need to include discussions of the European strategic nuclear environment in the MFR framework or to create a new forum for those discussions. Both SALT and the negotiations in Vienna over the conventional forces are increasingly complicated by the theater nuclear forces stationed outside the target area of the original MFR talks.

Thus the European military environment represents both a potential source for the disruption of pragmatic Soviet policies in Europe and an opportunity to manage cooperative relations. Given this study's assumptions about the policy environment likely to face a new Soviet leadership in the early 1980s, Europe constitutes a principal arena in which the political program of the modernists will be tested.

These four sources of disruption for the pragmatic syndrome of Soviet policy toward Europe might profoundly alter it. In particular, if two or more of them coincide, they might cause dangerous instability in Europe, but sensible Western policies should diminish the likelihood of such disruption. Thus, there are substantial Soviet interests in maintaining a stable interstate system for Europe into the 1990s. But the other side of Soviet policy toward Europe promises to be less predictable.

The Ideological Syndrome

We received a taste of the potential for difficulties between NATO and the Warsaw Pact during the mid-1970s. The web of issues engaged by ideological struggle is likely to spread in coming years, and it is unlikely that difficulties will be resolved by the 1980s. Whereas the traditional superpower interests of the Soviet Union point toward stability and cooperation in Europe, ideological problems point toward conflict. This conflict will not be simple and two-sided, as it often appeared during the 1950s, but will engage the many-sided conflicts of capitalism and socialism, Soviet socialism and Eastern European socialism, the communism of ruling and nonruling parties, the energies of political and economic integration within socialist and democratic blocs on the one hand, and integration that attempts to combine different political and economic systems on the other hand. Soviet policy toward Europe in the mid-1970s suggested some of the complexities which will characterize the future more than the past.

The optimistic mood of Soviet policy toward Europe in 1972 and the first half of 1973 sobered somewhat after the 1973 summit and the Middle East war. Soviet assessments of the balance of political forces were placed in the context of statements that the world situation had become ''complex'' and that reactionary circles in imperialist states had become more active.[6] Although

[6]The key to adjustments in Kremlin thinking was Brezhnev's speech at Alma Ata, ibid., March 16, 1974.

the CSCE was pressed to conclusion and trade with Western nations continued to develop, the evolution of the European Community must have looked less threatening, opportunities appeared for real political advances by socialist and communist parties, and tensions between the United States and its European allies must have offered tempting opportunities for a return to a policy actively promoting divisiveness in NATO.

Successes by "progressive forces" in Portugal, Italy, Greece, and even Spain created dual tensions for Soviet policy. On the one hand was the temptation to press for socialist advances. But these threatened détente and often involved the Soviet Union in conflict with Western European communist parties whose claims to power depended to some degree on being perceived as moderate and nationalist. Therefore, on the other hand, continuation of détente seemed to create the conditions for improvement in the fortunes of "progressive" elements in Europe, and this provoked a range of opinion and possibly some disagreement within the Soviet hierarchy on the proper course for Soviet policy toward Europe.

One line conceded that revolution moves through a bourgeois-democratic phase, but argued that the transition between the democratic and socialist phases of the revolution depended on the "hegemony of the proletariat."[7] It held that once the revolutionary process was begun, communist parties had to "carry out special measures intended to eliminate in the country political, social and economic conditions posing the threat of a bourgeois comeback." This was nothing more than a call for a "dictatorship of the proletariat and the peasantry as an indispensable condition for victory of a democratic revolution." The importance of this line could not have been lost on any literate socialist or communist. It amounted to a militant and orthodox call for communist parties to press their advantage, to recruit actively among the masses, and to play down cooperation with social democrats. In essence it amounted to a rejection of the policies being forged by the Italian and French communist parties.

---

[7]Konstantin Zarodov articulated this line in two pieces: *World Marxist Review,* April 1975, pp. 20–24; and *Pravda,* August 6, 1975.

A more moderate line also appeared in the Soviet discussion of these issues.[8] For revolution to succeed, this line held, there must be a sharp increase in democracy. This meant liberalized bourgeois democracy, within which communist parties could score gains with mass political work. While the dictatorship of the proletariat was not renounced, the emphasis of this second line was clearly on the role of communist parties during the transition to socialism, and this distinguished it from the impatience of the first position, which seemed to envision a compression of the two traditional phases of communist revolution under the "hegemony" of the party.

The policy importance of the debate was quite clear. Soviet reaction to events in Portugal during 1975 and the perception of Soviet encouragement for Cunhal's excesses there caused difficulties for Berlinguer in Italy and Marchais in France. This was brought out by the former's defiant insistence on an independent Italian line at, and the latter's conspicuous absence from, the CPSU's Twenty-Fifth Party Congress in February 1976.[9] Soviet relations with the two largest communist parties in Western Europe were obviously strained.

This dual temptation for Soviet policy toward Europe—supporting socialist advances but retaining cooperative relations with the pluralist states within which these socialist and communist parties compete for political power—may well become even stronger in future years and will pose difficult choices for American foreign policy in the 1980s. Of course, there are substantive issues concerning the response of the United States to the political claims of the European left, but they are not the focus of this study. The American response to Soviet policy alone poses questions requiring thoughtful answers.

Soviet policy since 1973 has revealed a division of mind within

[8]See A. I. Sabolev, "Leninism on Consolidating the Victory of the Revolution," *Rabochiy klassi sovremenny mir* (Working Class and the Contemporary World), no. 1, January 1975, pp. 3–20; Dr. S. Salychev, "Revolution and Democracy," *Kommunist,* no. 17, 1975, pp. 114–124.

[9]Berlinguer's speech on February 27, 1976, was carried in *Foreign Broadcast Information Service,* vol. III, no. 30, pp. 18–22. Gaston Plissonier delivered the French Party's speech, ibid., pp. 10–13.

the political leadership. Every Soviet Marxist-Leninist is torn to some degree between the nationalist/pragmatic and ideological/ revolutionary syndromes of that country's European foreign policy. The opportunities afforded by the economic crisis in the West after the OPEC embargo, by the overthrow of the colonels' regime in Greece, by communist electoral advances in Italy and France—all of these offered a chance for a "forward" line in Soviet foreign policy, seemed to confirm the powers of "scientific" prediction for their political beliefs, *and* promised gains for Soviet state interests. But such a line inevitably also complicated Soviet relations with the capitalist governments of the West. Soviet behavior in Portugal and Angola in particular revealed a willingness to take low-level and largely ideological risks with the détente policy to promote revolutionary gains once the opportunity had been created by local political forces. It is these risks that American policy must attempt to discourage. The success of Cunhal in Portugal would have run counter to the wishes of an overwhelming percentage of the population, as events subsequently demonstrated. That outcome by itself would have cut directly across important U.S. interests. Moreover, had the communist party succeeded in Portugal, Soviet ideological risktaking would surely have been reinforced and would have been given bureaucratic support in Moscow.

The pattern of 1973–1976 suggests an inevitable division of mind between the attractions of reducing East-West tensions in Europe and the ideological necessity of promoting the advance of rather orthodox conceptions of revolution. That division characterizes the entire Soviet leadership. It may, on occasion, also erupt in actual political divisions among groups within the leadership, depending on the different stresses individuals place on the separate and sometimes conflicting syndromes of Soviet policy.

Clearly, if the United States prefers détente and cooperation as features of Soviet foreign policy, the pragmatic/nationalist syndrome of Soviet foreign policy should be encouraged in Europe, as elsewhere. That judgment is separate from the question of communist or socialist participation in the governments of NATO allies, which essentially involves the political societies of the Western European countries concerned. The United States, in particular, should detach its conception of its European interests from the self-defeating notion that it is threatened by the very political pluralism and emphasis on the individual rights of social dissent that it has fostered and that constitute the genius of its own contribution to political history.

Soviet interventions in Western European politics to encourage the left by overt or covert means also threaten great power confrontation and a return to a more polemical style in East-West relations. Such a turn of events can produce only negative results: an increase in political and military tensions along the border dividing Eastern and Western Europe; consequent pressure on the Soviet Union's Warsaw Pact allies for greater conformity to a common political line; demands for increases in military expenditures by NATO; and further polarization of politics within NATO countries.

It could only serve orthodox Soviet interests to make narrow conceptions of ideological struggle the focus of European politics. A more open conception of Europe's future was implicit in the struggle over "freer movement of people and ideas" in the CSCE negotiations between late 1971 and the signature of the Final Act in August 1975. That conception holds that while a Europe characterized by widening exchange between East and West, by reduced political tensions, and by a lower level of military confrontation will not erase the political differences between state socialism and democratic pluralism or the mutually perceived need to retain powerful security forces, it will almost certainly lower the dangers of war and raise the chances that social and economic problems will receive humane and civilized solutions in both Eastern and Western Europe.

Soviet objectives in Europe will continue to include efforts to weaken NATO, promote socialist and communist causes in Western European countries, and reduce American influence on the Continent. But the Soviet leadership will also be required to address its own domestic economic problems and, therefore, will continue to be attracted to Western markets for technology and agricultural resources. Thus the possibility exists for coaxing the Soviet leadership into understanding that its interests will be served by a cooperative rather than conflictive policy in Europe.

At a minimum this general prescription implies two specific policy goals, both of which will require more coordination than NATO has yet achieved. First, Soviet leaders must be led to understand that the Warsaw Pact's preponderance in conventional arms is not the natural order of things in Europe. To achieve this end will require determination across time along two fronts. The stagnant mutual force reduction talks hold some prospect for an "interim agreement," after the pattern of SALT I, which would set at least some gross ceilings on forces and weapons and provide minimal collateral guarantees against destabilizing shifts in deployments of troops in Europe. That kind of agreement would have to be extended, as argued in Chapter 5, in subsequent rounds to include theater nuclear weapons like the SS-20, the Backfire bomber, and American forward based systems. Second, in the absence of a comprehensive European force reduction agreement, NATO's political leaders must continue to demonstrate the determination they had in their Washington meeting in the spring of 1978—a willingness to make steady, real improvements in the alliance's capacity to defend Western Europe without early introduction of nuclear weapons. Both goals must be aimed toward a reduced military posture in Europe, where technology has made war even more unthinkable today than in the past.

The Soviet Union has incentives for promoting a stable order, especially in Europe. It needs access to Western European technology. Its own energy crunch will provide at least the opportunity for Western industrialized nations to offer Eastern Europe an increased stake in access to reliable international energy and monetary markets. And, finally, changes in Western Europe itself—symbolized by the advances of the Italian and French communist parties—should make Moscow's 60-year image of "capitalist encirclement" less threatening.

On all these counts, opportunities exist to reduce the dangers of a politically antagonistic, economically divided and highly armed Europe. From NATO's perspective, the invasions of Hungary in 1956 and Czechoslovakia in 1968 represented real dangers of war and produced real deterioration in European security. A policy which patiently and firmly draws the U.S.S.R. and its WTO allies into an extended pattern of cooperation will promote adaptive trends in Eastern Europe and reduce Soviet incentives for conducting its Warsaw Pact and Comecon alliances as instruments for Moscow's control and for isolating Eastern Europe.

EAST ASIA

From the perspective of American foreign policy, East Asia has been among the most stable areas in the world since the close of the Korean war. This stability has emerged as the product of a quadrangular power relationship. Undoubtedly the keys to stability have been the assertion of an independent political line by the People's Republic of China (PRC) and the remarkable economic vitality of Japan. Both factors have reduced conflictive pressures in the relationship between the United States and the Soviet Union and strengthened the position of the United States in its competition with the U.S.S.R. Chinese independence has opened the Peking-Tokyo and Peking-Washington axes and has provided Soviet incentives for limited devolution in Eastern Europe and for détente as a means of limiting Chinese options. Japanese economic strength has led the Soviet Union to cultivate relations with Tokyo as an alternative to European and American markets and has thereby promoted modernist policy preferences.

But the balance may be fragile. It depends, in the first instance, on the continuation of Sino-Soviet hostility, and although that almost certainly will not be eliminated during the next decade, the situation may well be ameliorated. There have been persistent signs in Peking of alternatives to the harsh Maoist position on Chinese relations with Moscow. Changes were not dramatic following Mao's death in September 1976, but important shifts in policy could hardly have been expected during a period when the internal leadership was being sorted out.

Steadily a more pragmatic Chinese policy has emerged. The third plenum of the Tenth Central Committee in July 1977, followed by the Eleventh Party Congress in August and the Fifth National People's Congress in February 1978, set the path: eliminate the Gang of Four, bring back into political life party leaders disgraced in the Cultural Revolution, set new goals for modernizing the economy, and open China to foreign trade and to participation in the international system. Throughout these months the new policy has been symbolized by the reemergence of Teng Hsiao-ping as Vice Premier and Vice Chairman of the Chinese Communist Party, which process reached a symbolic culmination in his visit to Washington in late January 1979, following the normalization of relations between the United States and China in December. While these developments had not produced a parallel easing of Sino-Soviet tensions, they were not totally inconsistent with that development, and the prospect for deflation of Peking-Moscow animosities seemed brighter in 1979 than at any time since 1960.

The current balance in East Asia also depends on the maintenance of the Japanese-American alliance. That alliance was severely strained by the Nixon shocks (devaluation and his visit to China) in 1971–1972, the Lockheed scandal of 1976, and the continuation of economic rivalry, which has produced large American balance-of-trade deficits and continued pressure from the Carter administration for offsetting imports of U.S. goods to Japan.

The stability of the quadrangular relationship in the Far East, then, is delicate, and may well undergo important modifications in the 1980s. The striking thing about this balance is that changes in it, if they come at all, will probably originate within the Chinese and Japanese political systems, and that neither Moscow nor Washington is in a good position to influence those changes substantially. Thus, to some degree, both powers are prisoners of their rivalry along the East Asian rim.

While internal changes in Peking's power structure may eventually repair the Sino-Soviet relationship to some extent, it is difficult to imagine many issues in East Asia on which the two leading communist powers will have identical interests. The People's Republic of China will almost certainly want to retain the option of cooperation with the United States on issues where Chinese interests do not correspond with those of the U.S.S.R. As the ideological radicalism of Peking's leadership becomes more moderate, it is possible, although not likely given the positions of the Hua and Teng leadership, that the People's Republic of China and the U.S.S.R. will find an enlarged arena for co-operation in promoting the revolutionary process in Africa, Latin America, and even South Asia. But each is a large power in the Far East and has vital interests to protect there, and it is unlikely that either will defer to the political interests of the other in that region or be prepared to reduce its military posture. In fact, the very presence of large forces seems assured by past rivalry and technological trends.

As Chinese power grows, even under improved political relations, the Soviet Union will almost certainly not be able to thin out its forces east of the Urals in any substantial way. Even if relations were to improve in a manner that encouraged China to reposition some of its troops away from the border, geography and the distribution of population within the P.R.C. dictate maintaining large forces in the Shenyang (Manchuria) and Peking military regions. These can be quickly repositioned, and it is against them that Soviet troops are deployed.

Some opportunities exist for symbolic demilitarization of the Sinkiang–Kazakh border, but space and terrain worked to reduce the threat of each country to the other on that border to little more than an irritant even in 1969, when clashes erupted all along their frontier. Thus the perceived need to retain strong military forces along their borders is not likely to dissipate in either Moscow or Peking during the 1980s even if political relations improve. Military rivalry is a product of their emergence as great regional powers in the Far East.

Furthermore, Soviet apprehensions are likely to be fueled by the inevitable modernization of the Chinese armed forces. The present rivalry has developed, after all, during a period of overwhelming Soviet technological superiority, and while that will not vanish in this century, the gap between the technological capability of Soviet and Chinese forces may narrow, especially with the acquisition by the latter of longer-range missiles, a new fighter, a better tank, and a new generation of submarines—developments which could intrude on the relationship during the 1980s. Any improvements in China's capacity to project force will make Moscow more nervous about the exposed position of its Far Eastern military bases, its dependence on the Siberian railway, and even the need to defend the important cities of Irkutsk, Chita, Khabarovsk, and Vladivostok.

All of this is not to suggest that military hostilities between China and the U.S.S.R. are probable. On the contrary, future alterations in the policies of the Chinese political leadership toward pragmatic economic growth are likely to reduce the chances of war. But geopolitical realities place limits on the possibilities for military détente between the two communist powers. China is, therefore, very likely to maintain relations with capitalist industrial powers that will permit it to hedge against deterioration of its relationship with the Soviet Union and to increase its leverage in relations with Moscow.

There are other subtleties in this Far Eastern balance of power. American relations with the Soviet Union have not been greatly complicated either by the retention of 40,000 United States ground troops in South Korea or by the decision of the Carter administration to remove them, nor was there ever much pressure from Moscow for their withdrawal despite clear evidence that the regime of President Park was disinclined to reform and democratize. Moscow's low profile on the issue seemed to depend in part on the uncertain impact on Japanese policy of a further United States withdrawal. If an American withdrawal were to precipitate military conflict on the Korean peninsula or to fuel pressures in Tokyo for increased military efforts, both China and the Soviet Union, as well as many other countries that experienced Japanese domination in the 1930s and 1940s, would likely become quite apprehensive. In a sense, then, American troops and even the Seventh Fleet have served Chinese and Soviet interests in the Far East insofar as they have promoted Japanese military security, have reduced the perception in Japan that its interest requires larger defense efforts, and have helped maintain the regional balance in Korea.

The political balance in Tokyo was subjected to severe strains in 1976 by the Lockheed scandal and in 1978 by American pressure to reduce balance-of-payments surpluses, and this undoubtedly is not the best historical moment to project future developments. Still, the Liberal-Democratic Party (LDP) has suffered from both its severely tarnished image and the manner in which the scandals of the mid-1970s have lent credence to the claims of the socialists and communists that the LDP is an instrument of large and corrupt business in Japan. Its plurality has declined steadily in parliamentary elections. Cooperation in a united front between the Soviet Party and Communist Party of Japan (CPJ) was tried at the local level in 1975, and some effort has been made by the CPJ to cooperate with the 10 million-member religious organization Soka Gakkai to broaden its public appeal.[10] However, this attempt to construct a more vital left opposition in Japan has most recently worked decidedly against the interests of the CPJ and the Soviet Union. The formation of a "New Japan Society," which combines the Democratic Socialist, the Socialist, and the Komeito Parties and excludes the communists, represents an alternative formation on the left and promises to reduce sharply the gain which the CPJ might expect from the turmoil of the LDP. While it is possible that the CPJ will broaden its appeal during the 1980s, it is unlikely that it will become a major force in Japanese politics even if Japanese politics move toward the left, and it is certain that the U.S.S.R. will need to retain its traditional dual policy of encouraging the CPJ and maintaining good relations with whatever combination of political parties controls the government in Tokyo.

The impact of internal political developments in China on the Soviet-American rivalry in the Far East is far more difficult to project. The central question for Soviet-American relations is whether the successors to Mao will continue to pursue policies of open ideological and national rivalry with the Soviet Union and will continue to exercise the diplomatic option of limited cooperation with Japan and the United States. China initiated this latter policy only after the deterioration of Sino-Soviet relations in 1969, and its continuation is by no means inevitable.

Two separate tendencies in the Chinese leadership will clearly have an important impact on China's foreign policy, although it is not clear that either tendency will close entirely the option of

[10]See I. Ivkov, "Japan's Acute Problems," *International Affairs,* no. 8, 1976, pp. 98–108, and Soviet coverage of the 13th Congress of the Japanese Communist Party following the "Lockheed Scandal," *Pravda,* July 31, 1976.

limited cooperation with Japan and the United States. The pragmatic tendency in Chinese politics, identified with former Premier Chou En-lai, has been carried by Teng Hsiao-ping and Hua Kuofeng. This tendency, while it emphasizes economic development and deemphasizes ideological strife at home, does not support a single and obvious line in foreign and defense policies. On the contrary, adherents of pragmatic politics might well support reconciliation with the Soviet Union on grounds that economic growth would be facilitated, or they might support a continuation of quadrangular power policies to that same end. The ideological militants in Chinese politics—especially those associated with the Great Proletarian Cultural Revolution, like the ''Shanghai group,'' that had surrounded Mao's wife, Chiang Ching—have been discredited, purged, and in many cases arrested. Should they, or persons with lesser reputations who supported them, return to power, it seems unlikely that they could effect a rapprochement with the Soviets and it is not at all clear that even they would choose completely to reverse the policy of cooperation with Japan and the United States. Thus, the ''China opening'' seems based on objective considerations that are certainly supported by, but not limited to, the pragmatic swing in Peking internal politics.

Irrespective of internal political developments, which cannot be predicted with any certainty, Soviet military power will confront any political leadership that emerges in Peking. And China seems likely to seek to maintain an effective balance of power in the Far East and to develop its military power.

Thus Soviet security requirements and political objectives in the Far East are not likely to change dramatically in the 1980s. Although geopolitical rivalry with China will likely be muted, it seems almost certain that it will persist. Assuming that worst-case eventualities—for example, war or wide-scale Soviet intervention in Chinese domestic politics—do not occur, Soviet objectives in the Far East will retain their essential shape:

1. To avoid direct military confrontation with any of the quadrangular powers, which might upset the present balance in East Asia and encourage more vigorous Japanese defense efforts;

2. To expand Soviet military capabilities, especially naval forces of the Pacific Fleet, although not at a rate that threatens other political interests in the region;

3. To promote a reduction in United States presence and influence along the East Asian rim, although that objective may not include the removal of all American military forces;

4. To maintain cooperative relations with Japan as a source of advanced technology and economic credits (especially for the development of Siberia) and as a means of exercising some leverage over Japanese relations with the United States and the People's Republic of China;

5. To promote Soviet political influence by supporting the gradual leftward drift of Japanese politics and the fortunes of the Japanese Communist Party, but not to jeopardize Soviet relations with the Japanese government;

6. To moderate ideological differences with the Chinese Communist Party on terms acceptable to the CPSU;

7. To encourage the "peaceful" reunification of Korea under the domination of the communists.

All these policies suggest a low-risk profile for the Soviet Union in East Asia. They also mix cooperative and conflictive interests with the United States.

These Soviet objectives limit the possibilities for cooperation between the United States and the U.S.S.R. in East Asia, but they also suggest some general directions that United States policy should take. First, the quadrangular pattern of power seems more favorable to American interests than any mutation of it. The United States is not the major military actor in this pattern, and it should be possible to retain the balance with marginal United States military presence. That objective, however, will require the retention of effective United States forces in the Far East and the maintenance of political relations which make that objective feasible. It will also mean careful attention to power relations between the Soviet Union and the People's Republic of China. The acquisition by either country of naval forces adequate to threaten the political independence of American allies in Asia—Japan in particular—would clearly harm American interests and raise the possibility of Soviet-American military conflict in the region. While the Chinese navy is not a major threat now, it has increased its interdiction capabilities, and Soviet lines of communication in the Pacific are vulnerable.[11] Should the United States withdraw and/or the Soviet Union reposition its Pacific Fleet, the Chinese would clearly have a major regional role, and in some scenarios might prove dominant, at least until Japan responded with renewed naval programs.

Second, Japan is critical to an effective power balance in East Asia. The United States will need to acquire new habits encouraging Japan to take increasing regional leadership in political and economic affairs and trusting Japan's exercise of that leadership to secure many American interests. So important is Japan to the effective working of a quadrangular power balance in East Asia that unilateral actions by the United States in pursuit of specific national interests seem almost invariably counterproductive when these interests create tensions with Japan. The relationship is delicate because the United States must continue to cooperate with Japan on questions of defense and thereby to assist Japan in achieving a military course unique among great political and economic powers.

While some degree of rearmament might be "natural" for Japan, there are substantial political risks for both Japan and the United States in any major Japanese military program. The effects of a more aggressive Japanese defense policy on the Soviet and Chinese military postures in East Asia cannot be predicted with any certainty. It is difficult to see how Japan could rearm without a military response from China and the Soviet Union or without driving the two countries into closer relations. From the

[11]See Francis J. Romance, "Peking's Counter-Encirclement Strategy: The Maritime Element," *Orbis*, Summer 1976, pp. 437–460. For some suggestive indications of Soviet concerns, see Y. Semyonov, "The Bitter Fruit of Maoism," *International Affairs*, no. 9, September 1976, especially pp. 44–46; L. Latyshev, "Japan at a Diplomatic Crossroads," ibid., no. 10, October, 1975, especially pp. 61–64; V. Volodin, "Peking Maneuvers in South Asia," ibid., no. 11, November 1978, pp. 19–27; and comments on the Sino-Japanese Treaty, e.g., *Pravda*, October 15, 1978.

perspective of American interests, either development would be undesirable, and the effects of Japanese rearmament on American policy toward the Philippines, Indonesia, Australia, and Southeast Asia would create additional difficulties.

Continuation of the present security relationship between the United States and Japan is in the American interest. Japan's unique position is critical to maintaining the power balance of East Asia, and it may well be appropriate for the United States to cooperate more fully with Japan than it has in the past as a means of recognizing its political and economic leadership and of persuading it to avoid dramatic and destabilizing gestures of rearmament. Japanese rearmament on any significant scale would be so injurious to Soviet interests in Asia that the United States should be able to secure that country's tacit cooperation in encouraging Japanese restraint and in avoiding actions likely to threaten Japan sufficiently to make restraint nonviable.

While the United States cannot by any means dictate the choices of Japanese defense policy, it has even less influence over the third general direction of American policy suggested by Soviet objectives in East Asia. It is clear that the present balance has been improved by the ideological and national rivalry of the two major communist powers. This suggests that the United States must continue to walk the tightrope between them. It must cooperate with both powers, but must not be perceived by either to extend unilateral advantages to the other. Thus the "China opening" of 1972 and 1978–79 must be sustained, even enlarged. Both powers, however, are regional and global adversaries of the United States as well as occasional partners, and a one-sided policy of cooperation with either will certainly prove costly in the end. Still, so undesirable would more effective American-Chinese cooperation be to the Soviet Union that United States policy should be able to employ the tacit threat of that alternative to prevent the Kremlin from adventurist actions in Asia.

Fourth, President Carter has recognized that the United States has become a captive of its policy in South Korea. Its support for the Park regime raised broad questions of moral compromise and the conflict between long-term and short-term political interests. But with respect to Soviet-American relations in East Asia, the case is not so difficult. While Moscow has called for removal of American troops, withdrawal would serve Soviet objectives only if it did not lead to a war between North and South Korea into which it and the United States might be drawn. In addition, even if its objective of "peaceful reunification" were achieved under terms wholly acceptable to the North Korean communists, reunification would not be satisfactory if it either increased Chinese influence on the peninsula or so threatened Japan that it encouraged a more vigorous Japanese program for national defense. Thus, it would seem possible for the United States to cooperate with a moderate leadership in Moscow on the Korean issue. A continued American military presence supporting South Korea should prove tolerable to the Soviet Union, especially if the regime can be moderated after Park's assassination, and the United States should be able to count on the Soviets to exercise a restraining influence on North Korea's hegemonic ambitions.

THE MIDDLE EAST

Soviet-American relations in the Middle East are similar to those in the Far East in one important respect and dissimilar to them in another. As in the Far East, neither the Soviet Union nor the United States is able to exercise decisive influence, and the politics of both are captive to domestic developments in regional states. Unlike the Far East, where the two principal political dynamics—Chinese independence from Soviet influence and Japanese economic power—work to the American advantage in its competition with the Soviet Union, almost no political dynamic in the Middle East works substantially to the advantage of either superpower. Conversely, the economic dynamics of the region do work to the advantage of the industrialized and technological economies of Europe and North America. It is there that the markets for Middle Eastern petroleum exist and hard currencies can be found, by means of which the oil-rich states expect to modernize their societies during a period in which their favorable balance of trade makes importation of Western technology possible.

167

The one certainty of United States policy in the Middle East is that America's fundamental interests there conflict more sharply and dangerously with those of the Soviet Union than anywhere else. Thinking about the 1980s in this one geographic area, therefore, is especially important, but it is also almost uniquely obstructed by the universal myopia which makes the Israeli-Arab confrontation the focus of all discussion. The Israeli-Arab conflict has driven both Soviet and American policy in the Middle East for two decades, and it may continue to do so in the coming decade. But it would be a mistake to assume that the Israeli-Arab conflict will continue to do so, as events in Iran have so clearly demonstrated during the winter of 1978–79. In projecting toward the future of the region it is therefore necessary to think in terms of scenarios for the eastern end of the Mediterrean and the littorals of the Persian Gulf and Red Sea that involve various kinds of political conflict. It is possible that neither the United States nor the Soviet Union has defined its interests very sharply beyond the immediate problem of an Israeli-Arab settlement.

Although the issue of Kremlin policy in the Middle East is one of the most passionately ideological among American observers of the Soviet Union, there is surprising agreement among analysts of all political persuasions about the nature of Soviet regional interests. These have been, since 1956: (1) to promote the erosion of influence exercised by former colonial powers and the United States; (2) to support the Arabs' cause in their confrontations with Israel as a means of extending Soviet influence and diminishing that of the United States; (3) to support "national democratic" and "anti-imperialist" regimes even when that support has meant, as in the case of Egypt, sacrificing local communist parties; (4) partly as a consequence of these previous objectives and partly as a program for realizing ancient Russian and Soviet ambitions, to move Soviet naval forces gradually, but steadily, into the Mediterranean Sea and Indian Ocean; (5) to promote "neither war nor peace" strategies by the Arab belligerents along the Gaza and Golan lines of demarcation, or along the borders separating Jordan and Lebanon from their Jewish adversaries.

What is striking about these objectives is how closely they

parallel traditional superpower rules of rivalry and how little they seem influenced by Marxist-Leninist ideological considerations. Moreover, these policy objectives reveal few of the subtleties of cooperation and conflict found in Soviet policies toward the United States and Europe. While it is true that the Brezhnev leadership has developed an implicitly shared interest with the United States in containing the risks of a direct military confrontation between the superpowers in the Middle East, that interest has been limited and frequently sacrificed to the overall competitive thrust of the five objectives listed above.

The occasional coincidence of interests between Washington and Moscow was illustrated by Soviet reluctance to support Egyptian President Anwar Sadat's hardening position on the necessity for a military solution to the Egyptian-Israeli impasse during the winter of 1971–72, which hesitation finally led to the expulsion of the Soviets in July 1972, and by Secretary of State Kissinger's hurried and urgent flight to Moscow in October 1973, where the "cease-fire-in-place" was negotiated, which in turn eventually led to United Nations Security Council Resolution 338. But on both occasions the overlap of Soviet and American interests was narrow—to reduce the risks of outright military hostilities between the superpowers—and both powers continued to take actions that increased the risks of war between them. In fact, it can be argued that those risks actually reached their highest point since 1962 in the confrontation between elements of the Sixth Fleet and the Red Navy in the Eastern Mediterranean during the October War—a remarkable fact given the success of the two powers in containing the risks of military confrontation between them during the ten years of the Vietnam war.

The narrowness of these shared interests and the conflictive nature of Soviet objectives in the Middle East have led many observers to conclude that the Soviet Union prefers that the Israeli-Arab conflict not be resolved. It is easy, however, to confuse preferences with incidental profit. Prolonged conflict strengthens Soviet options, because some Arab clients will almost inevitably be dependent on the Soviet Union for arms and others will not risk closing the option of obtaining arms from Moscow.

The Soviet Union does profit from the irresolution of the conflict. But there is no substantial evidence to suggest that the Soviet Union has taken steps to obstruct an agreement thereby to retain its advantage. On the contrary, the Soviet position has been remarkably consistent throughout the 1970s: Israeli withdrawal from and return of occupied lands, Israel's right to exist as a sovereign state, and, more recently, the rights of the Palestinian people to a homeland.[12] These are, of course, the very issues that seem irresoluble, and the Soviet Union has profited from the dependence that fact creates for those Arab clients who see force as the only means of securing their interests. But the line is fine between prolonged conflict that breeds politically advantageous dependence and the risk of war brought on the Soviet Union by events over which it has little control, and some forces in Moscow would be willing to sacrifice some of the political advantage to reduce the risks of war.

American policy pressed toward a political resolution of the conflict—first in Kissinger's "step by step" diplomacy, then in the Carter administration's shift toward greater even-handedness in American treatment of Israel and Egypt, which was an important precondition for the Camp David success in the fall of 1978 and the treaty of 1979. These efforts have promoted an ambivalent reaction in the Soviet leadership. The Soviet Union can be expected to press for the return of the territories occupied in 1967 and for Palestinian rights, but it probably will not press for a "maximum solution" and may actually accept an agreement with substantial guarantees of Israeli security.

The picture that emerges from this analysis is that Soviet influence is severely proscribed in the Middle East. Following the 1967 war, the Soviets first worked to get Nasser's agreement to a negotiated settlement that would return occupied territories, then attempted to pressure Israel into political and territorial

[12]Compare, for example, Brezhnev's Reports to the Twenty-Fourth and Twenty-Fifth Party Congresses: *Pravda,* March 21, 1971 and February 25, 1976. The point is made in more exact parallel by examining the Soviet press during the 1971, 1973–1974, and 1978 American peace efforts: R. Petrov, "Arab Unity: Lessons and Prospects," *New Times* (Moscow), no. 18, May 1, 1971, p. 51; the Joint Communique following Podgorny's visit to Cairo in May 1971, *Pravda,* May 28, 1971; Gromyko's address at the Geneva Peace Talks, *Pravda,* December 22, 1973; A. Bovin's article in *Izvestia* on the Camp David meeting, September 20, 1978.

concessions. When the Soviet strategy came apart on the rock of Israeli intransigence, its Arab clients moved toward a military solution and the Soviet Union probably advised caution.[13] The July 1972 expulsion of the Soviets from their Egyptian bases almost certainly reflected Sadat's frustration with Soviet hesitation in supporting a military solution.

Although Egypt and the U.S.S.R. improved their relations after the 1972 low point, especially through the instrument of the Soviet airlift in the 1973 October War, Egypt has increasingly relied on improving its relations with the United States in the expectation that Secretary of State Kissinger and President Carter could deliver a political solution to the Israeli-Arab conflict. Thus, particularly when a partial political solution has been constructed in the Israeli–United States–Egyptian treaty, Soviet influence has been limited. Of course, that could change. A dramatic change in Egyptian domestic politics, failure to advance the 1979 treaty toward a more comprehensive settlement, or a return to reliance on a military solution by the militant Arabs might increase Soviet influence. One supposes that intensification of the United States role under Kissinger and Carter diplomacy has finite limitations in time. While the treaty represented an impressive achievement, it could come apart on the remaining issues of the West Bank, the Palestinians, the unsettled status of Lebanon and Jordan, and the continued hostility of Syria and Iraq. Still, conditions in the Middle East cannot be encouraging from Moscow's viewpoint. If the Arabs settle once again on a military solution, their chances are certainly much worse than they were in 1973, when the Soviet Union had to threaten direct intervention to save the Egyptian Third Army, and the risks of direct conflict with the United States would reappear. As long as all parties seem charted on a diplomatic course, even if there were a return to some kind of dependence on the Geneva mechanism, Arab moderates will need to rely on the United States to pressure Israel for a relatively favorable settlement. Only if Israel and the United States remain committed to negotiations and if Moscow can pose as a protector of the maximum Arab

[13]The evidence for this interpretation is mostly negative—Sadat's inability to get new Soviet arms in February and April 1972. See, for example, *Pravda*, March 17, 1972.

demands will Soviet influence be maximized. But these conditions are not likely. If the Soviet Union and the Arab states press too hard for complete withdrawal from all occupied territories and a Palestinian state, the Israelis will certainly break off the negotiations and the diplomatic wedge between Washington and Tel Aviv will dissipate. On the contrary, it is in Arab interests to seem reasonable and to focus on issues like the West Bank and Gaza settlements, where American support for Israeli positions is weak or nonexistent. Thus, from Moscow's perspective either a return to belligerency or continued resort to the diplomatic process limits Soviet influence.

Differences in the Soviet leadership on these questions may not be substantial. The issues of the Middle East do not seem to activate the fault line between modernist and orthodox impulses of Soviet political life. It is possible that most Soviet leaders share either the well-documented anti-Semitic bias of Russian political culture or an ideological distaste for the manner in which Israel seems so successfully to have defied the historical laws Marxists and Leninists have always stressed.

Thus, it is necessary to look beyond the immediate causes of Soviet-American conflict in the Middle East and ask whether there might be more substantial and long-standing interests of conflict or cooperation.

Energy and Oil

Changes in Soviet trading patterns for energy may constitute the most significant impetus behind shifts in foreign policy in the 1980s, and these will affect no region more than the Middle East.

Soviet requirements, which were analyzed in Chapter 2, will affect Soviet policy toward the Middle East greatly, but the nature of the changes cannot easily be predicted. It seems evident that access to Middle Eastern supplies will be a minimum requirement of Soviet policy. Its relations have not been good with the largest oil producers of the region, and one can expect added efforts to gain and maintain access to Saudi, Iranian, and Persian Gulf oil.

The basic fact is that substantial pressures will draw the Soviet Union into the Middle East region as an economic competitor with Western industrialized and consuming nations. On the one hand Soviet strategy might stress the conflictive aspect of its relations in the region and with other competitive powers. Such a strategy would include Soviet military presence, which enables the U.S.S.R. to exert pressure or establish influence, to keep open lines of communication and supply, and to dissuade competitors from asserting their interests by military means. The conflictive strategy will also attempt to arrange preferential treatment by a combination of political and economic means. On the other hand, the Soviet Union might be induced to develop a cooperative strategy in which it shares an interest with the United States and other oil-importing nations in maintaining free access to the region's resources and in permitting market forces to set prices without political or military pressure.

Clearly, American and Western interests will be far better served by the cooperative than by the conflictive Soviet approach to securing larger interests in the Middle East. The web of issues is tightly woven. A policy to reduce superpower military presence in the region would discourage assertion of conflictive interests by force, would encourage open market conditions for access to oil, and would enable all powers to exert some control over the risks of accidental or unintentional military entanglement. If the Soviet Union is encouraged to adopt market strategies for securing its oil requirements, it will need to earn hard currency, and that will increase the Soviet incentive to trade. That encouragement will require persistent and difficult efforts to accept the Soviet Union as an integral member of the international economic system and to foster the perception in Moscow that the Soviet Union has a stake in a stable economic order. Both Western strategies—to reduce the level of military presence in the Middle East and to encourage the Soviet Union to integrate its economic needs more closely with the international market system—will have the incidental effects of strengthening those political forces in Moscow whose programs include the latter and may, by implication, encourage the modernist tendency in Soviet domestic political and economic life.

Political Development

The radical shift in world economic power toward the Middle East in the 1970s has had, and will continue to have, destabilizing political effects. This instability cuts in two very different, but possibly mutually reinforcing ways. First, oil-rich states are modernizing on a scale and at a pace unprecedented in human history. The attendant social trends—urbanization, recruitment of new members to national elites, rapid expansion of economic and political participation, creation of internal demonstration effects, and exposure of wider segments of the population to the international demonstration effects by which the life style of individuals is contrasted with those of people far more "advanced" in the modernization process—have all been accompanied in less dramatic cases by political upheaval. It would be Pollyanna-ish, therefore, not to expect political instability, including revolution and the emergence of radical political groupings. Iran may simply have exhibited the first manifestation of the larger process.

Second, the distribution of oil wealth is exceptionally skewed. The ratio of wealth to population could hardly be less proportional. And pressures will probably grow for redistribution within the region. This mixture of rapid internal social, economic, and political changes and probable demands for redistribution of regional wealth is highly explosive. It might also be argued that the Israeli-Arab confrontation has kept the lid on these other regional conflicts, and that progress on that issue will loosen restraints on others.

Thus, there will be a temptation for the Soviet Union to extend its influence by traditional and orthodox means. Communist parties and leftist radicals will certainly play a role in exacerbated intraregional political conflicts, and, given the Soviet need to secure access to the region's resources, it will be tempted to support dissident and revolutionary factions. In fact, there will almost inevitably develop the classic ambivalence in Soviet foreign policy between the immediate interest of cooperation with national governments controlling resources and the encouragement of dissident elements seeking to overthrow them. Soviet ambivalence at the end of 1978 over the turmoil in Iran reflects the temptation and the hesitation. It was easy to warn the United States to keep "hands off" developments there, but impossible for Moscow to predict the course of events in Teheran or even to assess which outcome would be most satisfactory. Neither a fundamentalist Islamic state nor a military dictatorship seemed preferable to the Shah. And in its uncertainty, Moscow could do little more than snipe at American difficulties, protest the American role, and hope for a "revolutionary" outcome.

These two tendencies in Soviet policies toward the Middle East cut in contradictory directions. Immediate need for oil can increase the Soviet stake in cooperation and regional stability. Political upheaval in the region will tempt the Soviets to engage in conflictive behavior. This ambiguity in the international dimension of Soviet relations with the Middle East in the 1980s will activate the domestic ambivalence between the modernist and orthodox political tendencies. This study argued earlier that it is in American interests and the interests of international stability to encourage modernism in the Soviet Union and that Soviet requirements for oil would provide a lever to encourage it. But indigenous Middle Eastern political instability promotes orthodox responses in the Kremlin. If increased regional political instability is inevitable, two United States policy responses seem necessary. First, it is important to manage the superpower military balance in the region so that the Soviet Union does not find conditions favorable for the employment of force in support of factions or clients. Second, it will be necessary to encourage orderly change, including redistribution of regional economic and political power. This is easily said, but American leverage is not great, especially given its own short-term requirements for oil. It is almost predictable, then, that factional and even interstate conflict will occasionally erupt in the Middle East.

These dynamics seem to provide the best case for the contention that Soviet and American power to influence global political developments is diminished. It is not easy to see how developments in the Middle East can be anticipated with much precision or influenced by either superpower to any great degree. Still, the temptation will persist to employ military means to establish or retain influence and to back clients in political struggles in which the stakes are high. The limitations on superpower influence and the implicit risks to the primary interest of each—unobstructed access to resources—might make attractive policies designed to lower military presence and political competition. But such policies will be difficult at best and will require determined United States efforts in the face of probable setbacks.

The realistic question, however, is not whether efforts to lower the risks of superpower conflict in the region can be sustained, but rather, what the alternatives are. It is doubtful that either power has a greater chance of securing economic advantages by maintaining high-profile military and political policies, and efforts to advance competitive political and ideological claims will almost certainly increase the risks of disrupting access to resources. Thus, ultimately, the choice of strategy comes down to a determination of how pressing the primary economic interest in the region really is. If economic requirements are high, a mutual interest in promoting stability, and in acquiring the relatively more secure access to resources, can be established. From the point of view of American interests, a strategy that promotes cooperation and lowers the chances for political and military conflict promises the ancillary benefit of encouraging desirable political tendencies within the U.S.S.R.

The Military Powderkeg

Oil and political conflict have drawn vast quantities of arms into the Middle East. It has surpassed Europe as the region commanding the highest density of military forces. At the height of the October War in 1973, the Soviet Union had deployed over 90 ships in the Mediterranean, a force which probably outnumbered if it did not "outgun" American forces, and an additional force in the Indian Ocean.[14] Moreover, Soviet submarines had created conditions in the crowded eastern Mediterranean in which the "survivability" of American carriers became questionable. This concentration of forces underlines the extent to which the Red Navy had developed the capacity to challenge

[14]Senate Armed Services Committee Print, Congressional Reference Service, *United States/Soviet Military Balance,* Washington, D.C., 1976, p. 8.

American domination of the seas in selected environments. Even in less crisis-like conditions than prevailed during the 1973 war, the Soviet Black Sea Fleet maintains a substantial naval force on station in the Mediterranean that it can augment relatively quickly to challenge the Sixth Fleet.

These elements of superpower military confrontation, however, pale beside the concentration of indigenous military forces. Of course, much of this concentration of substantial and impressive military forces has been driven by the conflict between the Arab states and Israel. But the armaments of Iran and Saudi Arabia, for example, can be traced to petro-dollars, to the ambition to exercise greater influence in the region, and to the anticipation of the forces for instability discussed in the previous section. Should the Israeli-Arab conflict become less urgent in the 1980s, these forces might assume a quite different complexion. For example, several of the states have acquired the capability to place either superpower under considerable strain if it should choose to assert its regional interests by military means. Iran, Egypt, Syria, Saudi Arabia, and possibly even Iraq have acquired forces which might be employed to influence political outcomes in the region and even on its periphery. The instability of politics in the region makes these forces doubly dangerous. They may be used in a variety of ways and the superpowers may be drawn into conflict. Or, as events in Iran underline, political changes, by coup or revolution, may alter the balance of forces overnight. The transfer of high-technology military capabilities assumes substantial risks despite the lure of petro-dollars. Careful American military advisers have long been nervous about the direction in which Iranian F-14s might be pointed (see Table 5).

The combination of relative improvements in regional military forces vis-à-vis superpower forces in the region and the expectation of political instability might either increase the probability of superpower involvement or provide incentives to control these risks. The temptation to intervene as backers of local clients—either with materiel or supporting forces—will be real. Especially given the role of the United States and the Soviet Union as suppliers of military technology and the likelihood that balance-of-payments difficulties will encourage continued arms sales, it

TABLE 5

Military Forces and Equipment of Selected Middle East Countries, 1979

	Total Armed Forces	Tanks/ Most Modern Type	Combat Aircraft/ Most Modern Type
Egypt	395,000	1680/T-62, PT-76	563SU-20, MiG-23 Mirage III
Iran	415,000	1985/M-60	447 F-4, F-5, F-14
Iraq	222,000	1900/T-62, PT-76	339 MiG 23
Israel	165,000	5125/M-60, T-62, PT-76	576 F-15, F-4, Kfir, Mirage III
Jordan	67,200	500/M-60	73 F-5, F-104
Saudi Arabia	44,500	550/M-60	178 F-5
Syria	227,500	2700/T-62, PT-76	389 MiG-23

SOURCE International Institute for Strategic Studies, *Military Balance, 1979–1980,* London, 1979.

seems unlikely that they will be able to remain aloof from combat in the region irrespective of its political origins. There is a substantial difference, however, between the risk of supplying technology and the risks of actual military participation in hostilities. It is certainly in the interests of both powers to reduce the latter, even if economic necessity makes control of the former improbable.

The interaction between the United States and the Soviet Union in the Middle East has been dominated by the Israeli-Arab confrontation for over 20 years. As long as that conflict remains unresolved, the two powers will remain partially hostage to developments in this region. Their relative fortunes in the competition to affect outcomes there will undoubtedly fluctuate as they have throughout the 1970s, but they will remain fundamentally unable to control events or even the risks of their own involvement in direct hostilities. Thus, they seem to share an interest in reducing those risks, but their political positions on the return of territories, the Palestinian question, and Israeli requirements for security are basically divergent. Furthermore, the Soviet Union has advanced its influence in the region during the prolonged crisis and there no doubt exists considerable ambivalence in Moscow concerning the effects of a political settlement on long-range Soviet interests. The role for United States policy is delicate. It must continue to increase the credibility of its role as a mediator by correcting the perception of one-sided support for Israel, but it cannot exercise decisive influence in Tel Aviv and it has only recently established influence in Cairo and Damascus. The failure of these efforts, however, would strengthen the Soviet role once again, would drive the Arabs back into a more dependent relationship with Moscow, and would deflate whatever pressure exists inside the Kremlin to resolve the crisis or to contain the dangers of direct Soviet-American involvement.

This one feature of Middle East politics may not continue to drive all American and Soviet policy. Other conflicts may well appear, as they have in Iran, and assume relatively greater importance even if the Israeli-Arab confrontation is not ameliorated. Under either scenario—improvement in the fundamental Middle East conflict or the intrusion of other crises—the United States must transcend its traditional myopia of single-factor interest in the region. There are other issues of importance for Soviet-American relations in the 1980s.

First, the Soviet Union will quite possibly become a competitor for Middle Eastern oil by the mid-1980s. I argued earlier that it is in American interests to encourage the U.S.S.R. to participate in the international petroleum market. The implicit Soviet need for hard currency to finance an oil deficit in its balance of trade makes attractive orderly and expanded access to the markets of industrialized nations. The alternative is hardly attractive, since it would almost certainly increase the probability that a new Soviet leadership in the early 1980s would protect or advance its petroleum interests by a combination of backing political clients and exercising military pressure. The complementary benefit of encouraging a cooperative Soviet strategy to deal with the Soviet Union's probable oil requirements is that people in Moscow advocating modernist policy preferences will be in a position best to profit from them.

Second, the rapid transformation of regional political and economic cultures and the uneven distribution of the new wealth from oil will increase political instability in the Middle East during the 1980s, which almost inevitably will create pressures to secure Soviet interests by the traditional means of promoting revolution or supporting dissident factions. Such behavior is not in United States interests, although American options for shaping Soviet incentives in these matters are not numerous. Perhaps the United States can exercise some influence by promoting voluntary and peaceful changes in the region, but the record is not encouraging. Undoubtedly, the best American strategy will be to foster the perception in Moscow that its oil interests are best served by cooperative actions to maintain free and equal access to regional resources and the perception that the Soviet Union has an expanded stake in the undisrupted functioning of international economic mechanisms.

Finally, conflict in the Middle East has served as a lightning rod to attract concentrated bolts of military power. Again, the probability that the Soviet Union will develop new competitive interests in the region with the United States, combined with the military force that both powers have concentrated in the region, is potentially explosive. It is in the interests of both powers to defuse the powderkeg, and ideas like the creation of a nuclear-free zone in the Indian Ocean and arms control in the Mediterranean—both of which have received high-level Soviet support—hold promise for reducing the risks of direct military confrontation. The need to rethink the purpose of superpower military forces in the region is made more urgent by the heavy concentration of regional forces and the probability that these will be activated by the multidimensional political and economic conflicts of the Middle East. Neither power will probably be able to stop supplying arms, but there is a clear mutual interest in reducing the level of superpower forces that might be drawn into local conflicts.

These three regional interests exist outside the framework of the Israeli-Arab conflict and they combine to make an ambiguous picture for the 1980s. They can promote conflict or cooperation. It will take patient, coordinated, and determined policies by the West to reduce the potential for conflict and to encourage a new Kremlin leadership to perceive its interests as being served by cooperation in the Middle East. But the stakes are also high. The potential for military crisis in the Middle East is great, and flash points which draw in the United States and the Soviet Union on opposite sides will encourage orthodox and ideological tendencies in Moscow. With respect to such complicated international issues there are no guarantees that any policy will coax events in a desirable direction, but United States and Western policies have a greater chance of encouraging a stable and peaceful world order and domestic developments in the Soviet Union consistent with American interests if they: engage the Soviets in a system of cooperative efforts to decrease military forces, encourage extraregional powers to exercise restraint in local crises, and increase the confidence of the leadership in Moscow that its access to the region's resources is more reliably secured by reliance on international economic mechanisms and open markets than by manipulating clients and attempting to secure markets by military force.

AFRICA

Soviet foreign policy has probably experienced sharper fluctuations of success and failure in Africa than in any other region. This policy has also seemed more often to lead to precipitous strikes at "targets of opportunity" and to be based less on a long-range conception of Soviet interests. In Africa, too, Soviet behavior has revealed great ambivalence between traditional great-power geopolitical competition and ideological promotion of revolution and communism. Soviet support for Somalia seemed especially to be characterized by the "great power" motivation of acquiring base rights on the Horn of Africa until 1977, when that support was suddenly withdrawn and shifted to Ethiopia for reasons that were partly ideological. At times the policy has clearly indicated bureaucratic rivalry in Moscow. Altogether, Soviet behavior in Africa has reflected a mixture of motivations and has achieved very uneven results.

The Soviet Union has had two substantial assets in its efforts to establish and extend influence in Africa. First, its ideology provides an analytical framework that regards change as inevitable and justifies the exercise of violence to promote change. Marxism-Leninism is also explicitly anticolonial. These qualities inevitably appealed to the Continent when the first and overriding order of business was to liquidate the nineteenth century colonial empires. What was remarkable about Soviet policy in the 1960s and 1970s was how quickly this substantial advantage in its competition with the West and the United States was allowed to dissipate. The second advantage parallels the attraction of Soviet anticolonial philosophy. European powers and the United States have been tied in complicated ways to the white colonial outposts in southern Africa. While these regimes would have been targets of black African nationalism and the emerging sense of black identity in any case, Rhodesia and South Africa in particular have adopted racist policies almost perversely guaranteed to isolate them from the overwhelming majority of humankind. In both of these cases, Marxism-Leninism has served the Kremlin leadership well by anticipating the winds of change, while American identification with its Western European political, economic, and cultural foundations has led it to resist change and support regimes that otherwise embrace few principles that correspond to the American national experience.

Given these two substantial advantages for the Soviet Union in Africa, it is surprising how little durable success the Soviets have achieved there. The obstructions to Soviet policy are also deep-rooted and profound. First, Marxist-Leninist identification of the proletariat as the cutting edge of revolution has not fitted the facts of black Africa, where seasonal workers, peasants working small plots, petty traders, and businessmen have constituted the most alienated social groupings and in which tribal loyalties more often drive political events than do class antagonisms. Second, the shift in focus for international politics from East-West to North-South clearly identifies the difficulties of white, essentially European, industrialized, urban, and consumerist cultures in relating to what Lin Piao identified as the values of the countryside. The Soviet Union's policies in Africa have not been successful, have usually become unpopular, and have often revealed a persistent strain of racism.

There is another substantial reason for Soviet failures in Africa. Moscow was slow to shift from the decolonizing theme after much of sub-Saharan Africa had become independent. The Soviets attempted to stretch their successful anti-imperialist foreign policy into a more general identification of the new African states with a pro-Moscow and anti-Western orientation. While there were few outright supporters of the West and the United States among political leaders of the emerging African nations, almost all of them were wary of becoming too closely identified with any great power and most of them adopted a firm policy of keeping great-power rivalry out of Africa. They were willing to accept support from any source for their struggle for independence and, after that was accomplished, to accept aid from any nation, provided the strings were loose and few. Furthermore, the shift from anti-colonialism to economic and political development as the primary focus of African politics took place precisely as the Sino-Soviet dispute emerged as a major factor on the international political scene, and Soviet rivalry with China has been at least as significant a constraint on Soviet African policy as have the generic weaknesses of the Marxist-Leninist biases and Russian ethnocentrism.

Thus, both the United States and the Soviet Union suffer from substantial difficulties in their policies toward Africa. In projecting possible competition there into the 1980s, it would be sensible to distinguish between questions that are essentially political and economic on the one hand and those that are geographic and strategic on the other hand. Relations in the former case will undoubtedly continue to be characterized by very uneven performances on the part of both superpowers and will reveal a high degree of ideological conflict. In the latter case, Africa sits astride the central lines of communication between both powers and their principal allies and the oil of the Persian Gulf. Furthermore, in a resource-conscious future, Africa's own riches will increasingly become a prize for international competition.

Political and Economic Competition

Unless the United States moves its policy on Africa much closer to cooperation with that continent's black leadership and dissociates itself entirely from the white minority regimes, the United States will continue to forfeit the political competition. That is not to say that the United States will be left without influence, but the degree to which it equivocates on this primary issue will diminish its political influence throughout Africa. There can be no question that elimination of white minority regimes is the primary agenda of black African leadership, and possibly has been since the founding of the Organization of African Unity (OAU) at Addis Ababa in May 1963. It was the sole basis for the formation of the OAU's African Liberation Committee (ALC), which coordinates the armed resistance. The United States has attempted to walk a tightrope between support for majority rule in southern Africa and encouragement of peaceful means to that end. African leaders have been unanimous in their adoption of liberation as a unifying theme, but differences on the means by which this political objective might be accomplished go back to the roots of pan-African cooperation.

The split between the Casablanca and Monrovia groups in the early 1960s can be traced to this issue. The Lusaka Manifesto of April 1969 continued the tradition established by the latter group of pursuing political objectives by negotiation rather than violence. While the theme was muted during the disintegration of the Portuguese colonial system, it reemerged after the rebellion of the Portuguese army in 1974 and the establishment of a new government in Lisbon. Late in 1974, again at Lusaka, South Africa was offered a series of proposals by which the transfer of power from white minorities to black majorities might be accomplished. It is clear that former Prime Minister John Vorster had decided to abandon the recalcitrant Rhodesian regime and to compromise with black demands on South Africa's periphery while pulling his own defense of white rule back into the South African redoubt, and his significant tightening of the screws of racial control at home in 1977 may have reflected this badger-like strategy of white rule in South Africa.

But this process of steady southward pressure by black Africa and of determined retreat to defensible positions by white supremacists has tied American policy to a doubly losing strategy. The United States encouraged black African efforts at moderation, then urged the Rhodesians and South Africans to utilize the time gained by gestures of conciliation to negotiate peaceful change. When that strategy seemed to go aground on the intransigence of Rhodesian Prime Minister Ian Smith, the United States began to disassociate from the white Rhodesian regime's efforts at a "national" solution while it continued to make efforts at influencing the governments of former Prime Minister Vorster and then P. W. Botha in South Africa to moderate their domestic policies and to withdraw from Namibia. Thus, in the interests of nonviolent transition in southern Africa, the United States made its policies dependent on persuading the most racist regimes to moderate. In so doing, it earns the enmity of impatient black Africa by seeming to shore up the crumbling edifice of white rule and of Rhodesians and South Africans by seeming to exert pressure for solutions that are barely more acceptable to them than the demands of total surrender made by the most radical liberation movements.

The final irony of this American policy, of course, was the dilemma it faced after the election of a black African government in Rhodesia. Not only did the election of Bishop Abel Muzorewa's government seem to offer the kind of moderate alternative to which American policy had long been dedicated and thus to place the Carter administration in the position of backing "radical" solutions (at least in the minds of some Congressional leaders), but following the election of Margaret Thatcher's Conservative Party in Britain, Rhodesian policy threatened to produce a visible split between London and Washington.

Against this screen of political change, of course, must be projected the picture of the liberation movements themselves.

It is an incredible story of success: the African Party for the Independence of "Portuguese" Guinea and the Cape Verde Islands (PAIGC), the Front for the Liberation of Mozambique (FRELIMO), the Popular Movement for the Liberation of Angola (MPLA), the Zimbabwe African National Union (ZANU) and Zimbabwe African People's Union (ZAPU), the African National Congress and the South West African People's Organization (SWAPO). PAIGC achieved power in Guinea-Bissau, FRELIMO in Mozambique, and the MPLA in Angola in 1975. It seems only a matter of time before some combination of the Zimbabwe groups, possibly the Zimbabwe Liberation Army's (ZILA) High Command, attains power in Rhodesia, although the terms of that power and the cost of attaining it are far from settled. SWAPO will almost certainly establish rule in Namibia during the next several years. Only the "liberation" of South Africa itself seems unlikely to occur by the mid-1980s.

The Soviet Union has undoubtedly profited from its freedom to support this unraveling process in southern Africa and from its lack of constraints against early and full support for the liberation movements. But its political successes in sub-Saharan Africa have been surprisingly few and almost universally of short duration. The exceptions may be Angola, where Moscow nurtured a good relationship to its first President, Antonio Agostinho Neto, who visited Moscow in October 1976, again in 1978 amid reports of political difficulties at home, and for medical treatment before his death, and Ethiopia's radical Marxist leader, Mengistu Haile Mariam, who received Kosygin's visit in September 1979.[15]

The unfolding of events in Angola during 1974–1976 suggested three important features of African development that may influence Soviet policy toward that continent during the 1980s. First, guerrilla warfare can obtain its political ends without battlefield success. In driving the Portuguese from Africa, armed liberation movements wore down and demoralized their opponents just as the Vietcong and North Vietnamese did the Americans. While the parallels are limited between the experience of such outside

[15]*Pravda,* October 9, 1976; *ibid.,* Sept. 18, 1979.

military forces and that of the Rhodesian or South African forces fighting for what they regard as their homelands, the threat of prolonged guerrilla warfare will exert political pressure on the solutions of those conflicts just as certainly as it did in the Vietnamese and Portuguese cases.

Second, there have been subtle differences in tactics among the Front-Line Presidents—Julius Nyerere of Tanzania, Kenneth Kaunda of Zambia, Samora Machel of Mozambique, and Sir Seretse Khama of Botswana—and between them and the leaderships of ZILA and ZAPU. In Angola, Kaunda seemed to exercise more caution and to have supported forces opposing those backed by Nyerere and Machel. While there will continue to be unanimity about the final objective—black rule—and about resisting external interference, political disagreements will inevitably arise among the African principals in each dispute. Either an early resolution of political problems or prolonged warfare in southern Africa might increase political instability within Africa. Thus, there are two sources of potential complications in black African politics—differences over tactics and partially derivative internal political instability.

Finally, Sino-Soviet rivalry in Africa goes back to the early 1960s, and it will certainly persist. The Soviets demonstrated their determination and effectiveness with their support for the MPLA, and no doubt shifted the balance of Sino-Soviet influence among African liberation movements, but the Chinese have been more effective in support of Rhodesian guerrillas, have a longer and more consistent record of support for national liberation, and have closer relations with ZILA leaders. Therefore, China's rivalry with the Soviet Union in southern Africa will probably not diminish as political or military solutions emerge during the next decade. However, it is important to note how uncertain all these complicated developments are. No one would have predicted Soviet success in Angola as late as the winter of 1974–75, and events can obviously change very rapidly.

Nonetheless, Soviet policy will follow the pattern of the 1970s in Africa until the primary agenda item has been settled, and it is unlikely that the conflict of southern Africa will be resolved before the 1980s end. Therefore, the Soviet Union will almost certainly persist in its attempt to exercise political influence by:

- maintaining a highly visible, verbal identification with national liberation
- supporting radical and violent solutions to the black-white confrontation in southern Africa, including the supply of arms to military forces
- continued insistence on the distinction between "progressive and anti-imperialist" forces on the one hand and "racist and reactionary henchmen of world imperialism" on the other, by which Moscow will attempt to align the liberation struggle in Africa with its own global ambitions and with its cause in competition with the United States
- urging socialist political and economic models on the new states of the region, but retaining the flexibility of supporting "progressive" nationalist regimes when it suits Soviet purposes
- supporting the development of communist parties where that proves feasible, but not insisting on their control over political developments or even their participation in governments when they are not strong and when other political elements seem willing to cooperate with the Soviet Union or to accept Soviet aid and seem hostile or cautious with respect to the United States and its industrialized partners.

These Soviet predispositions will be shaped into reasonably flexible policies that have the distinct advantage of being identified with political change, but they will not serve as infallible guides through the complicated maze of African politics and will almost certainly become less effective as the agenda of black African leaders shifts from driving out the last vestiges of white colonialism and racist beachheads on the continent to political and economic modernization. There, the Soviet economy and the Soviet "model" for development will have to compete in a complicated environment, one in which the Soviet record cannot be viewed from Moscow as especially encouraging.

Soviet Leverage

The fact is, of course, that Soviet aid and trade with Africa have not been sufficiently large to support its extensive political ambitions. Data in Table 6 show that the concentration of Soviet economic aid has been to countries along its southern borders

TABLE 6
Soviet Economic Credits and Grants Extended to Less Developed Countries
(Millions U.S. $)

	1954–1976	1973	1974	1975	1976	1977	1978*
Total	11,769	661	580	1,299	945	392	2,010
Africa	1,800	14	22	67	369	21	
Algeria	715	0	0	0	290		
Angola	10	0	0	0	10		1
Benin	5	0	5	0	0		
Cameroon	8	0	0	0	0		
Central African Empire	2	0	0	0	0		
Chad	2	1	0	1	0		
Congo	14	4	0	0	0		
Equatorial Guinea	1	0	0	0	0		
Ethiopia	105	0	1	2	0		negl.
Ghana	93	0	0	0	0	1	
Guinea	201	0	2	0	0	1	
Guinea-Bissau	14	0	0	0	11		
Kenya	48	0	0	0	0		
Mali	86	0	12	0	0		1
Mauritania	5	5	0	0	0		
Morocco	98	0	0	0	0		2,000
Mozambique	3	0	0	0	3		
Niger	2	1	1	0	0		
Nigeria	7	0	0	0	0		
Rwanda	1	1	0	0	0		
Senegal	9	1	1	0	0		
Sierra Leone	28	0	0	0	0		
Somalia	154	0	0	63	0		
Sudan	64	0	0	0	0		
Tanzania	20	0	0	0	0	19	
Tunisia	82	0	0	0	55		

TABLE 6 (Continued)
Soviet Economic Credits and Grants Extended to Less Developed Countries
(Millions U.S. $)

	1954–1976	1973	1974	1975	1976	1977	1978
Uganda	16	0	0	0	0		
Upper Volta	1	1	0	0	0		negl.
Zambia	6	0	0	0	0		
East Asia	156	1	0	1	0		0
Indonesia	114	0	0	0	0		
Other	42	1	0	1	0		
Latin America	655	0	209	53	0	30	15
Argentina	245	0	200	0	0		
Bolivia	31	0	1	0	0		
Brazil	83	0	0	53	0		
Chile	238	0	0	0	0		
Jamaica	58	0	8	0	0		
Other						30	15
Middle East and South Asia	8,878	646	349	1,178	224	341	1,682
Afghanistan	1,251	0	0	425	0		
Bangladesh	300	35	28	46	0		
Egypt	1,300	0	0	0	0		
India	1,943	350	0	0	0	340	
Iran	750	188	0	0	0		
Iraq	699	0	0	0	150		
Nepal	0	0	0	0	0	1	
North Yemen	98	1	5	0	0		38
Pakistan	652	71	216	0	0		225
Sri Lanka	95	0	0	57	0		60
Syria	467	0	100	0	50		
Turkey	1,180	0	0	650	0		1,200
Other	143	1	0	0	24		159
Undistributed	280	0	0	0	280		

SOURCES: Orah Cooper, "Soviet Economic Aid to the Third World," in Joint Economic Committee, *Soviet Economy in a New Perspective, a Compendium of Papers*, Washington, D.C., 1976; CIA, *Handbook of Economic Statistics*, Washington, D.C., September 1977; CIA, *Communist Aid to Less Developed Countries of the Free World, 1977,* Washington, D.C., November 1978; CIA, *Handbook of Economic Statistics,* 1979, Wash., D.C. Aug. 1979.

and to those along the Mediterranean littoral. Africa has received relatively little economic attention. Chinese and American economic aid, in fact, have been larger. Furthermore, although annual commitments of Soviet aid have increased during the 1970s, nations in the Near East and South Asia continue to be the primary beneficiaries. This pattern of economic aid, moreover, parallels Soviet military aid [see Tables 7(a)–(c)].

Total Soviet trade turnover with less developed countries (LDCs) increased steadily from $2.0 billion to $11.1 billion between 1965 and 1977. By contrast, United States trade turnover with LDCs (excluding OPEC nations) amounted to $64.1 billion in 1977. Total gross capital flows (grants, loans, and loans repaid in recipient currencies) to LDCs between 1954 and 1976 amounted to $76.1 billion for the United States and $6.6 billion for the U.S.S.R.[16]

Thus, Soviet capacity for influencing the LDCs generally, and even Africa as a whole, is quite limited, but the picture provided by such gross statistics needs to be qualified in two ways. First, the overall level of Soviet aid and trade is low, and as Tables 6 and 7 make clear, it does tend to be concentrated in a few countries. Thus, Soviet support for Mali, Somalia, Guinea, or Ethiopia might prove relatively important in establishing or achieving political influence. Second, in many African states the economic requirements for establishing political influence cannot be judged by Western standards. Marginal injections of rubles might be decisive in making or breaking careers, in sustaining an economic project of high visibility, in tilting the balance in favor of one faction or another. Still, the contrast between the total trading efforts of the West and the East suggests that African political leaders have substantial interests in keeping open lines of communication with the former.

The Soviet Union may well establish considerable influence in isolated cases, as in Angola, by supporting national liberation and new African regimes. But there are severe limits on what the Soviets can achieve in Africa. Without the national liberation

[16]CIA, *Handbook of Economic Statistics, 1978*, Washington, D.C., October 1978, pp. 56, 62, 69.

TABLE 7(a)
Soviet Military Aid

	1955–1966	1967–1976	1970	1971	1972	1973	1974	1975	1976	1977	1978
Total Military Agreements to Less Developed Countries (LDCs) (millions of U.S. dollars)	4,500	16,375	1,150	1,590	1,635	2,810	4,125	2,010	2,890	3,990	1,765
Deliveries to LDCs (millions of U.S. dollars)	3,575	13,640	995	865	1,215	3,130	2,315	1,775	2,445	3,265	3,825

SOURCES: CIA, *Handbook of Economic Statistics, 1977*, Washington, D.C., September 1977; and *Communist Aid to Less Developed Countries of the Free World, 1977*, Washington, D.C., November 1978; Central Intelligence Agency, *Handbook of Economic Statistics, 1979*, Washington, D.C., August 1979.

TABLE 7(b)
Communist Military Technicians* in LDCs, 1977

	Total	U.S.S.R. and Eastern Europe	Cuba	China
Total	32,795	10,250	21,850	695
North Africa	1,615	1,600	15	0
Algeria	615	600	15	0
Libya	1,000	1,000	0	0
Sub-Saharan Africa	26,015	4,115	21,325	575
Angola	19,500	500	19,000	0
Equatorial Guinea	400	50	250	100
Ethiopia	600	500	100	0
Guinea	350	125	200	25
Guinea-Bissau	200	50	150	0
Mali	175	175	0	0
Mozambique	350	200	50	100
Other	4,440	2,515	1,575	350
Latin America	110	100	10	0
Peru	100	100	0	0
Other	10	0	10	0
Middle East	4,380	3,880	500	0
Iraq	1,300	1,150	150	0
North Yemen	100	100	0	0
South Yemen	700	350	350	0
Syria	2,175	2,175	0	0
Other	105	105	0	0
South Asia	675	555	0	120
Afghanistan	350	350	0	0
Bangladesh	120	50	0	70
India	150	150	0	0
Pakistan	50	0	0	50
Other	5	5	0	0

*Number present for one month or more, rounded to the nearest five.
SOURCE: CIA, *Communist Aid to Less Developed Countries of the Free World, 1977*, Washington, D.C., November 1978, pp. 3,4.

TABLE 7(c)
Military Personnel* from LDCs Trained in
Communist Countries, 1956–1977

	Total	U.S.S.R.	Eastern Europe	China
Total	50,050	41,875	5,100	3,075
Africa	15,850	11,975	1,200	2,675
Algeria	2,275	2,050	200	25
Benin	25	25	0	0
Burundi	75	75	0	0
Cameroon	125	0	0	125
Congo	850	350	75	425
Equatorial Guinea	200	200	0	0
Ghana	175	175	0	0
Guinea	1,250	850	50	350
Guinea-Bissau	100	100	0	0
Libya	1,275	1,250	25	0
Mali	400	350	Negl	50
Morocco	150	75	75	0
Nigeria	600	550	50	0
Sierra Leone	150	0	0	150
Somalia	2,575	2,400	150	25
Sudan	550	325	25	200
Tanzania	2,450	1,425	Negl	1,025
Togo	50	0	0	50
Zaire	75	0	0	75
Zambia	125	75	0	50
Other	2,375	1,700	550	125
East Asia	9,300	7,600	1,700	0
Cambodia	25	25	0	0
Indonesia	9,275	7,575	1,700	0
Latin America	625	625	0	0
Peru	625	625	0	0
Middle East and South Asia	24,275	21,675	2,200	400
Afghanistan	4,025	3,725	300	0
Bangladesh	475	450	0	25
Egypt	6,250	5,675	575	0
India	2,250	2,175	75	0
Iran	325	325	0	0
Iraq	4,075	3,550	525	0
North Yemen	1,175	1,175	0	0

TABLE 7(c)(Continued)
**Military Personnel* from LDCs Trained in
Communist Countries, 1956 –1977**

	Total	U.S.S.R.	Eastern Europe	China
Pakistan	425	50	0	375
South Yemen	875	850	25	0
Sri Lanka	Negl	Negl	0	Negl
Syria	4,350	3,650	700	0
Other	50	50	0	0

*Rounded to the nearest 25 persons. Data refer to the number of persons departing for or in training but not necessarily completing training.

issue, the Kremlin leadership would be hard pressed to exercise great influence and, even if that issue persists throughout the 1980s, as it well may in the case of South Africa, Soviet influence can be contained by means of an American policy that is not perceived in Africa as obstructing the transfer of power from white minority to black majority governments. Soviets have not been notably more successful than Americans in developing sensitivities to Africa, and both nations have been dramatically clumsy at times. Africans have a powerful interest in preventing the superpowers from intruding greatly into regional affairs; Sino-Soviet rivalry will obstruct Soviet influence; and the weight of economic interest will work to dissuade most African leaders from severing relations with the United States, Japan, and the European Community. No doubt ideological, political, and economic competition will persist between the superpowers in Africa, but neither side will have the option during the 1980s of excluding the other or of establishing decisive influence except in isolated cases. Even then, one-sided influence will probably last for only limited periods of time.

Geopolitical Competition

During the 1970s much attention has been focused on global Soviet ambitions, especially as these have been reflected by the

195

increased activity of the Red Navy. Soviet efforts to develop a base at Berbera in Somalia and fleet patrols in the Indian Ocean received especially wide public attention.[17] There was considerable talk after the MPLA's victory in Angola about Soviet base rights on the east coast of Africa.

There can be no doubt that the Soviet Union has demonstrated an interest in the Horn of Africa partly for strategic reasons, and increased activity by the Soviet Navy in the Indian Ocean reveals that strategists in Moscow have not missed the increased importance of the Persian Gulf. In fact, the demonstrated vulnerability of the Suez Canal and the resultant changes in the pattern of international petroleum trade have increased international attention to Africa as a strategic dagger pointed at the artery of Western Europe and the United States.

Geoffrey Kemp has argued the case for the increased strategic importance of coastal African states and of the islands that sit in the sea lanes by which supertankers now supply oil to the major industrial powers.[18] Whereas in 1965 0.9 million barrels per day (mbd) travelled around the Cape of Good Hope and four times that quantity moved through the Suez Canal, by 1976 18 mbd went around the Cape and only 2 mbd through the Suez. This shift in sea lanes undoubtedly increases the strategic importance of states on the African littoral, although it also decreases somewhat the importance of the Horn of Africa.

It is against this background that Soviet successes in Angola, Somalia, and Ethiopia have caused concern. In fact, the increased Soviet interest in Africa during 1973–74 may have reflected two primary motivations—to offset Chinese successes and to gain a geopolitical foothold along the Indian Ocean/South Atlantic sea lines of communication. The Chinese had been especially successful in establishing influence across the equatorial

[17]*Report to the Senate Committee on Appropriations by Members of the Fact-Finding Team Sent to Somalia at the Invitation of the President of Somalia,* 94th Congress, 1st Session, 1975, and *Soviet Military Capability in Berbera, Somalia: Report of Senator Bartlett to the Senate Committee on Armed Services,* 94th Congress, 1st Session, 1975.

[18]He has summarized a longer work on the subject in Geoffrey Kemp, "The New Strategic Map," *Survival,* March/April, 1977, pp. 50–59.

belt of Africa's waist—Mozambique/Tanzania/Zaire—and it may well have seemed in Moscow during the radical reorientation of international politics in 1973 that the U.S.S.R. might be dealt out of the new and intensified competition. The Soviet position has now been much strengthened. Not only has it achieved influence in Luanda, but it has encouraged Cuban military forces to meddle alongside Soviet advisers first in Angolan, then in Zairean politics, and then in the Somalian-Ethiopian struggle. Moscow's Angola gamble in 1975 not only got it in the African game, but also enabled it to take the first pot. It has considerable chips with which to play African poker throughout the 1980s, but the game will remain one of high risks.

Yet this scenario is not completely persuasive as an explanation for Soviet African policy. No doubt such geopolitical considerations do play a role among Soviet motivations, but they are not sufficient to explain the risks the Soviet Union has already taken nor those attendant on prolonged entanglement in a very unstable region. The notion that the Soviet Union has extended its influence into Angola as a means of establishing sea and air basing rights, for example, has a doubly archaic ring. This kind of reasoning attributes to the Kremlin leadership balance-of-power motivations of a kind that oversimplified even nineteenth century behavior of Western and imperialist states operating under the influence of Metternich or Bismarck and which bears even less relationship to the political and technological complexity of the current balance in Africa and to the motivations of Lenin's heirs.

First, there is no evidence that any segment of the leadership in Moscow thinks in such purely mechanistic terms. On the contrary, the Marxist-Leninist framework within which world events are perceived and by which policy prescriptions are formed, explicitly rejects conceptions of world politics based on metaphors taken from the physical sciences. While notions of "power vacuum," "counterweight" and even "balance" pervade discussions of international affairs in the West (especially since the 1940s and under the profound influence of Hans Morgenthau, Nicholas Spulbuhr, Raymond Aron, and Henry Kissinger), one must greatly stretch Soviet statements and analysis almost to the limits of self-delusion to find parallels. Moreover, vacuums have never existed, and influence in Africa, as in the Third World generally, is both fragile and temporary. While the above analysis argued that the Soviets were slow in the early 1960s to realize that the popular and inevitable themes of decolonization and anti-imperialism could not be extended into permanent anti-Americanism or anti-Westernism, Moscow has been and will be sensitive enough to avoid assuming an imperialist role of its own. It has good reason to understand how transient influence can be. It has been burned in Algeria, Egypt, Ghana, Togo, Guinea, Mali, the Congo, and other states whose national politics proved unpredictable and whose leaders proved more independent than the Soviet Union anticipated. This is simply to argue that Soviet efforts to establish exclusive influence in an entire region of Africa or even in individual states for a prolonged period of time will not achieve easy success. Such an outcome is in the interest of only those African political leaders most vulnerable to domestic overthrow, and even if weak leaders should invite superpower intervention, leaders in surrounding states will almost certainly be prepared to take whatever actions are required to contain or counter the intrusions.

In cases where its adversary does intrude, either superpower will probably be better served by patience, by encouraging the African state to retain its independence of action through keeping open relations with both superpowers, and by encouraging other African political leaderships, when all else fails, to offset the influence of the intruding foreign power. In fact, it is the essence of a devolving American foreign policy to use its resources to encourage subtle changes in regional balances by applying marginal economic and political incentives by which friendly indigenous leaders themselves will contain Soviet or Chinese influence. It will also serve United States policy well if it defers to Britain, France, Spain, or even Portugal where these European allies maintain effective political relations with former colonial territories.

There are, in addition, military and technological reasons why the image of intrusive Soviet influence along the African littoral should not cause alarm in Washington. First, sea lanes are vulnerable to littoral powers. The military forces required to threaten large tankers on the high seas are widely available. The interdiction of sea lanes for limited periods of time does not require superpower forces. It can be accomplished by air strikes, wire-guided shore-to-ship missiles, or fast-moving patrol boats. To do so in the face of armed NATO resistance is quite another matter, and it is almost inconceivable that any state along the African littoral would do so. Furthermore, limited Soviet support would mean relatively little in the calculation of such a state. No African state, or combination of African states, now or for the remainder of this century, has or will have the capability to interdict NATO's sea lanes of communication. Nor is Soviet interdiction any more likely, although it is possible to imagine that Soviet forces might be positioned to establish air and sea interdiction for a time. But such imagined conflicts border on the fulminations of cuckooland. Is the threat one of limited war? Does anyone really believe that the Soviets would undertake a limited war at sea from bases exposed on the shores of Africa to the combined NATO naval strength? And does anyone suppose that any Kremlin leadership would calculate that it could cut NATO's sea lines of communication short of general war? Such scenarios originate in thinking about the current military balance in terms of World War II's struggle for control of the seas. No doubt in a prolonged and general conventional war—an unlikely event in any case—there would be an intense struggle for control of the seas between NATO and its adversaries. But that struggle would not be appreciably affected by exposed Soviet bases along the African coast.

The simple fact is that Western ruminations about the threat of Soviet bases in Angola or Mozambique derive from apprehensions over the expanding power of the Soviet navy. It has steadily extended its range for the past 15 years and has acquired a global mission. In the context of this general "threat," basing rights along the coast of Africa might be seen as symbols, but they would not add significantly to the wartime capabilities of the Red Navy. In peacetime the United States can do little, and should do little, to obstruct the Soviets from using whatever ports they choose. To focus on the alleged military threat of

Soviet presence in sub-Saharan Africa can confuse the strategic issues of the current global military environment with those of the past and detract from the primary interests of both powers in Africa, which are economic and political.

Soviet penetration along Africa's northern coast has long been linked to competition in the Mediterranean, and efforts to interfere and to establish bases on the Horn of Africa are better understood in the context of Middle Eastern conflicts and control of the Persian Gulf. This is not to argue that the extension of Soviet naval power globally should not concern the United States. Rather, it seems that Soviet military presence in Africa during the 1980s will not add appreciably to the kinds of military threats that exist from local military forces or to the general dangers of military confrontation between the superpowers.

In fact, it might be argued that Africa is uniquely suited to a strategy of arms restraint between the superpowers. There are few strategic advantages to be gained by maintaining large American or Soviet forces there, and general political instability certainly increases the risks of accidental and escalating entanglement. The military risks between the superpowers are certainly greater in terms of conventional arms transfers and, possibly, nuclear proliferation, than in terms of basing and direct military conflict.

It is precisely because political alignments are so complicated that Africa seems a region destined to draw superpower competition during the 1980s. The possibilities for political cooperation appear limited, and the risks of drawing military conflict on the shirttail of political conflict are substantial. It may make sense in both Washington and Moscow to forge agreements limiting the transfer of arms by which Africans will kill Africans and defining superpower interests that seem to require some military presence. Limiting Soviet and American forces in Africa is made attractive by the uncertainties of political gains to be achieved by such means, by the widespread regional interest in preventing the intrusion of either superpower, by the near certainty that any gains will be temporary, and by the mutual interest of the superpowers in avoiding escalating military conflict in a region where influence is so tenuous.

Furthermore, an American policy that actively presses the Soviets to avoid militarization of inevitable political conflicts in Africa promises two substantial tangential benefits. First, the United States has to overcome its image as an ally of colonial powers and racist regimes and its image as an obstructor of change on the continent. The Kissinger trip to Africa in 1976 and the Carter administration's efforts to reverse the tilt of United States policy in southern Africa away from Rhodesia and South Africa represent first steps in this direction. The mistakes of a generation cannot be corrected overnight, but substantial resources are available to American leaders with the will to use them. The United States has a large population of African descent. Its relations with African states will depend in part on how well the United States meets the challenge of equal opportunity and human dignity at home. If the momentum of the past decade can be maintained, the themes of freedom and human rights will be effective instruments for American political influence in Africa. The United States and China share an interest in limiting Soviet intrusion into Africa, and a peaceful triangular competition by political and economic means will certainly not favor the Soviets across the long term.

Africa will retain substantial interests in trade with the industrialized and advanced technological economies of the United States, Europe, and Japan. These interests will almost certainly increase as the agenda of black Africa shifts from eliminating colonial and minority regimes to modernization. While the United States has much to learn about African cultural sensitivities, which will be engaged by the modernization process, the Soviet model of development is even further from native cultural patterns than the American.

Second, there are few areas in which modest and peaceful superpower competition seems more appropriate. Neither has a solid foothold in Africa and neither has good prospects for establishing substantial political or military influence. Thus, a strategy that presses the Soviet Union to join the United States in restraint will probably be well received by African states and will encourage those modernist policies in Moscow that stress domestic development, that advocate cooperation with the West for economic ends, and that may be attracted to reductions in military competition between the superpowers. The alternative of engaging in African geopolitical competition will encourage the most orthodox impulses in Moscow.

Africa is not likely to prove decisive in the Soviet-American relationship in any event, but there is little to lose and some marginal advantages to gain from a United States policy that (a) deemphasizes superpower competition, especially for military presence, (b) relies on regional political leaders to understand their own interests in containing the intrusion of Soviet influence onto the continent, (c) encourages American allies with historical ties to Africa to take the leadership in supporting American interests, (d) promotes open access to economic resources and trade with African states on the principles of mutual and comparative advantage, (e) stresses traditional American themes of equality and freedom, provided that progress toward realization of racial justice within the United States can stand as its own example. Not only will such policies improve American relations with Africa, but they will coax the development of Soviet-American relations in a direction of mutual interest to the superpowers and, incidentally, promote the evolution of Soviet politics that is most favorable to a stable and peaceful international political environment.

OTHER REGIONS AND ISSUES

Many of the political and economic pressures in Europe, East Asia, the Middle East, and Africa are found in other regions as well. They appear in different combinations and with different emphases in each particular context, but some general patterns do emerge. The pressures of the changing international system seem, in these cases particularly, to haul and veer the foreign policies of both the United States and the Soviet Union. There is simply no way of avoiding the contradictions of contemporary world affairs, and political leaders will continue to have difficulty steering a steady course.

The pressures of their divergent interests will continue to create stress in the relationship of the superpowers. The Soviet conception of international affairs retains its zero-sum, your-loss-is-our-gain character. Moscow continues to promote "revolution" and to support "radical" regimes. This Soviet support for factions or states committed to change does not constitute the primary threat to world peace or to the United States. That idea was the nightmare of the cold war, and it prompted the efforts of John Foster Dulles to encircle the U.S.S.R. with interconnecting alliances. It is an old nightmare, one best left behind, as adults outgrow the scares of monsters in the night.

Of course, to say that Soviet support for political forces favoring socioeconomic change is no longer a worthy fear is not to say that there are no legitimate fears. On the contrary, the efforts of the Third World to modernize have contributed to economic inequities that constitute real threats to peace in the 1980s and beyond. Americans, too, must find ways of orienting their foreign policy toward support of forces for change within the Third World and in relations between the industrialized and modernizing states. The central threat from the Soviet Union, however, is not that it has perceived this need, but that its conception of these dynamics is too unidimensional, too undifferentiated, and insufficiently flexible to adapt to rapid environmental changes.

We live in a time when old conceptions of the world order have come under serious attack but during which no substantial consensus concerning a new order has yet emerged. Indeed, one explanation for the apparent contradictions and reversals in American foreign policy during the 1960s and 1970s lies in the need to construct new policies to cope with a variety of problems still only dimly perceived. And it can be argued that even the frequent changes in presidential leadership during the past 18 years derive from the impossibly high demands that we place on presidents to "solve" the complicated issues facing us.

The "human rights" issue, made prominent during the Carter administration, illustrates the point. It was impossible to reconcile easily America's support for Park's South Korea and the Shah's Iran as allies in the Soviet-American geopolitical competition with a general policy opposed to the violation of values fundamental to the American conception of freedom and justice. This basic contradiction was complicated by the domestic political interests that supported both "human rights" and the "alliances" with Teheran and Seoul.

In most regions of the world the Soviet Union and the United States will find some interests in common and others in conflict. But the strains of the bilateral relationship in the Mediterranean Sea or Indian Ocean, in Latin America, in the Law of the Sea Conference, or in the United Nations Conferences on Disarmament and on Science and Technology are not likely to be of primary concern to the two countries. Rather, each will need to adjust to local political and economic conditions and to general pressures for transformation of the international order. In such circumstances other interests and policy issues will take precedence over the requirements of the superpower relationship. Nonetheless, these regions and issues may provide opportunities for marginal adjustments in relations between the superpowers, leading eventually to more substantive changes in the overall relationship.

It seems to me that superpower interaction in these regions and on these issues will conform largely to five distinct patterns:

▪ First, both superpowers have sometimes asserted their interests in a region, have concentrated military forces to protect those interests, and have, therefore, acknowledged their rivalry. The clearest examples, of course, are Europe and the Eastern Mediterranean. In both cases the concentration of Soviet and American forces is not primarily a product of superpower rivalry, but derives from the assertion of significant local interests that exist independently of the Soviet-American relationship. It will not be easy to adjust the superpower relationship in such cases. The United States and the Soviet Union have conflicting political and economic stakes in the Middle East and on the Mediterranean littoral. These, too, are not likely to be adjusted.

However, the concentration of forces itself can become a superpower interest. During the 1967 and 1973 outbreaks of war in the Middle East, the Mediterranean naturally became a critical theater, one in which the danger of a major confrontation between the superpowers was significant. There have been hints, on the American side at least, that a clash between the Sixth Fleet and the Soviet Navy hung by a hair's breadth for many hours in October 1973. Such an occurrence was hardly in the interest of either superpower, and represents a classic example of a regional conflict that might have upset the central relationship. Thus, there emerges a shared interest in controlling the dangers of concentrated military forces.

The Soviets have long suggested that the Mediterranean might be converted into a "zone of peace," but that vague idea seemed in its earliest formulations to be aimed at reducing the strategic role of the Sixth Fleet. It was partly to reduce the dangers of the concentrated naval forces in the Mediterranean that the United States and the Soviet Union initiated discussions that led to the agreement in May 1972 to prevent incidents on or over the high seas.

The general case in which each superpower has vital regional interests and in which together they have placed a heavy concentration of forces need not be assumed to preclude adjustments. On the contrary, it may be precisely the concentration of forces that creates a mutual interest in their reduction or control. Some evidence suggests that one motivation for the Soviet naval-building program in the 1960s and 1970s was the desire to match the United States Navy and to provide incentives, in particular regions, for mutual abstention, withdrawal, or reduction.

. There are other regions in which shared superpower interests seem less well defined but on the increase, and in which, to date, the deployment of military forces has been limited. The Indian Ocean is an example. Here the political interests of the two sides are fluid, and the use of military force has been probing, cautious, and tentative. It is not likely that many powers bordering the Indian Ocean would welcome competition between the superpowers, and, therefore, the prospects for limitations on the use of force in this region seem good.

Bilateral negotiations on the Indian Ocean began in June 1977. The United States presented a draft agreement in the second meeting of the Working Group in Washington that September, and the Soviet Union countered with a draft of its own in the third Working Group meeting in Berne the following December.

The combination of political and economic interests—which, while substantial, are not as clearly defined or as historically established as those in Europe or the Mediterranean—may increase the likelihood that the superpowers will make agreements defining the levels and functions of their military forces. Such agreements offer two distinct benefits. First, they reinforce the cooperative reflex in the central relationship and thereby strengthen the arguments of modernists in the Kremlin. Second, they reduce the probability that political conflicts will develop into military ones involving the superpowers. The latter benefit cannot be exaggerated in cases where the status of clients is inevitably unstable. The shift of Soviet support from Somalia to Ethiopia, for example, has changed the nature of American interests in the Horn of Africa in ways not yet entirely clear. Once again a superpower could not resist the temptation to use force in protecting or establishing local clients. In this case, the Soviets intervened on both sides, albeit *seriatim*. Such uses of force are dangerous. That the Soviets were unopposed by the United States was to some extent a product of very special circumstances. They should not count on similar American abstention in the future. Even when one superpower succeeds in asserting its interests in this fashion, it may damage its long-term interests by drawing the attention of other regional states to its ambitions and by creating opposition in the other superpower, which inevitably washes over onto other issues and affects behavior in other regions. The risks of superpower conflict might be made more acceptable by agreements defining the levels and deployment of military forces. The very lack of definitions of political intentions in such regions increases the attractiveness to the superpowers of defining as many military variables as possible.

There is a serious qualification, of course, to this prescription. Agreements to define military variables in cases of dynamic political and economic rivalry may be misunderstood by important publics within either or both superpowers or by regional states. Such misunderstandings can create political pressures for an even more militant assertion of political interests than might have been demanded had no agreements to control military forces been made. It may be necessary to take this risk, however, while at the same time recognizing the need for public education. The fear of angering publics should not be permitted to blind policy makers to the benefits of controlling critical military variables in what will inevitably at times be rapidly changing regional conditions involving substantial competition between the United States and the Soviet Union.

. A third pattern of superpower interaction might be found in regions where one has had a dominant influence and the other can be seen as a challenging power, or where the dominant power faces its primary rival in a third power. In the latter case, the "excluded superpower" might be tempted to create trouble for the dominant one by its support of the third-party rival. Such cases exist in two regions in particular: (1) in Latin America, where traditional American dominance has been challenged directly by the Soviet Union and also through the proxies of its Cuban and even Eastern European allies and (2) in Southeast Asia, where Soviet influence and American exclusion are far more recent phenomena but where the shifting configuration of political forces among Vietnam, the People's Republic of China, and the Soviet Union seems to offer an opportunity for reestablishing an American role at the margins of power.

Latin America represents an interesting example of asymmetrical Soviet-American influence. Between 1954 and 1976 only 2 percent of military aid and 9 percent of economic aid extended to the Third World by all communist states was directed toward Latin America. There is some evidence, however, that following the overthrow of Allende in September 1973, Soviet and Eastern European aid increased noticeably to Latin American regimes that were favorably regarded. Still, United States aid greatly outweighs that of the Soviet Union, and the level of total American economic activity in the region dwarfs that of the socialist states.

Such regions seem especially unpromising for superpower cooperation. The dominant power has little incentive to invite participation by its rival, and the challenging power has very little to offer to induce condominium. These cases are likely to remain areas in which the excluded superpower will attempt to extend its influence on a selective basis and in which the incentives for cooperation will remain weak.

. Fourth, the superpowers will interact on other issues in which their interests are ambiguous and in which the immediate question will be tangential to others of greater importance. For example, the United States negotiators were somewhat surprised at how cooperative the Soviets seemed to be once the two sides began to discuss conventional arms transfers in late 1977. It had been assumed that arms transfers on both sides were primarily the product of each nation's efforts to deal with its balance-of-payments difficulties or to influence factions and client states in regional conflicts. Neither motivation for arms transfers suggests much room for cooperation between the United States and the Soviet Union. Traditional wisdom would have predicted that the immediate and specific national interests in supporting the balance of payments and in extending influence among recipient states would outweigh the ambiguous and diffuse interest in restraining arms proliferation. But the negotiations have proved more substantive throughout the first four sessions of the bilateral Soviet-American working group than the American participants had anticipated. While it is too early to determine if substantial common interests can be defined in the transfer of conventional arms to third parties, other cases in which superpower interests are ambiguous and tangential may offer greater opportunities for adjusting the risks of conflict than has generally been supposed.

It is precisely on issues such as conventional arms transfers or chemical warfare—where a number of interests point in quite different directions and where "national interest" might therefore be said to constitute an ambiguous guide to diplomatic behavior—that it makes sense to consider longer-range and more indirect benefits of cooperation, such as possible effects on the distribution of power among general political tendencies in the Kremlin. Soviet cooperation on conventional arms control will, of course, be discouraged by the costs of lost sales and by a reduced capacity to support clients with certain types of weapons, but the risks to the U.S.S.R. that the United States will back its clients with countervailing technology and the uncertainty of both military and political outcomes make cooperation more attractive. On the American side, similar conflicting interests exist. Generally, decisions about arms transfers themselves are tangential to decisions about other political and economic goals. In most circumstances in which the incentives toward cooperative behavior and toward conflictive behavior are roughly balanced, it is probably safe to assume that cooperation in specific areas will be difficult to arrange. At least thus far in the history of Soviet-American relations the benefits of cooperation have had to be both immediate and concrete, the costs longer range and uncertain, to produce cooperative agreements. However, there may be a category of cases, like arms transfers, in which careful diplomacy can induce both sides to assume concrete immediate costs in the hope that their actions will produce some immediate benefits and the prospect of a more stable future relationship. In fact, if an administration in Washington were looking for symbols with which to communicate its desire to cooperate with a new Kremlin leadership, or vice versa, initiatives in this fourth category of interaction would probably create the fewest domestic difficulties and offer marginal chances to influence the broader selection of policies on the other side.

▪ The fifth and final pattern of interaction—condominium—has caused the most speculation but is the least substantial in terms of superpower behavior, given current assumptions of the two political and economic systems. There has long been speculation that the superpowers might take joint action, say, to punish miscreant actors in the international system, such as a terrorist group or regional powers whose conflict threatens to spread to the central military balance. The general Soviet-American relationship does not yet offer such bases for cooperation. In almost every case conflictive interests are sufficient to prohibit such dramatic cooperation, and the day of joint operations by the Marines and Soviet paramilitary forces still seems far removed.

However, a number of changes in the international system

might be thought to make condominium more likely in the future. Demands by the Group of 77 in the United Nations are sometimes equally disadvantageous to industrialized socialist and capitalist states alike. A considerable distance may lie between sharing verbal attacks from the South and planning combined actions against other actors in the international system; but the sphere of shared interests between the Soviet Union and the United States with respect to the demand for a new international economic order will undoubtedly grow. Especially on issues like access to resources, or others like nuclear proliferation, objective bases for increasing cooperation seem to exist. The degree to which Soviet and American positions have corresponded in the Law of the Sea Conference and in the preparatory commissions for the United Nations' Special Sessions on Disarmament and on Science and Technology suggests that cooperation may become a more important theme in the 1980s and beyond.

Thus, while condominium does not appear to be a realistic expectation in the foreseeable future, it is probable that the Soviet Union and the United States will find more issues susceptible to cooperation as the international system as a whole changes. While such shared interests will not alter the fundamental Soviet-American relationship, they clearly have the capacity to reinforce more general tendencies toward cooperation or conflict, depending on how each side conducts its diplomacy outside the spotlight of summitry and on issues not yet central to either power.

There exists, then, a series of other issues and other regions that offer more opportunities than have generally been recognized to support the more central objectives of the superpowers for their relationship. On none of these is the bilateral relationship primary. An aggressive program to identify cooperative interests and to secure them by patient construction of agreements in these regions and on these issues will provide a powerful accelerator for whatever influence the United States seeks to exert on the foreign and security policies of the Soviet Union.

SEVEN

Conclusion

The power of the Soviet Union and the United States will undoubtedly continue to make them critical actors in international affairs throughout the 1980s. Their bilateral relationship will remain an important, possibly even the central, preoccupation in Washington and Moscow. Other actors will assume relatively greater importance for prolonged periods of time and other issues will demand the attention of the Politburo, Congress, and the President, but Soviet-American relations simply cannot be neglected. The political and economic health of both societies and their survival and that of the world as well depend on this one relationship to a degree they depend on no other.

The relationship also combines cooperative and conflictive interests, and policy discussion will inevitably center on their appropriate mix. I believe the international system and American interests will be better served in the 1980s by policies that attempt to coax the American-Soviet relationship toward cooperation. The case for this argument can be simply summarized.

The Soviet Union has emerged during the 1970s as a global superpower. No wishful thinking will make that fact go away. The United States has been a global superpower since the early 1940s. It can choose between strategies of fighting brushfires or of environmental management. It has the resources to contain Soviet influence by rushing to each scene where Moscow asserts its interests and by trying to counter each advance of Soviet power. This brushfire strategy would condemn United States policy to constant reaction and would abdicate initiative in world affairs to the Soviet Union. Or, the United States can join with the Soviet Union to manage the environment created by their shared and conflicting interests. This strategy will not dissolve all conflicts. Rather, its purpose would be to define areas of cooperation and of conflict—patiently to enlarge the former and to delimit the latter. The strategy of managing the environment of Soviet-American relations will not eliminate the dangers of war between them, but it promises to reduce them.

The international system has become much more complicated in the 1970s. American confidence, born in the extraordinary and ultimately enviable wartime conditions from which it emerged as the only power commanding functioning and major economic, political, and military resources, has been shaken. New actors have become prominent in world affairs, and the system of international relations has become multipolar. New issues have also emerged, and the international system now functions on many separate planes—superpower military balance, multinational corporate economic power, regional alliances, North-South issues of redistribution and resource supply, population pressure on food supplies, domestic-constituency influence on foreign policy. The United States must learn to exercise responsible leadership in a multipolar and multiplanar world. As these new issues and actors intrude on the consciousness of policy makers in Moscow and Washington, real dangers will arise that the necessity to manage the environment of superpower relations may slip out of focus and increase the risks of war.

Nonetheless, if the political will exists within the Soviet Union and the United States, sufficient opportunities exist for enlarging cooperation and containing conflict between them.

In the Soviet Union, the 1980s may produce strong incentives for cooperation with the United States. It is probable that economic growth will slow, and possible that it will decline to such levels that major economic and political issues will be forced to the surface. Furthermore, the leadership of the Soviet Politburo will have to be replaced before the end of that decade. Three lines of critical policy choices may thus converge in a relatively compressed time frame—the need to sort out questions of succession to the Brezhnev leadership, the need to address sharply reduced rates of economic growth, and the perceived requirement to respond to developments in American military capabilities that have just emerged in the late 1970s. The compression of these three developments into a relatively short period of time—say, 12 to 18 months—would create major instabilities in the Kremlin leadership.

Even if these separate policy requirements can be drawn out across a longer time frame, they will reactivate a system of complicated fissures in the Soviet leadership between impulses to modernize policies and adapt structures on the one hand and orthodox, relatively ideological impulses on the other. This conflict between modernism and orthodoxy in Soviet politics does not represent factionalism in the sense we are accustomed to in pluralist political systems, but it carries absolutely vital implications for personalities and policy preferences just the same.

The modernist orientation, based on relatively greater confidence in Soviet power and in that country's position in international relations, advocates trade as a means of promoting Soviet economic development and prefers a more stable and open system of world politics. It may, incidentally and across time, permit adaptation of Soviet political and social institutions, and it may also tolerate less comprehensive controls on Soviet intellectual activity, especially in those sectors in which it anticipates payoffs in the acquisition of technology and productivity. While I have argued that attempts to interfere with Soviet domestic policy constitute an inappropriate and counterproductive short-term objective of American foreign policy, and that policies that link established cooperative interests to conflictive ones are shortsighted, it is appropriate and sensible for the United States to conduct itself in world affairs in a manner that cooperates with, and nourishes, the modernist orientation in Soviet politics.

Modernism implies greater Soviet confidence in the international system and a greater willingness to cooperate with the United States to manage conflicts and to build a stable order from which both powers will profit. A future "modernist" leadership may also prove more willing to accept modest adaptation of the Soviet political system than has any political leadership since 1917. I believe that there is a qualitative difference between two expectations of United States policy. On the one hand, it is unrealistic to expect that the United States can force changes in Soviet political practices by threatening to sacrifice cooperative interests (e.g., the assumptions behind the Jackson-Vanik Amendment in 1974) or alter particular foreign policies not to our liking (e.g., Soviet involvement in the Ogaden) by threatening to abandon established arenas of cooperation (SALT II). On the other hand, a foreign policy that mixes steady progress toward cooperation where it is feasible, and firm assertion of our separate interests where it is not, rests on the more modest expectation that such policies across time might encourage amelioration of the most repressive features of the Soviet system. The latter expectation strikes me as wiser because it quite clearly falls more nearly within our capacity and because it implies fewer risks in cases of irreducible conflict.

Even this more modest objective of attempting to influence Soviet selection of foreign and security policies and of avoiding interference in Soviet domestic politics, will strain American political resources. We can identify members of the Soviet elite who exercise power and whose attitudes we would like to influence in promoting a more cooperative relationship. We can also predict with more accuracy for the Soviet system than for our own the pool from which the next generation of top leaders will be drawn. But our access to those people is limited and most efforts to influence them by direct means would prove counterproductive. It seems more sensible to conduct American foreign and security policies in a manner that creates incentives for cooperation and disincentives for risk taking in the assertion of Soviet interests when those conflict with our own. The results may be the emergence of personalities in the Soviet leadership and the selection of policies relatively more favorable to cooperation between the superpowers, but more overt efforts to influence the selection of policy and the attitudes of particular members of the Soviet elite would almost certainly complicate those very aims to which they are addressed.

The relationship between the United States and the Soviet Union offers considerable opportunities for cooperation and substantial risks of conflict. The case I have made for American policies that stress cooperation in Soviet-American relations ultimately rests on the analysis of particular areas of functional and geopolitical interaction between them, but it also contains the bias that the international effort of each superpower affects the entire structure of political and economic choices of the other.

Modernist forces in Moscow find that their cause suffers by aggressive assertions of American power because such actions fit the perceptual framework of the most ideological and orthodox members of the Soviet elite and because actions to counter such assertions of American power are a part of the orthodox Marxist-Leninist-Stalinist political program. It is probably less well recognized in Moscow, however, that the modernist policy program, which promotes cooperation, also suffers when there is a successful assertion of Soviet power. Such actions, although they may appeal broadly within the Soviet elite, also induce a reaction in Washington that makes cooperative relations less tenable. The reciprocal effect in Moscow is probably reinforcing.

For example, the successful assertion of new Soviet interests in Angola in late 1975 caused the mood in Washington to become very unfavorable to Soviet-American relations, and moderate, pro-détente forces found themselves on the defensive for many months. Similarly, the aggressive use of United States power in Vietnam in 1965 strengthened the hand of elements in the CPSU least congenial to economic and political reform. In a more subtle case, the Nixon opening toward China in 1972 may have strained Brezhnev's policy of détente. Thus, on both sides, superpower behavior is complicated by the effect that assertions of influence by one can have on the internal political forces operating within the other and within its own leadership.

This is not to argue that attention to guidelines like those put forward in Chapter 6 will eliminate competition between the United States and the Soviet Union, or that it will provide guarantees even against the risks of war. But such rules can be helpful in reducing conflict, or in defining interests when conflict proves intractable. Managing conflicting interests in such a manner may enlarge the arena of cooperation, promote political interests in both Washington and Moscow that prefer it, and render the international system more stable and safe. While such a strategy will not assure the dominance of modernist political and economic forces in the Kremlin, it will increase the chances that the Soviet Union will perceive its interests to be served by relatively open access to markets and resources of the international economic system. Foreign policies relying on cooperative participation in world affairs would almost certainly across time provide incentives for adaptation of Soviet domestic policies as well.

Chapter References

CHAPTER 1:
THE SOVIET-AMERICAN RELATIONSHIP AND THE
INTERNATIONAL SYSTEM

The literature on Soviet foreign policy in general and on Soviet-American relations specifically is extensive. But of these works, those which are based on a serious effort to use Soviet analysis of international affairs and even official Soviet party and government pronouncements constitute a much more selective list, despite the widespread availability of Soviet materials in English. Among serious scholars the works of E. H. Carr have long set

BIBLIOGRAPHIC NOTE: This note has been prepared for the general reader as a guide to some of the materials that have proved useful to the author. It is, therefore, selective in two senses. The scope of this essay is so great that only a fraction of the relevant literature can be commented upon here. More importantly, each of the chapters in this study engages a body of scholarship in which work on Soviet policy constitutes only a tangential part—for example, literature on Africa, the Middle East, Europe, and Asia is obviously important for Chapter 6, and literature on military strategy and arms control for Chapter 5, but I limit my comments here to studies which deal directly with Soviet policy on these broader subjects. Finally, my knowledge about many of the components in a project bearing this scope is obviously limited and derivative. While I have tried to acknowledge my principal debts to the work of colleagues, either in footnotes or in this note, these thoughts on Soviet-American relations in the 1980s reach beyond my knowledge in greater degree than modesty or wisdom would recommend, and my dependence on the work of others is correspondingly larger than space permits me to acknowledge.

a standard for Russian language research, and volume three of this multivolume study of the Russian Revolution—*The Bolshevik Revolution, 1917–1923* (New York, Macmillan, 1961)—was a pathbreaking work on the sources of Soviet foreign policy. In the United States, Philip E. Mosely played a particularly significant role in training both scholars and government officials in analysis of Soviet foreign policy, and a collection of his work was published in 1960: *The Kremlin in World Politics* (New York, Vintage Books, 1960). In this tradition, Marshall D. Shulman's *Stalin's Foreign Policy Reappraised* (Cambridge, Mass., Harvard University Press, 1963) has had an important role.

Perhaps the best historical overviews of Soviet foreign policy from 1917 to the present can be found in Adam Ulam, *Expansion and Coexistence* (New York, Praeger, 1968), and Alvin Rubinstein's collection of source material, *The Foreign Policy of the Soviet Union*, 3d ed., (New York, Random House, 1972). For the postwar period, J. M. Mackintosh, *Strategy and Tactics of Soviet Foreign Policy* (New York, Oxford University Press, 1963) and Thomas W. Wolfe, *Soviet Power and Europe, 1945–1970* (for the RAND Corporation, Baltimore, Johns Hopkins University Press, 1970), and W. W. Kulski, *The Soviet Union in World Affairs: A Documented Analysis, 1964–1972* (Syracuse University Press, 1973), provide chronological coverage across a variety of issues, but vary considerably in style and method. I have long recommended the Wolfe book for its careful documentation and attention to the relationship of military power to foreign policy.

A number of works attempt to address the problem of Soviet motivations in international politics in ways less strictly historical than the studies mentioned above. Arnold L. Horelick and Myron Rush provided a work which had profound impact on the field by its examination of the relationship between power and policy during Khrushchev's years: *Strategic Power and Soviet Foreign Policy* (Chicago, University of Chicago Press, 1965); Jan F. Triska and David Finley attempted one of the most ambitious and interesting efforts to conceptualize the making of Soviet foreign policy in *Soviet Foreign Policy* (New York, Macmillan,

1968); Morton Schwartz has made a pioneering effort to examine systematically the relationship between foreign and domestic policy: *The Foreign Policy of the USSR: Domestic Factors* (Encino, Calif., Dickenson, 1975); and Vernon Aspaturian has collected the most comprehensive selection of articles, in which his own work stands out, summarizing the state of scholarship in the study of Soviet foreign policy today: *Process and Power in Soviet Foreign Policy* (Boston, Little, Brown, 1971). Alexander Dallin's work has been of exceptional variety and scope, among which his *The Soviet Union at the United Nations* (New York, Praeger, 1962) remains useful and provides an analysis of Soviet behavior in a multilateral context.

Despite the apparent challenge to the superpowers of changes which have taken place in the international system during the 1970s, little analytical work of book length has yet appeared on the relevant subjects. However, a number of authors have contributed useful essays: Robert H. Legvold, "The Nature of Soviet Power," *Foreign Affairs,* October 1977, pp. 49–71, and "The Super Rivals: Conflict in the Third World," ibid., Spring, 1979, pp. 755–778; Richard Lowenthal, "Soviet 'Counterimperialism'," *Problems of Communism,* November-December, 1976, pp. 52–63; and Elizabeth K. Valkenier, "The USSR and the Third World," *Survey,* Summer, 1973, pp. 41–49. Two congressional documents provide helpful analysis and data: Report to the Committee on International Relations, *The Soviet Union and the Third World: A Watershed in Great Power Policy?,* Washington, D.C., 1977; and Subcommittee on Europe and the Middle East, Committee on International Relations, *Hearings,* United States-Soviet Relations, 1978, Washington, D.C., 1978.

A number of volumes in the Council on Foreign Relations 1980s Project, of course, are relevant to Soviet and American adjustments to changes in the international system: *Enhancing Global Human Rights; Reducing Global Inequities; Rich and Poor Nations in the World Economy; Controlling Future Arms Trade; Nuclear Weapons and World Politics; Nuclear Proliferation: Motivations, Capabilities, and Strategies for Control.* All are published by McGraw-Hill in New York. Each touches on Soviet behavior in the international system and contains analysis salient to Soviet options for the 1980s.

Selected Soviet Sources

It is impossible, of course, to suggest the wealth of Soviet writing on contemporary international politics and on Soviet-American relations. However, the Institute of the USA and Canada in Moscow is one especially good source of these materials, and it publishes a monthly journal: *S.Sh.A.: ekonomika, politika, ideologiia* (The USA: Economics, Politics, and Ideology). A sister institute under the Academy of Science, The Institute of World Economics and International Affairs, publishes a monthly entitled *Mirovaia ekonomika i mezhdunarodnye otnosheniia* (World Economics and International Affairs). These are supplemented by another Moscow journal published monthly in English, among other languages: *International Affairs*. For an excellent discussion of Soviet work on the United States, see Morton Schwartz, *Soviet Perception of the United States* (Berkeley, University of California Press, 1978).

CHAPTER 2:
ELEMENTS OF SOVIET POWER IN THE 1980s

Soviet materials on economic questions are generally available more often than materials on foreign policy and domestic political questions. In addition to the Central Intelligence Agency and congressional studies cited in the footnotes, there are a variety of good texts on Soviet economic issues and performance. Among these, the following are generally available: Alec Nove, *An Economic History of the USSR* (Baltimore, Penguin Press, 1972); Robert W. Campbell, *Soviet Economic Power* (Boston, Houghton Mifflin, 1966); and Paul R. Gregory and Robert C. Stuart, *Soviet Economic Structure and Performance* (New York, Harper and Row, 1974).

Two recent articles by Gregory Grossman provide a persuasive analysis of the Soviet economy in the 1970s: "An Economy at

Middle Age," *Problems of Communism,* March-April, 1976, pp. 18–33, and "The Second Economy," ibid., September-October, 1977, pp. 25–40. The Office of Economic Research in the CIA continues to provide analysis among the most sophisticated in the world of Soviet economic developments. Two recent econometric studies include: *SOVSIM: A Model of the Soviet Economy,* ER 79–10001, February 1979, and *Simulations of Soviet Growth Options to 1985,* ER 79–10131, March 1979.

American and Western scholarship on Soviet military power has been in decline for several years. This development coincides ironically with the emergence of the U.S.S.R. as a global superpower with persuasive credentials of military parity with the United States. Standard works, dealing principally with the revision of Stalinist doctrine after 1953, include: Thomas W. Wolfe, *Soviet Strategy at the Crossroads* (Cambridge, Mass., Harvard University Press, 1964); Raymond L. Garthoff, *Soviet Strategy in the Nuclear Age* (New York, Praeger, 1962); Raymond L. Garthoff, *Soviet Military Policy* (New York, Praeger, 1966); Herbert S. Dinerstein, *War and the Soviet Union* (New York, Praeger, 1962); and John Erikson, ed., *The Military Technical Revolution* (New York, Praeger, 1966).

More recently, Michael McGwire has put together three provocative collections of articles on the Soviet Navy, the most recent of which he edited with John McDonnell: *Soviet Naval Influence: Domestic and Foreign Dimensions* (New York, Praeger, 1977). Two recent books have reviewed the role of the military in Soviet society: Edward L. Warner, *The Military in Contemporary Soviet Politics: An Institutional Analysis* (New York, Praeger, 1977), and William E. Odom, *The Soviet Volunteers: Modernization and Bureaucracy in a Public Mass Organization* (Princeton, Princeton University Press, 1973).

Several shorter articles have been useful in the very recent past: William E. Odom, "Militarization of Soviety," *Problems of Communism,* September-October, 1976, pp. 34–51; Raymond L. Garthoff, "SALT and the Soviet Military," ibid., January-February, 1975, pp. 21–37; John Erikson, "Soviet Military Power," *Strategic Review,* Spring, 1973, pp. iv–127; Jack L. Snyder, "The Soviet Strategic Culture: Implications for Limited

Nuclear Operations,'' (Santa Monica, RAND, R–2154–AF, September 1977); and Douglas F. Garthoff, "The Soviet Military and Arms Control,'' (UCLA: Center for Arms Control and International Security, 1978).

There are a number of sources commonly used by all analysts working in this field. The most authoritative discussion of Soviet military capabilities has come in the annual reports by the Secretary of Defense to the Congress, of which the most recent is: Harold Brown, *Department of Defense Annual Report, FY 1980* (Washington, D.C., January 25, 1979). These are included in the multi-volumed hearings held before a subcommittee of the Committee on Appropriations each year, of which the most recent is *Department of Defense Appropriations for 1979* (Washington, D.C., 1978). The most convenient single source on military developments is the annual review published by the International Institute for Strategic Studies each September, of which the most recent is: *The Military Balance, 1979–80* (London, 1979). Finally, a new source has begun to appear: David R. Jones, ed., *Soviet Armed Forces Review Annual* (Gulf Breeze, Florida, International Press, 1977).

Selected Soviet Sources

The most useful Soviet work on military strategy in the past two decades has been V. D. Sokolovskiy's *Soviet Military Strategy*. While this work first appeared in 1962, the third edition has recently had a good translation by Harriet Fast Scott (New York, Crane, Russak, 1975). A more recent and very important translated work is: A. A. Grechko, *The Armed Forces of the Soviet State* (Washington, D.C., 1977). The United States Air Force has sponsored the translation and publication of a series entitled *Soviet Military Thought*, now in fourteen volumes and available through the United States Government Printing Office. William F. Scott has compiled a useful guide to these materials: *Soviet Sources of Military Doctrine and Strategy* (for the National Strategy Information Center, Inc., New York, Crane, Russak, 1975). Finally, the U.S. government's Joint Publication Research Service publishes a weekly series, *Translations of Soviet Military*

Affairs, which represents a very rich and underutilized source in English of Soviet military writing.

CHAPTER 3:
SOVIET POLICY MAKING IN THE 1980s

The study of Soviet internal politics has flourished in recent years. However, the Communist Party of the Soviet Union (CPSU) has treated its inner workings, especially political disagreement within its elite, as a state secret to be protected from the public with no less diligence than military secrets. Thus, the study of Soviet politics produces a variety of methodologies.

Two primarily historical studies of Soviet political life since 1917 have long been considered standard: Merle Fainsod, *How Russia Is Ruled* (Cambridge, Mass., Harvard University Press, 1963), and Leonard Schapiro, *The Communist Party of the Soviet Union* (New York, Vintage Books, 1960). The former of these two classics has been wholly revised and updated by one of Professor Fainsod's most able students: Jerry F. Hough and Merle Fainsod, *How the Soviet Union Is Governed* (Cambridge, Mass., Harvard University Press, 1979). This new edition explores Soviet politics with fresh analysis and new data. It has proven very successful in my first effort to use it in the classroom. Mr. Hough gives questions perennially difficult for students—like Stalin's successive political struggles in the 1920s and the return to repression in 1946—a clear and persuasive analysis.

Shorter books that provide excellent overviews of the Soviet system and the history of Soviet politics include: John A. Armstrong, *Ideology, Politics and Government in the Soviet Union* (New York, Praeger, 1974); John S. Reshetar, Jr., *The Soviet Polity* (New York, Dodd, Mead, 1971). Alfred G. Meyer has provided a book which makes an effort to bring the study of Soviet politics into closer relationship with the broader field of comparative politics: *The Soviet Political System* (New York, Random House, 1965), an objective shared in the more recent study by Darrell P. Hammer, *USSR: The Politics of Oligarchy* (Hinsdale, Dryden Press, 1974).

Reading textbooks on Soviet politics may not be everyone's notion of how to spend an enjoyable summer day on the beach or a transcontinental plane flight. However, two former reporters in the Soviet Union, for the *New York Times* and *Washington Post* respectively, have produced readable and excellent descriptions of contemporary Soviet life: Hedrick Smith, *The Russians* (New York, Ballantine, 1976), and Robert G. Kaiser, *Russia: The People and the Power* (New York, Atheneum, 1976). My students have found them sufficiently enjoyable to carry them to the beach, and both books provide clear, reliable insights into Soviet politics and society.

Unfortunately, the careful study of relationships within the current Soviet political elite and the issues with which its members are engaged has fallen into disrepair. Michel Tatu, former *Le Monde* correspondent in Moscow, set a standard for this kind of work which no one else has matched in the past decade. But persons interested in the politics of the last years of the Khrushchev leadership and the first years of Brezhnev's could do no better than to turn to his *Power in the Kremlin* (New York, The Viking Press, 1970).

Problems of the Brezhnev succession were admirably discussed before the Twenty-Fifth Party Congress by Grey Hodnett, "Soviet Succession Contingencies," *Problems of Communism*, March-April, 1975, pp. 1–21. Paul Cocks, of Stanford University, has been doing interesting work, much of which has not yet been published, on the politics of Soviet scientific issues, but the volume which he, Robert W. Daniels, and Nancy W. Heer put together in 1976, *The Dynamics of Soviet Politics* (Cambridge, Mass., Harvard University Press, 1976), still has useful essays on various aspects of Soviet politics—science and technology, nationalities, industry, education.

Of course, the past decade has brought an enormous wealth of work by Soviet emigres and dissidents, of which the views of Alexander Solzhenitsyn, Vladimir Bukovsky, Andrei Sakharov, Roy and Zhores Medvedev, Peter Grigorenko, Edward Kuznetsov, and Anatoly Marchenko, are only the best known. These materials are important, if of vastly different literary quality, but it is difficult to know just how to treat their relevance to the broader picture of Soviet life. Two early collections of material on dissent retain their usefulness: Peter Reddaway, *Uncensored Russia* (London, Jonathan Cape, 1972), and Abraham Brumberg, *In Quest of Justice* (New York, Praeger, 1970). The Reddaway book collects the first eleven issues of *A Chronicle of Human Rights,* a periodical of *samizdat* (underground, "self-published" materials from the U.S.S.R.) which is still published in New York by Khronika Press.

CHAPTER 4:
STRATEGIES OF ECONOMIC INTERACTION

The most convenient single source is, of course, the series published every three years by the Joint Economic Committee of the Congress, a new volume of which has appeared in 1979: *Soviet Economy in a Time of Change* (two volumes), Washington, October 10, 1979. It covers trade among many other dimensions of the Soviet economy. A more limited study was published by the Committee on Commerce in 1977: Committee on Commerce, *Hearings,* "American Role in East-West Trade," Washington, D.C. 1977.

Two collections contain useful essays on Soviet-American trade and others that place such trade in a broader political and economic framework: William E. Griffith, ed., *The Soviet Empire: Expansion and Détente, Critical Choices for Americans,* volume IX (Lexington, Lexington Books, 1976); and Charles Gati, ed., *The International Politics of Eastern Europe* (New York, Praeger, 1976). An excellent article, contributed in a volume devoted to the changing international economic order by Franklyn D. Holzman and Robert Legvold, still has relevance: "The Economics and Politics of East-West Relations," *International Organization,* Winter, 1975, pp. 275–322. Franklyn Holzman's own *International Trade Under Communism: Politics and Economics* (New York, Basic Books, 1976) contains a useful discussion.

Finally, just as in the case of Chapter 2, the output of the Office of Economic Research at the CIA is generally available and invaluable for anyone trying to understand Soviet motives and constraints in trade. A representative selection of recent studies would include: *USSR: Hard Currency Trade and Payments, 1977–78* (ER 77–10035U, March 1977); *Reconciliation of Soviet and Western Foreign Trade Statistics* (ER 77–10132, May 1977); *Soviet Chemical Equipment Purchases from the West: Impact on Production and Foreign Trade* (ER 78–10554, October 1978); *USSR: Long-Term Outlook for Grain Imports* (ER 79–10057, January 1979).

CHAPTER 5:
STABILITY IN THE STRATEGIC RELATIONSHIP

In addition to the references cited for Soviet military power in Chapter 2, there has been a vigorous debate over Soviet-American strategic military relations during the years since SALT I. Three volumes summarize the SALT process: John Newhouse, *Cold Dawn: The Story of SALT* (New York, Holt, Rinehart and Winston, 1973); Mason Willrich and John B. Rhinelander, eds., *SALT: The Moscow Agreements and Beyond* (New York, Free Press, 1975).

Since SALT I, the debate in the United States has tended to become polarized between two schools of analysis. There are analysts who view Soviet intentions with relative skepticism and partly for that reason assess the military balance between the superpowers as relatively unfavorable to the United States. Representatives of these views can be found in the following sources: Lawrence Whetten, ed., *The Future of Soviet Military Power* (New York, Crane, Russak, 1976), especially the contribution by William Van Cleave, "Soviet Doctrine and Strategy: A Developing American View"; Leon Goure, Foy Kohler, and Mose Harvey, *The Role of Nuclear Forces in Current Soviet Strategy* (Miami, University of Miami Press, 1974); William T. Lee, *Understanding the Soviet Military Threat: How CIA Estimates Went Astray* (National Strategy Information Center, Agenda Paper, 1977); John M. Collins, *American and Soviet Military Trends Since the Cuban Missile Crisis* (Washington, D.C., Center for

Strategic and International Studies, Georgetown University, 1978).

A number of influential voices have expressed skepticism about the American position in the strategic arms balance with the Soviet Union: Albert Wohlstetter, "Is There a Strategic Arms Race?", *Foreign Policy,* Summer, 1974, pp. 3–20, and "Rivals, But No 'Race'," ibid., Fall, 1974, pp. 48–81; Paul Nitze, "Assuring Strategic Stability," *Foreign Affairs,* January 1976, pp. 207–232; Colin S. Gray, "The Strategic Forces Triad: End of the Road?", ibid., July 1978, pp. 771–789.

Contrasted with this view, a number of authors have attempted to construct a less alarmed conception of the strategic military balance: Richard Burt, "The Scope and Limits of SALT," ibid., pp. 751–770; Jan M. Lodal, "Assuring Strategic Stability: An Alternative View," ibid., April 1976, and "SALT II and American Security," ibid., Winter, 1978–79, pp. 245–268; Paul Doty, Albert Carnesale, and Michael Nacht, "The Race to Control Nuclear Arms," ibid., October 1976, pp. 119–132; much of the Winter, 1978–79 issue of *International Security* is devoted to balanced analysis of the arms race and deterrence between the United States and U.S.S.R.; Aaron L. Friedberg, "What SALT Can (and Cannot) Do," *Foreign Policy,* Winter, 1978–79, pp. 92–100; Michael L. Nacht, "The Delicate Balance of Error," and Johan Jorgen Holst, "What Is Really Going On?", both in ibid., Summer, 1975, pp. 155–177; and Les Aspin, "How to Look At the Soviet-American Balance," ibid., Spring, 1976, pp. 96–106. Congressman Aspin released a detailed study entitled "What Are the Russians Up To?" in November 1977, a version of which is published in Fred Warner Neal, ed., *Détente or Debacle: Common Sense in U.S.–Soviet Relations* (New York, W. W. Norton, 1979), pp. 87–108. Finally, the Brookings Institution has published several analytical studies of the military balance, including Barry M. Blechman, et al., *The Soviet Military Build-up and U.S. Defense Spending* (Washington, D.C., Brookings Institution, 1977).

Several interesting papers have appeared which attempt to break out of the traditional terms and number counting which characterize this debate over Soviet-American military balance.

The Center for Arms Control and International Security at UCLA has published a number of useful working papers: Dennis Ross, "Rethinking Soviet Strategic Policy: Inputs and Implications" (June 1977); Douglas Garthoff, "The Soviet Military and Arms Control" (November 1977); Bernard Brodie, "The Development of Nuclear Strategy," (February 1978); and Robert Jervis, "Deterrence Theory Revisited" (May 1978). A number of RAND studies attempt to divide the problem into constituent parts and to provide micro-analysis in an effort to influence the broader political debate, of which the work of Arnold Horelick, Abraham Becker, Thomas Wolfe, and recently the monograph by Jack Snyder cited in the note for Chapter 2 are excellent examples.

CHAPTER 6:
GEOPOLITICAL COMPETITION

No section of this study has depended more heavily on the work of other scholars than Chapter 6, and my debt to other scholars, particularly to those who have contributed articles and monographs, simply cannot adequately be acknowledged. However, there are a number of works not previously cited to which the reader may wish to turn for additional analysis, much of it less sanguine than I am about the prospects for stability in Soviet-American competition in many regions of the globe. A particularly useful overview was provided by Marshall D. Shulman to the Subcommittee on Europe and the Middle East, House International Relations Committee, *Hearings,* "United States–Soviet Relations, 1978," Washington, D.C., 1978, pp. 131–153.

Two earlier works that treat Soviet foreign policy globally still have relevance: W. Raymond Duncan, *Soviet Policy in Developing Countries* (Waltham, Mass., Ginn-Blaisdell, 1970), and Uri Ra'anan, *The USSR Arms the Third World* (Cambridge, Mass., MIT Press, 1969). More recently, Alvin Z. Rubinstein, *Soviet and Chinese Influence in the Third World* (New York, Praeger, 1975), and Roger E. Kanet, *The Soviet Union and Developing Nations* (Baltimore, Johns Hopkins University Press, 1974) have surveyed Soviet foreign policy on the North-South axis. In addition to those articles cited in the bibliographic note for Chapter 1, I have found two especially thoughtful: Curt Gasteyger, "Soviet Global Strategy," *Survival,* July-August, 1978, pp. 159–169, and Richard Lowenthal, "Continuity and Change in Soviet Foreign Policy," ibid., January-February, 1972, pp. 2–7.

A rich literature exists on Soviet policy in geographical areas, and only a very limited selection of those can be listed here. Among general works on Europe two cited earlier stand out: Thomas W. Wolfe, *Soviet Power and Europe, 1945–1970,* and Charles Gati, ed., *The International Politics of Eastern Europe.* Zbigniew Brzezinski's *The Soviet Bloc: Unity and Conflict* (Cambridge, Mass., Harvard University Press, 1967) remains a standard work in the field. For a good recent summary of East Europe–Soviet relations, J. F. Brown's "Relations Between the Soviet Union and Its Eastern Allies: A Survey" (Santa Monica, RAND, R–1742–PR, November 1975) is useful, as is Robert Legvold's "Four Policy Perspectives: The Soviet Union and Western Europe" (Cambridge, Mass., Russian Research Center, Harvard University, 1976), and a work by the unrivaled Pierre Hassner, "The Left in Europe: Security Implications and International Dimensions" (Santa Monica, Calif., Arms Control and Foreign Policy Seminar, 1979). Two additional works on Eurocommunism and its implications for Soviet leadership among communist parties are important: Donald L. M. Blackmer and Sidney Tarrow, eds., *Communism in Italy and France* (Princeton, Princeton University Press, 1975), and Donald L. M. Blackmer and Annie Kriegel, *The International Role of the Communist Parties of Italy and France* (Cambridge, Mass., Harvard University Press, 1975).

Writing on Soviet policy in the Middle East and Africa is as rich as exists for any region: Jon Glassman, *Arms for the Arabs* (Baltimore, Johns Hopkins University Press, 1976); Alvin Z. Rubinstein, *Red Star on the Nile: The Soviet-Egyptian Influence Relationship Since the June War* (Princeton, Princeton University Press, 1977); Charles B. McLane, *Soviet Middle East Relations* (New York, Columbia University Press, 1973); Walter Laqueur, *The Struggle for the Middle East* (New York, Macmillan, 1969); Robert O. Freedman, *Soviet Policy Toward the Middle East Since 1970* (New York, Praeger, 1975); David Morison, *The USSR and Africa, 1945–1963* (London, Oxford University Press, 1964); Robert Legvold, *Soviet Policy in West Africa* (Cambridge, Mass., Harvard University Press, 1970); John J. Stremlau, *The International Politics of the Nigerian Civil War, 1967–1970* (Princeton, Princeton University Press, 1977).

There is, of course, a large and varied literature on Soviet foreign policy in other regions. James Theberge's *The Soviet Presence in Latin America* (New York, Crane, Russak, 1974) is a good introduction to that region. Charles B. McLane has done a number of excellent works on the relatively neglected region of Southeast Asia in Soviet foreign policy, for example, *Soviet Strategies in Southeast Asia* (Princeton, Princeton University Press, 1966). Bhabani Sen Gupta's *Soviet-Asian Relations in the 1970s and Beyond* (New York, Praeger, 1976) is helpful. Soviet relations with China have been followed with particular skill for almost two decades by William E. Griffith, and his *Sino-Soviet Relations, 1964–65* (Cambridge, Mass., MIT Press, 1967) is representative of this work. I have used the works of Allen S. Whiting, A. Doak Barnett, and Robert A. Scalapino in my approach to Soviet policy in East Asia, especially Barnett's "Peking and the Asian Power Balance," *Problems of Communism,* July-August, 1976, pp. 36–78.

Other volumes in the 1980s Project assess Soviet policy toward particular areas, or engage questions which inevitably will help shape Soviet policy: Allen S. Whiting, *China's Future: Foreign Policy and Economic Development in the Post-Mao Era* (New York, McGraw-Hill, 1977); Colin Legum et al., *Africa in the 1980s* (1979); Guy J. Pauker et al., *Diversity and Development in Southeast Asia* (1978); John Waterbury and Ragaei El Mallakh, *The Middle East in the Coming Decade* (1978).

East European Countries
in the World Economy

William Diebold, Jr.

ONE

Directions of Change

The communist world was outside the mainstream of international economic cooperation in the postwar period largely for political reasons. It is not to be assumed, however, that even in their absence the communist world would have been in the mainstream. The cooperative structure was mostly concerned with relations among market economies and, while the problems of fitting in state-controlled economies were recognized, they were not adequately dealt with. In spite of this, a substantial amount of East-West trade developed. More important, economic relations took on some new forms in which the state trading element was less important. The recasting or refurbishing of parts of the international economic system that has marked the 1970s and the effort to find new approaches to some major issues provide an opportunity (and a need) to consider whether the communist countries can take a fuller part in the system than before. The question has to be looked at in a fairly long perspective—say, 15 years—and even then it is best to think in terms of the conditions toward which it would be worth trying to move rather than stipulating precise arrangements that should be made.

Such an effort has to be speculative. Prediction aside, this essay cannot discuss in detail what changes are most likely or most desirable in the international economic order. Some directions are described, a combination of analysis and prescription based on other work.[1] Then we try to see how the Soviet Union

[1]The background and much of the underlying analysis about the future of international economic cooperation is to be found in my book, *The United*

and the countries of Eastern Europe might relate to such changes—if they want to. Yugoslavia and the People's Republic of China are to be regarded as special cases not covered by the body of this essay. Even so, generalizations about the remaining countries, East and West, though perhaps especially East, are difficult to make and a little strained. The resulting statements are naturally schematic and imprecise; the basis is factual, but the facts, too, are often generalizations and sometimes rough approximations; the conclusions are suggestive and impressionistic. This discussion as a whole should be treated as a personal, interpretive essay, not a carefully reasoned piece of scholarship leading to balanced conclusions. Partly for that reason, there are few references to the work of others, which has been vital to my understanding of these matters.[2]

It is impossible to discuss the economic issues on which this essay centers without regard to political and security questions (to use the conventional terminology). It was equally impossible to put everything in this analysis. Therefore, the next section of this chapter sets out some political assumptions intended to free the author and the reader to think about economic issues. The assumptions establish some constraints, but not very severe

States and the Industrial World. Praeger for the Council on Foreign Relations, New York, 1972. A refinement and further projection of some of the issues will be found in *Industrial Policy as an International Issue,* McGraw-Hill, 1980s Project, N.Y., 1979. Other studies for this project, included and listed in this volume or forthcoming, have helped me understand a number of relevant issues.

[2]The justification for publishing this essay at all is that an earlier version provoked interesting discussions among people of quite different backgrounds from socialist and capitalist countries, and so a wider audience may find something of interest. The essay was first discussed by a group on the principles of international trade policy, chaired by Lawrence McQuade as part of the 1980s Project. Subsequent discussions have taken place with Western experts on socialist economies and with economists from the U.S.S.R., Poland, Hungary, and the German Democratic Republic. I am extremely grateful to all these people as well as to my colleagues at the Council, especially John C. Campbell and Miriam Camps, and the directors of the 1980s Project, Richard Ullman, Edward Morse, and Catherine Gwin, all of whom have been exceptionally encouraging about an effort that sometimes seemed rather idiosyncratic. The present modestly revised version of the original text was completed in September 1978.

ones. While they do not permit unqualified optimism, they allow us to take seriously the possibility that the communist countries and the rest of the world might make a greater effort in the 1980s than they have in the past to bring the communist countries more fully into the processes of economic cooperation. Whether either group of countries, or some of them, will really want to do this is, of course, another matter. Some points in the analysis have a bearing on the question but I draw no conclusions, either predictive or prescriptive. Instead, the emphasis is on what might be done in various economic fields if circumstances—political or other—encouraged governments to try.

It follows that this is not an essay on policy. That seems peculiar in a field in which policy, at least that of the United States or the Soviet Union, does so much to shape the circumstances. But to reach conclusions on policy one must do exactly the kind of balancing of factors and careful drawing together of elements that this free-ranging paper eschews.[3] Probably the clearest link I make with United States policy or that of any other Western country is in the laying out of possibilities. These are put in terms of the international system as a whole and consider the interests of the Eastern countries. It is inevitable, though, that issues should mostly be looked at from a Western point of view, partly because of obscurity about what Eastern points of view might be, partly as the result of bias, and partly because I assume that the democratic industrial countries will continue to play the major parts in organizing the system. It will become increasingly disorganized if they do not.

POLITICAL ASSUMPTIONS

1. Global peace continues to depend primarily on the Soviet-American strategic balance. Economic developments must not be allowed to endanger this balance. Contributions that economic arrangements may make toward maintaining it are

[3]In a book under way for the Council on Foreign Relations, I focus on United States economic policy toward the U.S.S.R. and Eastern Europe, taking into account systemic issues of this sort.

welcome, but we do not assume that good economic relations ensure peace.

2. East-West relations—and particularly Soviet-American re-lations—may range from fairly high levels of friction to greater détente than has so far been experienced. It would be straining credibility to assume harmonious relations be-tween the two superpowers through thick and thin. Although it can be dangerous, quite a lot of cold-warism on both sides can probably be tolerated without upsetting the strategic balance. At such times, however, economic relations would undoubtedly deteriorate, and one of the most troublesome problems is how to make the system capable of dealing with this. We leave aside the question of what contribution eco-nomic relations can make to holding down the level of tension or friction.

3. Because of the foregoing, American-Soviet relations inevita-bly dominate East-West relations, even when bilateral economic relations are limited. However, one needs to bear in mind certain facts that can coexist with this assumption and that may be of crucial importance for some economic ar-rangements. (a) At any given time, some Western countries' relations with the U.S.S.R. may not be completely aligned with those of the United States. (b) The United States may wish and be able to differentiate among the communist coun-tries both in its direct treatment of them and with regard to their ability to fit into the international economic system. (c) The freedom of action of the smaller European communist countries in these matters is limited but not altogether absent. (d) Good East-West economic relations are economically more important to the smaller countries on each side than to the United States and the U.S.S.R.

4. There will be no radical change in the character of the Soviet economy and polity. That is to say, the U.S.S.R. will remain an authoritarian, centrally controlled country with a centrally planned economy. Within this framework, there may be con-siderable changes in economic organization and methods, but we will assume that they will not be on such a scale as to alter the general appearance of the country.

5. The U.S.S.R. will continue to be the dominant influence over the general character of the smaller European communist countries and their position in the world. The membership of that group will not change. This assumption is not incompatible with the continuing growth of varying degrees of political and economic differentiation among the smaller countries. Such experimentation and differentiation should be allowed to take place when indigenous forces support it.

6. The emphasis of this essay makes it unnecessary to set out political assumptions about China in any detail. However, we assume that the international system of the 1980s should be able to accommodate: (a) a China that increases its participation in world affairs or one that holds itself largely aloof; (b) something like a normalization of Soviet-Chinese relations or a continuation of the strained relations of recent years; (c) the reappearance of a close alliance of Moscow and Peking, provided this is not followed by the two countries acting together in ways that are aggressive, that inflict major damage to the system as it has evolved, or that are internally disruptive to many countries.

7. An increase in individual liberty and respect for human rights in the communist world would be desirable. The international system should foster these developments. A concern for them should be reflected in the policies of some outside countries. This will have a bearing on what those countries are willing to do in economic matters. Our assumptions, however, are that the Western countries do not have the ability, by economic policy, to bring about a complete change in communist practice in these respects, and that they will not let their effort to influence communist behavior in these matters lead either to a complete severance of economic relations or to all-out economic warfare.

8. The Western countries are assumed not to alter their character in any drastic way. Whatever additional measures of "socialism" or government intervention and "planning" may develop, they will remain democratic countries with mixed but largely market-oriented economies. They will be more like one another than like communist countries and

most of them will continue to adhere to a view of security in which the United States is of central importance. The violation of this assumption in a few cases would not completely undermine the discussion that follows but the seriousness of the consequences would depend on the cases.

9. The Third World as a whole will continue to be "nonaligned," but its diversity will be such that a number of countries will undoubtedly be closely attached to one side or the other. Some will probably be more or less "communist" and some markedly anticommunist. These political attachments or professions will not necessarily correspond to types of economic organization or degrees of central control and planning. While East-West (or Soviet-American) rivalry for influence in the Third World will sometimes be sharp and significant, these difficulties will be local rather than general. That is to say, neither side will let its economic or foreign policy be dominated by a general struggle for influence in the Third World, nor will it act there so as to violate the assumptions made here about East-West relations.

10. East-West economic relations will continue to be a matter of controversy on both sides. From that one may deduce that continuity and coherence in policy will not always be attainable. The arrangements for economic relations must be compatible with that fact and capable of surviving it.

THE ECONOMIC ISSUES

While these political assumptions allow for periods of considerable friction between East and West and even something resembling cold war, the discussion that follows does not deal with the kinds of economic relations that would be natural to those periods. This does not imply a belief that the Soviet Union or America could (or should) keep their economic relations from being influenced by political quarrels. But if the communist countries are to become more fully engaged in the world economy, the arrangements of the 1980s have to be made capable of surviving such periods of strain. One cannot reasonably expect to insulate East-West economic relations from current political issues to the degree that economic transactions among Western nations were insulated in the 1950s and 1960s. It should be possible, however, to fashion some safeguards so that what is agreed to in the "best" days is not always destroyed in the "worst." How this can best be done is a matter we must leave aside, though some hints may be found in what follows.

A necessary working hypothesis, however, is that both the East and the West perceive a common advantage in making a serious effort to maximize the economic benefits of increased cooperation. This implies a preference for conditions that can loosely be called "détente." How much the one necessarily promotes the other is another question that must be left aside. Neither superpower will be willing to sacrifice any major interests for economic advantage. But of course this says nothing about how they will interpret the words "major," "sacrifice," or "economic advantage."

Chapter 2—the longest—deals with trade, payments, and industrial cooperation, the East-West equivalent of direct investment. The basic question is whether changes in the Eastern economies or the Western pattern of cooperation offer new opportunities to overcome the recalcitrant problems of past times that arose from basic differences in economic systems. Then we turn our attention to rather different kinds of problems—food, energy, raw materials, and technology—in which systemic differences are less crucial but the prospects of cooperation are beset by other uncertainties. Comecon and its possible evolution, the agenda of so-called North-South issues and the possible evolution of international economic organizations—or the creation of new ones—are briefly looked at before this essay closes with a few reflections on the basic issue and its relative importance in the scheme of things.

TWO

Trade, Payments, and Industrial Cooperation— The Systemic Problems

When the postwar structure of international cooperation was being built, the best understood but least effectively resolved problems of East-West trade relations concerned the difficulty of applying to a centrally planned state-trading economy rules and procedures that had evolved in predominantly market economies. The principal trade policy issues involved were the quid pro quo for most-favored-nation status (m-f-n), state-trading rules, and dumping.

There has never been much doubt in Western minds that an exchange of promises to accord most-favored-nation treatment was a one-sided bargain if the other party controlled its foreign trade according to a central plan and conducted it through state trading. Tariffs, if they were present at all, would mean little and would certainly not determine the flow of trade as they are supposed to do in market countries. That was true whether one was concerned about discrimination that favored one supplier over another or about the height of the tariff, which would either affect the buyer's choice between domestic and foreign suppliers, or narrow the market by raising the price of the goods, or take money away from the foreign supplier (or importer) and give it to the domestic fisc. To cope with this imbalance, a number of formulas were used or suggested (some of which could be combined). Each has salient weaknesses.

Purchasing commitments may take the form of amounts of goods (as in the Soviet-American agreements of the 1930s), annual percentage increases (Poland's protocol with the General Agreement on Tariffs and Trade [GATT]), increases in proportion to those of total imports (Rumania's GATT protocol), or commitments on specific products (Canadian wheat in the 1950s and 1960s). There is also the vague commitment implicit in statements of intent or expectation (common to many trade agreements and discernible in the American-Soviet arrangements of 1972). One weakness of these arrangements as long-run commitments is that, if the amount is small enough for the buyer to sustain it conveniently, there is little clear advantage to the seller. Larger amounts may create difficulties about payments, raise doubts about the value of the agreement to the buyer, and are certainly not in keeping with the economic principles of the market countries. If the agreements are bilateral, they are apt to lead to discrimination against the trade of third countries. Even a multilateral commitment may raise questions of fair allocation among suppliers. When purchase commitments become general, they either lead to a rigid pattern of world trade or break down.

State-trading rules in GATT, following some earlier practices in bilateral agreements, call for the conduct of state-trading entities according to "commercial considerations" (thus not ruling out discrimination of a sort that a private monopolist might find advantageous). State trading is not to be used to frustrate trade liberalization. Though these rules apply to all state trading, not just that of the communist countries, little has been done to build around them bodies of law and practice, so they tend to be all but unenforceable except perhaps in cases of flagrant abuse (or when other countries want to take drastic action). Consequently, they can hardly be thought good value as the quid pro quo for the most-favored-nation treatment that gives the state-trading country favorable access to a market economy. Still, the rule is probably worth retaining for the principle it embodies and if an effort is made to put it into practice.

The Havana Charter for an International Trade Organization (ITO) of 1948 had a further provision concerning negotiation of the markup between the external buying price and the internal selling price. An additional commitment was to import enough to clear the market at the agreed internal price unless there was rationing. Untried, these principles hardly seem compatible with the pricing and supply practices of most communist countries and do not sound very enforceable.

Access provisions. Beginning with the abortive legislative proposals of the Johnson administration, United States policy about a quid pro quo for m-f-n has concentrated on arrangements intended to improve the ability of American firms to sell to communist government trading agencies and to assure fair treatment of them. Under the American foreign trade act adopted in 1974, the result of negotiations must satisfy the United States government as to the balance of reciprocity as well as meet a number of specific conditions. The whole approach leaves a good deal to judgment and discretion, which is probably inevitable and sensible but which makes it difficult to write down international rules and principles.

No formula? Yugoslavia became a regular member of GATT with no purchase commitment on the ground that its degree of decentralization and the introduction of market features made its tariff meaningful. The decision to allow Yugoslavia to join may have been colored by political considerations but was not altogether implausible. Years later, Hungary obtained a somewhat similar arrangement; there was no purchase commitment, but under a protocol a variety of considerations about the operation of its foreign trade system can be discussed. The political considerations involved were less weighty than those in the Yugoslav case and Hungary's argument rested largely on the decentralization of decisions about buying and selling to enterprises, the expanded use of the price mechanism, and the introduction of a three-column tariff. It was clear that at least in some cases the height of the Hungarian tariff could determine whether an enterprise would buy abroad (and how much) and that differential tariff treatment could determine the source. What was not clear—and still is not—is how long these arrangements would operate as well as their designers hoped, how large a share of the economy they would cover, and to what extent the allocation of foreign exchange or other control measures would minimize or offset these "market" elements. In principle, at least, a communist country appeared to have found a possible way to provide an adequate quid pro quo in the form of m-f-n and little else.[1]

From this limited experience, I draw the following conclusions about m-f-n in the 1980s. Purchase commitments should be avoided. State-trading rules along GATT lines should be kept but regarded as pointing a direction rather than reliably regulating behavior. More attention should be given to the development of practice and interpretations of rules that offer possibilities of becoming a code or at least a kind of common law. This is all the more important as state trading will almost certainly become more prevalent in noncommunist countries.

Major reliance should be put on access provisions that should be formulated and revised in the light of practice and set up as the obligation of the communist country to all who give it m-f-n, not just as a series of bilateral (and sometimes variant) commitments. Incorporated in the access provisions—whether granted bilaterally or multilaterally—should be commitments of equal treatment. While it is not easy to stipulate precisely in what way this is to be interpreted (every set of circumstances having unique features), some boundaries and standards are possible. Most of all, the principle of equal treatment will provide the focus for negotiations about its application. The situation will in some respects be similar to the arrangements being worked out under some concession agreements in developing countries whereby the foreign company is assured of treatment as good as that subsequently achieved by someone else. Thus all gains are generalized much in the manner of m-f-n. These uncertainties will have their Western parallels as efforts are made by other countries to deal effectively with nontariff barriers and various kinds of governmental measures of industrial policy that affect trade.

---

[1]Czechoslovakia, a founding member of GATT, had its m-f-n treatment withdrawn by the U.S. in the early 1950s when U.S. legislation required that. Other countries did not follow suit but often establish quantitative limits on imports from Czechoslovakia when they deem it necessary. Czech protests seem absent or muted, perhaps for fear of being charged with nullifying past tariff concessions by state trading, which could lead to losing the rest of its m-f-n advantages.

The communist countries have an interest in these barriers and, while they have only a few counterparts on which they could offer true reciprocity, it is not unreasonable to suppose that some relation between the two kinds of negotiations would make sense.

As the foregoing has made clear, more is involved than simply m-f-n in its traditional and largely tariff-related application. However, m-f-n, as such, should also be part of trading arrangements. To the extent that tariffs and related measures come to have any meaning in a specific communist country's system, the basic principle of reciprocity via m-f-n will make sense. In addition, the communist countries have—perhaps rightly—attached a good deal of symbolic importance to m-f-n status. Those who have (and give) m-f-n status are part of the system; those to whom it is denied do not belong.

Equal treatment is not the whole story; there is also the question of the removal of trade barriers. The m-f-n formula gives the Eastern countries the benefit of the extensive tariff reductions (and many related concessions) of the whole postwar period as well as of those to come. There is no escaping this and the Western countries simply have to assure themselves that the bargain is worth it. The same is true of the communist countries. (Most communist countries, however, would have no difficulty in making it clear that they would spend all the hard currency that they earned.) But how can they be sure that the Western countries will in the future reduce trade barriers of special interest to them? This leads back to the previous question of what kind of quid pro quo for m-f-n can be given by a state-trading system. The possible answers run along the lines already discussed.[2]

The problem may not be very serious by the 1980s. If trade barriers are low, Eastern countries may not find them a great

---

[2]Presumably most Western countries have already made satisfactory bargains, as the U.S. denial of m-f-n to the U.S.S.R. and some other countries is exceptional. However, Western European countries generally, and perhaps others, use quantitative restrictions or bilateral understandings to limit the amounts of some products imported from communist countries. The latter would have a right to ask for the removal of restraints under the formula suggested here. This connects with the dumping issue discussed in the next chapter.

problem, or Western countries may be willing to reduce them on the assumption that not too much protection is lost and that exports may increase. Perhaps, however, some trade barriers will have been kept so as to offer preferences to developing countries. Then attention will focus on which communist countries would be eligible to receive such preferences and also on how restrictions on imports receiving preferences are related to industrial adjustment in the importing countries. Further developments along that line depend on how far the Western governments go in improving the international handling of problems arising from national industrial policies. If they rely heavily on consultation to apply broad principles to complex cases it is not inconceivable that the communist countries should sometimes take part in these processes.

Subject to these many caveats, can one find a general formula? It is tempting to say that, so long as the access provisions work satisfactorily and there are safeguards against market disruption (see below), it is hard to see why imports from communist countries should not be treated in the West on an equal footing with imports from industrial countries with market economies. Certainly Western consumers have no interest in denying communist countries equal treatment. The use of such denial for bargaining purposes can be set aside here, as we are discussing the results of the negotiating, not the bargaining process.

There is, however, no escaping the fact that, even with an equal-treatment formula fully in place, state-controlled economies will still have discretion in the placing of orders in the West. Thus, they have bargaining power. The equal-treatment formula can do something to regularize relations, to reduce the sources of friction, and to increase the transparency of the situation. It can, to a degree, be made multilateral instead of bilateral. But it cannot turn communist countries into market economies. And unless the Western governments of the 1980s are very different from those we know, they will be concerned with how communist countries use their bargaining power and how their own exports fare. Whatever advantages we ascribe to the kinds of arrangements suggested here, they cannot settle all questions. One would expect that export credits and export controls might be drawn into the arrangements. Even within itself the proposed formula of equal treatment is not as precise as standard m-f-n commitments. Practice and negotiation will determine the meaning of the formula (as is likely to be the case with arrangements concerning nontariff barriers and other practices).

Once granted, m-f-n status ought to be regarded as likely to be permanent and not as something that has to be renewed or reaffirmed every few years. To be sure, the right to withdraw it is essential, as it is under Western agreements, but the presumption ought to be, as it is in the West, that m-f-n is the normal way of doing business and is changed only under severe provocation. The reason for this is simply that uncertainty about tariffs or other import barriers can greatly reduce the mutual benefits of trade over time. If m-f-n is to be semipermanent, Western governments must have some other measures they can use when they feel that Eastern governments are not living up to the principles of the agreement.[3] It is not immediately apparent what these mechanisms might be, but they should not be impossible to devise. The more the situation is one in which all trade negotiations are about specifics because general barriers such as tariffs are minimized, the more likely it is that there will be ways of graduating reaction to circumstances.

DUMPING AND MARKET DISRUPTION

One of the oldest worries in the book, "Soviet dumping," poses questions about intersystemic difficulties of the most fundamental sort. When an economy has a pricing system that, to meet

[3]The need to say "feel" shows the fragility of the arrangements we are discussing. Naturally one ought to try to institutionalize such matters in ways that produce as objective and regularized results as possible (international supervision, boards of experts, etc.), as will also have to be done for other trade. But this possibility is limited by our necessary assumption that the political cast to East-West trade will continue for as long ahead as we can see and because the nature of the trade dictates that flat rules will have to give way to a certain reliance on ad hoc measures.

its special needs, severs any logical relation between internal and external prices, counts costs in ways wholly alien to the capitalist world, and has an arbitrary exchange rate, how can laws intended to offset unfair price competition apply? As the government can determine when and where to offer goods for sale abroad at whatever prices it pleases, for political or economic reasons, how can capitalist competitors—or even the market system itself—be protected?

While the discussion of these issues over 50 years has often been inflamed by emotion and exaggerated because of competitive conditions, there is no doubt that the basic objections are valid. It is difficult to see a solution or reconciliation that is intellectually satisfactory. But in the 20 years up to the recession the problem was minor.[4] That was not because of changes in the Eastern pricing system or of any improvement in the sophistication of Western laws to cope with these outré cases. It was more because the U.S.S.R. and the other communist countries formally or informally accepted Western conditions about the prices and quantities of goods marketed. Whether they did this to maximize their own foreign exchange earnings on a given volume of sales or for fear of restrictive measures that would leave them worse off is a secondary matter. During the recession, complaints about dumping grew in number and sharpness (and not only in East-West trade). That was hardly surprising considering the sag in Western demand and the increased difficulty Eastern countries had in earning foreign exchange. Nevertheless, the Western protective devices continued to work.

Though these arrangements contain the problem of dumping, they are not satisfactory as a long-run solution. From the point of view of the Eastern countries, the conditions are inequitable because they rest on the ability of the Western countries to impose restraints unilaterally. From the point of view of everyone in the Western countries except the producers who would be affected by the competition, the arrangement is unsatisfactory because it simply protects the existing price structure and denies

---

[4]There were many antidumping cases but whether judged by the amount of trade involved or the international friction the issue was not a major factor in East-West relations.

the country the benefit of lower costs of production in the socialist countries even when there is no unfair competition. Even otherwise competitive producers can be hurt if one of them gets exceptional profits from the markup of the dumping price.

It can be assumed that an increase in East-West trade, and especially in the shipment of manufactured goods from the East, will increase the number of antidumping claims. Decentralization of economic decisions—as has been introduced in some of the smaller Eastern countries—would reduce the risk of politically motivated dumping but might increase incentives for individual enterprises to dump while making less plausible the Eastern governments' assurance that this would not happen. While in a few cases economic reforms may reach the point where both transparency and the pricing system make possible an application of Western tests of whether dumping has in fact occurred, these will surely be exceptional, leaving the basic problem as it was. Moreover, such reforms are likely to involve arrangements that, from a Western point of view, amount to subsidies. (For present purposes, it will be simplest to lump together all practices that result in low-priced imports as "unfair competition.")

In the West, too, the dumping issue will become more important. The more open the economies of the industrial countries are to one another, the greater their concern about fair competition, including pricing practices. Further elaboration of existing antidumping rules is unpromising; they have become more and more arbitrary. For reasons that cannot be dealt with fully here, discriminatory pricing, rules about subsidies, questions of market disruption, and increased international surveillance of national adjustment processes will all have to be related to one another— though not necessarily dealt with in the same agencies or covered by a single set of rules. Working out acceptable arrangements is likely to be slow and piecemeal. Cases will have to be dealt with as well as principles. The best approach to "dumping" from the East—which probably should be translated "price competition"—will be to try to include it in this process. This will not always be possible. For example, certain arrangements dealing with intra-Western trade may rely partly on the play of market forces; others may use estimates of true cost advantages or comparisons of actual domestic prices. Sometimes a special formula may have to be applied to communist products, but the aim ought to be to approximate the results that are sought by the intra-Western arrangement. A multilateral framework is preferable to a bilateral one.

This is not a neat solution, and not altogether satisfactory intellectually, but I know of none better. Note that it involves a departure from established Western ideas about "antidumping" rather than reform of the socialist pricing systems, and that this is to be undertaken primarily for reasons of good order in the West, not as a way of dealing with East-West relations. The more realistic pricing in the East becomes, the narrower the gap is likely to be. How large or small the dumping issue may become is impossible to say. But even if progress is made along the lines suggested, two problems will remain unsolved.

The first is the tendency of existing arrangements to deprive Western economies of some of the benefits of trade with the socialist countries. Roughly the same problem exists within the West where antidumping has always been subject to protectionist abuse. The best approach appears to be to adopt antidumping procedures that go as far as possible toward giving consumer interests representation and access and that put government officials—and perhaps sometimes international officials—under obligation to guard against the abuses. Competitive markets, to which sellers from a number of countries have access with low or no trade barriers, also reduce the loss from using antidumping procedures to protect an existing price structure.

The second problem is that of dumping in third markets—i.e., unfair export competition. The problem here is that the dumping may be regarded as a boon by the importing country (so long as there are no domestic producers to complain). When the recipient of the dumped goods is a developing country, there is the added difficulty of distinguishing between unfair competition and development assistance. This problem is inadequately dealt with in the West, so perhaps its East-West manifestation can also be drawn into the larger process of working out new standards and methods.

INDUSTRIAL COOPERATION

This term covers a wide variety of arrangements between Western firms and Eastern governments or enterprises. There were forerunners of importance in the 1920s and 1930s, but our concern is with the new wave that began in the 1960s and still involves far more European than American firms. Industrial cooperation exists in all communist countries but varies in importance and method. The introduction of true foreign private investment in a few socialist countries—i.e., foreign ownership of up to 49 percent of some enterprises—is ideologically striking but I would not myself see this as a major watershed. Others disagree and believe that the future of East-West industrial cooperation depends on the growth of these practices. That may prove true, but I suspect that this form of cooperation is self-limiting, partly because it makes an overt, radical break with socialist concepts. In any case, for working purposes I find it preferable to treat "true" ownership as only one of a number of forms in which Western partners can operate, control, or influence decisions, and draw their profit—whatever it is called.

Our concern here is not mainly with the forms of industrial cooperation but with two of their most important consequences. First, they can overcome—or at least modify—some of the difficulties in trade and payments arising out of differences in the systems. Second, and perhaps most important of all for the focus of the 1980s, is the potential that industrial cooperation has for tying the communist countries more closely to the rest of the world economy, and particularly the Western industrial world, than they have been before.

Many ventures in industrial cooperation, including some of the biggest, offer little that is of long-run systemic interest. This includes those that principally involve the design and construction by Western companies of plants and other facilities in communist countries, the equipping of such plants, turnkey projects generally, the one-time sale or licensing of technology, and so on. These activities may be important in that they increase productivity of Eastern economies and improve their export capacities. They are undoubtedly significant with respect to the substantial increase in human contacts they involve and the accompanying exposure of societies to one another (thousands of Westerners live in China and the Soviet Union; hundreds of Russians are in training in American industry). Then they may help bring change and have other substantial consequences. Our concern, however, is with lasting commercial connections. Of course, what start off as single transactions may become lasting, especially if they involve patent licensing and other forms of technological transfer. It is also true that in number and volume the limited arrangements may well be more important for a long time to come than the more intimate kinds of industrial cooperation on which this section concentrates. But not very much can be said about them that is new.

Of special interest are those arrangements in which the Western partner has a continuing responsibility to supply technology, equipment, training, and know-how and takes payment in the form of products from the plants he has helped establish. Both arms of the transaction have a number of forms and there are important long-run differences among them. On the supplying side, for example, there is a significant difference between receiving flat contract fees worked out by negotiation and receiving a return that is geared in some fashion to the successful operation of the enterprise in the communist country. Arrangements that permit true Western equity or create joint ventures conform to Western practice, but the same results can be approximated by other means (for example, payments in proportion to the volume of output or some other measure of activity.) No arrangement ensures that the Western partner will have the influence on efficiency and costs that is ordinarily counted on, but such influence is sometimes possible, especially if there are local people who want that improvement.

On the payments side, the major distinction focuses on the reasons the Western partner takes goods. If he does so only because that is the one form in which he can get his proceeds—or a share of them—he has discovered the disadvantages of barter. The picture of East-West economics in the 1980s would be more promising if such arrangements were on their way out.

However, in the mid-1970s Eastern countries, and especially the Soviet Union, put a new emphasis on "buy back" or "compensatory" arrangements. Given their debts and the difficulties of selling in the West, that was understandable enough. Western firms that would have liked something better went along to beat out competition, keep up production, and make what profits they could (sometimes by charging higher prices than they would have for cash transactions). Such considerations might help perpetuate the practice and the benefits it brings to the East, but these compensatory agreements promise little for an improved linking of two different economic systems.

If the Western partner takes goods it is glad to have, then the situation is entirely different. A good new source of the products it already markets in the West may be welcome. Prices may be lower, and new items may conveniently fill out product lines or supplement some existing activity. An even closer tie is established when the Western company takes raw materials, semifinished goods, or components for use in its own processing operations in the West. In these circumstances we have a familiar arrangement resembling some of the functions of multinational corporations in the rest of the world. Plainly, there are also important differences, but the main point lies in the lasting links based on mutual advantages, which tie the Eastern countries closer to the outside world's economy than ordinary trade would be likely to do for a long time to come. Further embellishments include joint marketing ventures in some or all of the world outside the communist countries; distribution and service activities that will eventually be run by the Eastern partner alone; and activities in developing countries. These contractual arrangements lack some of the flexibility usually attributed to the activities of multinationals, however major, and a troublesome example is the persistence of the obligation to buy even when demand falls and the goods cannot be sold.

More important than the proliferation of forms is the extent to which this kind of industrial cooperation overcomes some of the chief obstacles to the growth of East-West trade. While these arrangements do not by themselves altogether eliminate the disadvantages of not having m-f-n treatment, they permit the companies to absorb some of the discrimination internally, just as multinational corporations (MNCs) can overcome tariff obstacles more easily than two merchants dealing with one another from opposite sides of the customs fence. The same is true of other trade barriers. Moreover, the creation of an interest in the Western country in importing may lead to the lowering or removal of these obstacles. The risk of antidumping action is reduced. Much more important, marketing, long one of the weaknesses of the Eastern countries, is made the responsibility of a Westerner who in some cases also provides the market. Sometimes the Western partner is responsible for the hard-currency financing or at least can help obtain or reduce the amount needed by its own contribution in kind. What in principle are formidable obstacles to the linking of market economies and centrally controlled ones fade in importance in industrial cooperation. The discrepancy in pricing systems, fictitious exchange rates, and other distorting factors are not allowed to stand in the way of realistic arrangements that have to be beneficial to both partners to be acceptable. Whether the proliferation of such ad hoc arrangements will in the long run have an influence on the pricing and exchange rate systems of the Eastern countries is another matter.

As to whether industrial cooperation should be allowed to tie the communist countries into the world economy, there are two views in the East. One is that closer relations with Western firms should not be allowed to disturb internal arrangements. This usually means keeping the Westerner as an external partner, a deliverer of equipment and technology. When he has done his job, he has no further connection except as an outlet for goods which he continues to take in payment or may even buy for hard currency. The other view is that the Eastern benefits are greater when the Western partner has a continuing incentive to keep up the quality and effectiveness of his activity and that it is therefore desirable to keep him deeply and continuously engaged. There are also differences of opinion about the desirability of changes that new methods and productivity encourage. If different socialist countries come to different conclusions on these matters, greater diversification than we have known will result. Strains may also develop in intra-Eastern relations. It is impossible to say whether the future division will be that of the recent past, with the small countries proving more flexible in these matters than Russia—or what the consequences would be if the division changed.

The communist countries do not have an altogether free choice, as their ability to attract the Western businessman depends in part on their ability to be flexible enough internally to permit him to work well. Again the question of size is important, because businessmen are willing to put up with more inconvenience for a chance at the huge orders of Russia and China than for what the smaller countries have to offer. There was a time when Western businessmen thought that activities abroad were of little interest unless they were based on the ownership of true equity and probably majority control. Now, however, the forms of industrial cooperation being developed in communist countries sometimes resemble the terms which less developed countries (and others) have set for foreigners doing business in their countries. Some businessmen welcome the change because they fear the vulnerability of what might almost be called old-fashioned investment. Thus the difference between investing in various parts of the world and becoming a partner in industrial cooperation in the East is narrowing. There is even the much-touted— by Easterners as well as businessmen—advantage of political stability in the East (and no strikes). Are the incentives to businessmen to make arrangements with the East great enough to suggest that there may be an increase in East-West integration accompanying a reduction in North-South integration?

During the 1980s the number of internationally agreed-upon rules applying to international investment and the activities of MNCs is likely to increase considerably. There are likely to be different sets of rules and different kinds of limitations—on host governments, home governments, and companies. Not all will be accepted by all countries. As in the case of dumping and related matters, the possibility will suggest itself of drawing East-West industrial cooperation into this system of rules. Several considerations argue against the desirability of doing that (apart from the probability that socialist countries will be unwilling to subject themselves to international limitations and that their attitude may reduce the willingness of others to agree to rules). Some of these concern systemic differences: legal, monetary, and the like. Others stem from the undoubted power of the communist governments, which make irrelevant any arrangements intended to assure governments that they have control over multinationals. The need to let experiment play is a major reason to avoid codification for some time to come. Moreover, codes tend toward uniformity, and differentiation among communist countries in their treatment of industrial cooperation and in other relations wtih Western countries is not to be discouraged.

Payments and Money

The inconvertibility of the communist currencies and the gap between the internal and external financial or pricing arrangements raise fundamental questions about the relation of these countries to the rest of the world economy. While inconvertibility is not a systemic difference, no one is quite sure how much and what kind of convertibility would be tolerable under the communist system. There is a chicken-and-egg aspect to the convertibility question and the price problems frequently referred to in this essay. There can be no realistic exchange rates without major changes in the communist pricing system; full convertibility would make impossible the kind of price differences that now exist.

At one end of the scale one can start with the existing system: communist currencies have internal functions only; foreign transactions are carried on entirely in foreign currencies. The arrangement is awkward, though workable. Most of the other difficulties can be expressed as balance-of-payments problems. From the chronic pressure for foreign exchange stems the need for compensation arrangements and the special attraction of industrial cooperation. Bilateral balancing of one sort or another has long been a besetting problem of East-West trade. While much of the original need came from the Eastern side, the process was strongly abetted by Western countries, especially in Europe, which treated the Eastern market primarily as a place to promote exports. To modify bilateralism, there grew up switch trading, modern alchemy that turns barter into coin, but is really a poor and costly substitute for money. Recent years have seen a marked improvement in these matters, mostly as a result of the freer use by Eastern banks and governments of Western credit in various forms, and especially their discovery that they could do quite well in the Eurocurrency markets.

Then came some sharp reminders that inconvertibility, credit, price discrepancies, and central "control" do not altogether insulate the communist countries from the rest of the world. Western inflation raised their import bills for food and machinery. The rise in oil and raw materials prices benefitted the U.S.S.R. and, on balance, probably Poland, but hurt the others. Recession in the West damaged exports. The resulting balance-of-payments difficulties brought several of the communist countries to the edge of their creditworthiness. There has since been some turnaround, partly as a result of measures taken in the East and partly through the drop in raw materials prices and the beginnings of recovery in the West. Highly liquid Western bankers kept lending. Nevertheless, barter has had a renaissance. We are not concerned here with current events, but the episode showed that, in spite of the impediments this essay stresses, communist countries are already involved in the world economy to a considerable degree. The forces that have brought them this far may continue to be the major factors determining their position in the late 1980s even if no drastic changes are made in the relations discussed here. Alternatively, these trends may not be able to continue without some major changes in such matters as price policies and exchange rates. (It is also possible that they will not be allowed to continue—but we shall return to that later.)

The disjunction of domestic and foreign prices is not between the communist countries as a group on the one hand and the rest of the world on the other, but between each communist country and the rest of the world. Though trade within Comecon uses world prices as guideposts (in varying ways), the prices at which goods are traded within Comecon and the internal price structures of the member countries have no meaningful connection. Similarly, the degree to which prices are permitted to move in response to market forces—or generally how they are adjusted or administered by governments—differs greatly from country to country. Finally, the differences among internal price structures and the responsiveness of each to world prices vary both according to the amount of external (Western) trade and also according to the domestic economic system. There arises, therefore, the difficult question of whether increased linkage with the world will be easier or more useful if it is established on a country-by-country basis or through a process that calls for internal Comecon adjustment (if not alignment) first—which would cover the larger share of each country's trade.

The determination of that issue, along with many others that affect the economic evolution of the communist countries, is less likely to be settled by outside forces than by internal developments within the countries or in their relations with the U.S.S.R. That may also be true of the question of future relations with the International Monetary Fund, a potential avenue of significant interconnection with the outside world. Though the Soviet Union could have been a founding member of the Bretton Woods institutions, it turned away, and the belief grew that a communist country could not join them. Two main reasons were usually given: a communist country could not achieve convertibility with its managed system, and it could not provide the information the Fund requires because of its stress on secrecy. The first objection is subject to a qualification; noncommunist countries were members of the Fund for a long time before making their currencies convertible; the degrees and types of convertibility of many currencies of the less developed countries still fall short of what the simple word suggests. Some people see a difference in principle between postponement of the possible (or conceivable) and a modus vivendi with a system one believes could never permit convertibility. Others would not boggle. Rumania has joined the Fund and, while its currency can be expected to remain in limbo for some time (it considers itself a developing country and is accepted as such in various parts of the world), it must have satisfied Fund members and itself that some workable arrangement on information could be achieved. This may or may not work, but it is worth noting that, quite apart from the Fund, the increased recourse to Western private capital by communist countries has entailed unprecedented publication of facts and figures. Other forces work in the same direction, so the secrecy problem may lose much of its importance by the late 1980s.

What will remain crucial will be the advantage any Eastern country sees in joining the Fund, the Soviet Union's view of the matter, and the view of Fund members about the usefulness of admitting countries with substantially different systems.

Whether the clear advantages of Fund membership will be thought to outweigh the costs will depend on circumstances. Poles and Hungarians were once very interested; their interest was diminished by the troubles of the international monetary system. The outer world seemed a dangerous place. But their balance-of-payments difficulties helped make a good case for the view that not only they but the U.S.S.R. would be helped by their access to the Fund (not to mention World Bank loans). But for the U.S.S.R. to see matters this way would require a number of judgments that do not seem to have been made. One involves weighted voting arrangements that give capitalist countries control of the Fund (in contrast to GATT, in which each country has one vote). The Russians may also prefer to have the smaller countries dependent on them because they lack outside resources. Judgment on the third point depends on what one assumes the Fund's future functions will be and how seriously they would be weakened by the participation of some fairly small communist countries whose methods fit imperfectly into the system. One would guess that the issue would be a secondary one in almost all the reasonably predictable futures of the Fund.

Soviet membership in the Fund would be quite a different matter. Indeed, that possibility cannot be seriously considered without envisioning either a massive transformation of the U.S.S.R. or of the Fund and with it the international monetary system. Even in a speculative essay this possibility would carry us too far afield. In the terms in which it is recurrently raised it is the wrong question, and so is the one about making the ruble convertible. In less simplistic terms, however, ruble convertibility is worth some attention.

If one were to accept the comprehensive program of Comecon as a credible guide, a good bit of progress toward ruble convertibility might be made before the end of the 1980s. The world is full of skeptics on the matter, and the internal debate in the communist countries is too muted to provide a basis for anything but speculation. There is, however, some piecemeal evidence worth noting and a few considerations one ought to have in mind. When it was introduced in 1963, the transferable ruble was put forward as a major step toward convertibility. (Westerners saw the analogy with the European Payments Union of 1950 that helped European currencies along the road to general convertibility). But the analogy was false and the claims made in the East invalid. The transferable ruble is still not a very liquid commodity and works mostly to offset balances negotiated bilaterally. What is transferable, when, and at what rate depends on circumstances too complicated to go into here. However, credit arrangements within Comecon have improved so that imbalances can exist for longer than in the past. Bilateral negotiations among Comecon countries are said to take increasing account of the outside world. There has been a large increase in the amount of hard-currency trade among Comecon members (i.e., transactions in goods that, because they are easy to sell outside, are not only priced in world terms but paid for in convertible currencies when traded in more than an agreed-on volume). A limited agreement among some countries permits part of the persistent credit balances to be paid in convertible currencies (an echo of the idea pressed some years ago by Poles and Hungarians that a share of debts within the group should be paid for in convertible currencies, more or less in the manner of the European Payments Union). One can easily imagine further modifications of the system arising, as these must have, from its inconvenience to members. It is not so easy to imagine how far the modifications will be allowed to go.

A second source of pressure—much less important, I should guess—is external. Some Third World countries have been allowed to make some limited transfers of ruble balances within Comecon and are pressing for more. The possibility of such an arrangement for Western countries was held out in announcements about changed rules in 1976. But the practical results were negligible. Some broadening or limited transferability for outsiders or Comecon members is not inconceivable. On any scale, however, either this kind of arrangement requires a high degree of solidarity (voluntary or dictated) within Comecon—as would some pooling of foreign exchange—or it invites internal friction, with members refusing to buy from others so as to earn hard currencies by running export surpluses.

Not true convertibility, this kind of arrangement is a reminder that there are degrees of convertibility and limited measures that achieve some of its features. There can be distinctions according to who holds the currency, to whom it is paid, for what, and what the recipient does with it. It is easier to imagine a ruble that can change hands among those who need rubles than one that can be spent freely on Soviet goods. Demand could be created by requiring Western partners to put up cash as well as kind; supply could come through some payment of profits in the same way. But then a new exchange rate might appear. The field is a rich one for scenarios.

Internal, not external, forces seem likely to be the decisive factors in this matter. It is the communist countries that have the most difficulty on account of convertibility, not the rest of the world. While the rest of the world ought to be prepared to help along a development of convertibility or other forms of easing communist countries into world monetary cooperation, it is not a matter of high priority. Consequently, no elaborate preparations need be made until possible avenues of approach are more apparent. Certainly no serious inconveniences to the operation of the Western system—whatever it is by the 1980s—should be accepted for the sake of accommodating a possible change in the communist currency system.

Perhaps the same general principle applies to the larger issue of increased communist participation in the remodeling or managing of the monetary system in the 1980s. Some years ago, when it seemed as if the world's monetary system was to be refashioned and reformed with a certain deliberation and sense of purpose, one had to think whether it would be sensible to invite the communist countries—really the Russians, that is—to interest themselves in the process. If they did not actually take part they might, at least, let their views be known so that they could be taken into account. To do all this publicly would have been chancy. Most of what is known about Soviet thought on monetary affairs—at least the officially approved part—has more to do with gold, fixed exchange rates, and "sound money" than was altogether fashionable at the time. Perhaps nothing was done; private efforts to draw attention to the subject by trailing it in front of some Soviet economists usually drew no serious response. Now that reform is on the shelf and adaptation is in order, there is no urgent need to pursue the question—but that may allow opportunities for quiet discussions that would bear some fruit by the 1980s, when a new generation of Soviet economists will have moved ahead. The gold question, at least, is in a new phase and has aspects of interest to the Russians. Stability, highly valued in controlled economies, is not without its admirers in the West, especially after a period in which flexible exchange rates were supposed to make for a better balance in the world than was possible under the Bretton Woods system of fixed rates (as they were called, not altogether correctly).

Apart from the broad issues, two specific ones might be acted on sooner that directly involve the communist countries. These are the international regulation of banking and efforts to control or at least influence the Eurocurrency market. It is not clear whether any special problems affect communist banks that function abroad or how the regulation of borrowing and lending in the Eurocurrency markets would affect them. There is no doubt, though, that any measures taken to narrow the freedom of borrowers or lenders in the Eurodollar market would be highly relevant to the fortunes of the East.

THREE

Food, Energy, Raw Materials, and Technology Transfer

Systemic difficulties of the sort discussed in the last section arise mainly from the differences between market and nonmarket methods of economic organization and the building of cooperative mechanisms for them. Some of the most important international activities of the 1980s pose problems that are quite different. They have to be dealt with by governmental commitments that do not depend on each economy's internal system. In food, energy, raw materials, and technology transfer, however, there will continue to be markets that will have greater or less freedom. Therefore, problems will continue to arise from the relation of state trading and central planning to these markets even though the major disagreements about market forces and how markets ought to be organized do not arise.[1] Since the cooperative system of the past quarter-century was weak in dealing with issues being discussed in this section, there is little historical record to draw on. The belief that major, positive steps

[1]For instance, some respectable opinion shows that with a little luck and good sense world food production can be expected to respond well enough to demand and additional support so as not to require major government-to-government commitments about delivery, production, etc. It can be argued that national, not international, policies will prove adequate to promote production, provided incomes are raised to the point where hunger becomes a problem that can be taken care of by disaster relief. In raw materials, too, there are serious arguments not only that market forces will bring about adjustments that will obviate large-scale international management of major problems, but that measures that resist market forces will break down in the long run.

will have to be taken to deal with these problems in the 1980s may be distorted by the worries about shortages indicated by OPEC and the Club of Rome's *Limits to Growth,* but let us assume that an effort will be made to manage these problems better through intergovernmental arrangements. To cover the range of possibilities with any precision is impossible in an essay of this length, so the discussion in this chapter will be sketchier than in the last.

A major element of uncertainty is the extent to which the U.S.S.R. is likely to be willing to take part in international efforts to deal with food, energy, and raw materials problems—and let its allies do so. The record of the 1970s is not clear. Some increased involvement has taken place; there are signs of increased willingness to go further, and others that point in the opposite direction. For the Western countries, there are questions like those raised above about the reform of the international monetary system. However, in all four of the subjects named in the title of this chapter, the U.S.S.R. is more important in the world economy than in trade and payments generally. For that reason, the first premise of the discussion that follows is that the international system of the 1980s would benefit if the U.S.S.R. took a responsible part in handling these matters, provided there was a sufficient area of agreement as to the purposes to be served. The second premise derives from uncertainty: Methods should be devised for dealing with food, energy, and other problems that do not depend on the U.S.S.R.'s taking part, whether because of its unwillingness to do so or because its participation would impede the operation of the arrangement. How much these two premises might conflict and how difficult it would be for Western countries to pursue a two-track policy are matters that it is perhaps best not to generalize about.

FOOD

A relatively small share of the world's grain moves in international trade. Because the U.S.S.R. produces and consumes so much, shifts in its internal demand and supply have accounted for a high proportion of the fluctuations in world markets for some time. No one doubts that one of the most substantial contributions the U.S.S.R. could make to stabilize the world food economy in the 1980s would be to internalize the adjustments required by annual variations. This would mean carrying large stocks and more or less regularizing purchases on world markets. Whether adequate stocks can be maintained physically or financially is partly a question of the expansion of productivity and production. Efforts to improve Soviet agriculture have been going on for decades, not without progress but never producing the expected results. Whether this will change by the late 1980s is a matter no one can feel certain about, but it is a prospect the international system ought to encourage. If an international effort is made to expand production, the U.S.S.R. ought to be part of it. The United States and other Western countries should see technological and scientific cooperation with the U.S.S.R. in fields relevant to agriculture in more than bilateral terms. It may well be, however, that high agricultural productivity in the U.S.S.R. can be advanced only by internal changes of a sort that outsiders cannot contribute to.

According to one view of the world food economy, national efforts are not likely to meet world needs. International efforts will be required to assure minimum supplies or to pursue more ambitious goals, such as minimum nutritional standards for all. These will require stockpiling under some form of international agreement. Whether the stocks are held nationally or internationally, what formulas govern their accumulation and disposal, and how they are financed are important questions that need not detain us now; it is enough that the framework is international. All countries above a certain level of income would be expected to contribute to these stockpiles in kind or cash. That would include the U.S.S.R. and, presumably, the other communist countries. If the U.S.S.R. had food to export beyond Comecon's needs—as has been true in the past and, some Russians believe, is likely over the next few decades—it might be able (or compelled) to sell to the stockpiles if they had a stabilization function. Access to the stockpiles would presumably be limited to those who had contributed to their accumulation (or were too poor to), and this seems the main incentive for the U.S.S.R. to participate. But if supplies elsewhere were adequate, it might be to the advantage of the system to supply the U.S.S.R. even if it had not participated.

Variations on this possibility suggest some of the difficulties of constructing a satisfactory international system when important countries remain outside. It might well be of some importance to the U.S.S.R. whether decisions on such questions were to be made by an international agency (perhaps in accord with principles agreed on in advance) or were left to the countries producing or holding surpluses. This last condition raises the question of what the suppliers—mainly the United States and Canada—would do and what they might be obliged to do, either by the general international agreement or by commitments made bilaterally. The existing American-Soviet grains agreement is something of a substitute for a broader agreement but could be closely geared to one so that the U.S.S.R. became a kind of associate member. It might, however, give the U.S.S.R. a good deal of assurance of supply with few obligations, and could conceivably put the United States in a position in which its bilateral commitments pulled against—or actually conflicted with—the international arrangement.

Further questions arise about the extent to which an outsider willing to make commitments to buy in quantity could, by dealing with a number of countries, assure itself of the benefits of the scheme without obligations as well as what commitments it would have to make about exporting at the same time it imported. In the case of the U.S.S.R., further questions arise about the extent to which it would take over the supplying of grain for the smaller Comecon countries or let them take part in an international reserve system. Finally, there is the whole set of questions about information as to supplies, needs, crops, and the like, which can do much to alter the substance of any arrangement about world supply and demand, whether the U.S.S.R. is in or out of the system.

An alternative view of the world food economy is that no elaborate international arrangements are needed because market forces and national policies assure adequate supplies and reasonable distribution so long as the purchasing power is provided. That is the kind of world in which the disturbingly large and secretive Soviet purchases of the early 1970s took place. The bilateral agreement with the United States provides some assurance against a repetition; a Soviet need at a time when American grain bins were empty would produce quite different results. Again, bilateral arrangements—which could involve other suppliers and consumers as well—become crucial. It is not hard to see why the case for broader international arrangements is strong or why the interest in Soviet participation remains ambivalent, whether seen from Moscow or Washington.

ENERGY

With regard to oil and coal, the situation of the U.S.S.R. is the reverse of that concerning food. Still an exporter, it may either lose its position or expand it, depending largely on how fast sizable internal resources are developed. The issue is important to the Eastern European countries, for whom the U.S.S.R. is the principal supplier. It can also be significant to the Western European countries and Japan, who have a special interest in expanding and diversifying their sources. Other consumers, including the United States and Canada, have an interest in all expansion of energy production, even if they are not direct recipients of the Soviet products. Whether that interest could be said to be so great as to warrant the expenditure of capital to help develop Soviet energy resources is another matter, and one that depends in part on alternative possibilities and the existence of more secure sources of supply. But considerations that might keep public American funds out of Siberia might not apply to public Japanese funds or private funds of any nationality. The provision of some international public capital to expand Soviet energy production might be a reasonable feature of an arrangement under which the U.S.S.R. participated in world energy development or gave credible assurances of security of supply.

In other words, if producing and consuming countries were to work out some kind of multilateral energy regime, it is not hard to imagine the U.S.S.R. becoming part of it. More complex issues arise if the general pattern persists of division between a producing group centering on a cartel (but with some producers outside it) and a consumer interest—not necessarily highly organized—with various supply arrangements. An OPEC with the U.S.S.R. as a member would be politically a very different thing—internally and externally—from the OPEC we know. A U.S.S.R. that is a free rider on OPEC price policy is no more unthinkable, in the future than in the present, but the uneasiness that cartels must feel about important outsiders would grow if the Soviet supply were greatly expanded with the capital and, perhaps, technology of consuming countries.

On the Soviet side, a question of considerable importance with regard to the country's relation to the world energy economy is whether Moscow will take major responsibility for the energy supplies of Eastern Europe or will carry further the approach (which predates the crisis) of pressing the smaller countries to look for a growing part of their own supplies in the rest of the world—and on what terms.

On the question of what part nuclear energy comes to play in the world energy economy, the U.S.S.R. is again a country of considerable potential influence, mostly on the supply side. Its potential depends to an important degree on technical advance. What it chooses to do in this field will inevitably be much affected by concern over security and proliferation and by the action of the United States and other Western countries. The systemic concern with these matters is obvious and so is the matter of international cooperation in research and the dissemination of information.

RAW MATERIALS

The U.S.S.R. is both a major supplier and a major consumer of raw materials. It exports more than it imports but, of course, the situation differs from product to product. One can assume that the U.S.S.R. would look benevolently on any arrangements to hold up world prices and stabilize markets for the products it exports. How far it would go in participating in these arrangements is not clear, nor is its position on measures focused on products of which it is a net importer. During the next two decades internal demand may also rise to a level that forces the country to import some things it now exports. While the U.S.S.R. endorses the rhetoric of the Group of 77 in the United Nations Conference on Trade and Development (UNCTAD), how far it will go in practical policies remains untested. Some statements and discussions by Soviet citizens show a reasonable degree of pragmatism in these matters.

Without a better idea of what Soviet attitudes and practices might be, it is hard to say a great deal about the difficulties or advantages of Soviet participation in the many kinds of raw materials arrangements that might be undertaken in the 1980s. What has been said about food and energy has some analogies. Long-run contracts fit Soviet methods very well and have a place in both existing international arrangements and some of those envisaged as resulting from the breaking up of the vertical integration practiced by many multinational producers. If consumer countries are to pay part of the cost of stockpiles or other stabilization arrangements, the U.S.S.R. could reasonably share in this activity for products it imports. There are, however, difficult problems of judgment in administering the less automatic features of commodity arrangements, so how the Soviet influence would be directed would make a difference to the meaning of its participation. There are some indications that the Russians have yet to make up their minds as to how far they want to be associated with activities that may force them to choose between the rhetoric of the less developed countries and a national economic interest, which would sometimes lead them to take a position on the side of the industrial countries. Whether other countries should try to push for the resolution of that issue (or could do much if they tried) is far from certain. Most of the kinds of measures being discussed with regard to raw materials could probably work without Soviet participation, while an uncertain Soviet voice might be a good deal more trouble than it was worth. This is not true of those products of which the U.S.S.R. is a major supplier, or, probably, several products in which its import position is significant.

That lame conclusion is one more demonstration of the need to look at raw materials individually instead of collectively.

TECHNOLOGY TRANSFER

While much contemporary discussion of technological transfer is cast in North-South terms, the East-West dimension has always been of major importance and is likely to remain so. If it does not, that diminished importance could be the result of either of two developments. The first would be the generation in the East of a technology-producing process that would put it on something like an equal export-import footing with the West. This is not very likely, though the appreciation of some technological developments arising from Eastern and especially Soviet conditions is greater than it once was.

The second possible development would be the triumph in the U.S.S.R. of the school of thought that holds that when once a certain amount of foreign technology has been imported the process should stop for the time being. Where the first possibility would create a balance, this one would create a vacuum. Such a development is not inconceivable but both material factors and several schools of thought work against it in the Soviet Union.

Assuming neither of these eventualities, there will continue to be a flow of technology. Some of the issues this involves have been taken up in the discussion of industrial cooperation and of the reasons Westerners might have to keep the most modern technology flowing and even why they might prefer East-West to North-South activities. Perhaps a word should be added about the considerations, public and private, that argue for seeking commercial advantage by restraining exports of technology at least until the next stage is ready to be introduced. That hardly seems the way to promote the efficiency of the international economy of the 1980s.[2] And for the present it is enough to say

[2]It does not follow that the speediest possible diffusion is desirable. Account has to be taken of concern for the pace of change, dislocation, disturbance, and the kinds of things that are considered in industrial policy and related matters.

that when such a course is followed there is no reason to discriminate against the Eastern countries in favor of other Western countries or those in the developing part of the world.

Past and present discrimination against the Eastern countries in the export of technology has been based mostly on security and a set of views about it that merge with looser political and economic warfare arguments. To call for the end of such discrimination in the 1980s would be to postulate far more East-West harmony than we have known or can consider very likely. As long as countries have allies, export controls based on security may be discriminatory. It cannot be sensible to say that there should be no discrimination against the communist countries if that would increase insecurity. (See the assumptions in Chapter 1.)[3] It is not likely that this issue can be confined to purely military technology. Strength is too complex for that. Good economic arguments (based on fungibility) support a belief that technological denial is not a good way of restraining the long-run growth of military strength, though it has obvious short-term uses. Still, as true détente must rest on security, the control of exports of direct military technology and a bit more will remain a national or alliance matter. It is worth noting that the situation is asymmetrical. In the West, national export rivalry plus differences of view about the treatment of dual-purpose technology (and probably about some security issues) tend to reduce the range of controls, whereas Soviet officials undoubtedly face no such challenge from their allies in deciding what not to export. Within this framework, one can suggest that East-West relations in the 1980s could be improved if export controls on technology were limited as much as possible to clearly military matters, made as predictable as possible, and handled by a simple and speedy process.[4] Emphasis should also be put on the fact that sustained

[3]However, if security lies in strategic balance, one can conceive of circumstances in which technological transfer would help to keep the military balance instead of stimulating an unbalancing stage of the arms race.

[4]This is not the correct conclusion if export licensing is to be used for bargaining or political pressure or if it is believed that a fairly modulated control by the West is useful. Then uncertainty and murky but controllable procedures are the order of the day. However, for this essay we have left aside that range

industrial cooperation reduces security risks by providing a built-in surveillance over dual-purpose technology. Even in the absence of a Western partner, inspection can be extended by various means to major technological installations of professedly civilian purposes but with military potential.

The international system of the 1980s would benefit from two kinds of East-West technological cooperation. Combined research and the sharing of discoveries in new fields or arenas of common interest make sense on both economic and political grounds. All the problems of international management of such projects have to be taken into account. Often bilateral arrangements will seem superior to multilateral ones. Problems of focus, duplication, and inadequate dissemination will arise, however, if too many pairs of countries act separately.

Joint East-West ventures in dealing with Third World countries are more talked about than practiced. They may, however, have special value in technology transfer and we should learn more about this during the 1980s. It is said that some technology in use in the Eastern countries is better suited to developing countries than that commonly found in the richer Western countries, although the latter have advantages in design and management. A combination of Western design and finance with equipment and labor from the East (to hold down costs) might sometimes seem both politically and economically advantageous to all concerned, including the developing countries. However, recalling what Bernard Shaw said to Ellen Terry in another connection, one would want to be sure that the joint venture did not produce a combination of Eastern management and Western prices.

---

of issues just as we have not entered into the argument that anything that "strengthens" the Soviet economy beyond a certain point is a risk to security because it increases the possibility for independent action and thus plays into the hands of those who favor pressing ahead to extend Soviet power wherever possible. The debate in the United States in 1978 and 1979 about the denial of export licenses for large computers and bits for drilling oil wells echoed the arguments of earlier years about oil pipe, aircraft, electronic equipment, and some machine parts.

FOUR

Comecon

There is a tendency in the West to see Comecon as only a riposte to or mirror image of events in the West (the formation of OEEC, OECD, European Community, etc.), and that is a significant element of its history. But Comecon also has an internal reality that affects the behavior of its members not only in relation to one another but to the rest of the world as well. It may also have more of a dynamic than is generally allowed for. Whether it will develop a common approach to the rest of the world is an open question that may be quite important for the 1980s.

Inevitably, the Soviet Union dominates Comecon, which could once be seen largely as one of the methods by which Moscow exploited smaller countries. The domination is still there but there are benefits for the small countries as well. For one thing, assured access to the Soviet markets makes possible economies of scale which they could not attain by themselves. Similar gains may be obtained through specialization agreements. For a long time the major asset of Comecon was the stability of supply of relatively cheap raw materials and energy. This advantage has been somewhat reduced since 1973, but the disturbances have been less than in the world outside, and this has not gone unnoticed in Eastern Europe. Earlier, the use of world prices for intra-Comecon trade probably gave the smaller countries an advantage in the terms of trade when buying raw materials from the U.S.S.R.

The advantages of Comecon membership are understood in the smaller countries and the organization seems to be accepted as permanent. If what the smaller countries can achieve by co-operation with the Western countries or through multilateral organizations seems to be limited—or if the way is not open because the U.S.S.R. forbids it—then the important question will be what relation Comecon might have to the world economy of the 1980s. The question of whether the Eastern countries are to become more fully involved in the world economy than in the past opens two lines of inquiry. One is about the effect of Comecon on the member countries' economies and their external relations. The other is about the fitting of Comecon as a unit into the world economy.

On the first score, one would take account of all the advantages the Eastern economies gain from stable supplies of raw materials and energy, economies of scale, and the like. However, not all Comecon arrangements strengthen the member countries in dealing with the rest of the world. There is some tolerance of poor-quality production for a sheltered market and some acceptance of high costs when partners are easier (but not better) sources than other suppliers. Sometimes a certain conflict occurs between intra-Comecon trade and a member's trade with the West. One obvious bridge to technological and economic gain—linking East-West industrial cooperation with specialization for the large internal Comecon market—has been used less than one would expect. There are no clashes of principle and some progress may be expected. The complexity of negotiation is one factor that might yield to persistent attack. Rivalry among the Eastern countries for the technology that comes with the Western "investment" may be a more durable source of difficulty, though a sufficient increase in the volume of cooperation might help by spreading the benefits. However, unless the Eastern economies become much more flexible, specialization arrangements introduce rigidities and not just the economies they might achieve in competitive markets.

What was said above about monetary and payments issues indicated a useful influence of Comecon, especially if steps were taken toward transferability within the system, more multilateralism, and even partial convertibility. All of these steps tend to stimulate competition within Comecon and thus give the more efficient countries some advantages in dealing with the outside world. This advantage, however, generates its own opposition within the system. It would be a mistake to expect a process comparable to that which took place in Western Europe in the 1950s, by which competition and currency transferability within the group paved the way for convertibility and effective competition in world markets. The discrepancies in national prices and pricing systems are important here. In spite of these difficulties some attention has to be given to the possibility of Comecon as a monetary area within the international monetary system.

Another source of national economic strength from Comecon arrangements ought to be found in the rather free transfer of technology, combined research, and the like. It is hard for an outsider to know how much weight to give this but one notices that these possibilities are given less vocal attention in the East than is technological cooperation with the West.

The whole question of the possible gains from Comecon integration is clouded for the smaller countries by the link between the strength of Comecon and the U.S.S.R.'s dominant place. Nowhere is the dilemma seen more sharply than in the conduct of external trade. Facing the European Community, Hungary, Poland, and the rest feel themselves at a substantial disadvantage as individual nations because so much of their Western trade is with a group that now wants to negotiate as a bloc. Joined together in Comecon, the Eastern countries would offer a better balance. But the price would be a stronger voice for the U.S.S.R. than when each negotiates separately and unending compromises (at best) as to what should be sought in the negotiations, a matter on which national priorities differ quite a bit. In-between courses are imaginable; both the Community and Comecon have proposed formulas; but the dilemma illustrates an important point that exists in other fields as well. It is moderated in the trade case by the fact that industrial cooperation and a number of other trade-related matters are covered by arrangements that remain bilateral—but these are troublesome from the point of view of

Community solidarity (as in the continuing national control of export credits). A third possible course for the Eastern countries is to put their national negotiations with the Community as firmly as possible in the framework of GATT. At present they are still having trouble there with the Community's insistence on keeping quantitative restrictions on their products, but in principle the alternative seems a possible way out of at least some problems.

By most standards it would appear that the Western and systemic interest lies in moderating the impact of Soviet dominance on the smaller countries and of giving them as much freedom of action and as many opportunities to use it as is reasonably possible. It follows that international economic arrangements should not be such as to force those countries to deal with the outside world through Comecon when there is a reasonable alternative. They should have as many opportunities as possible to fit into global or multilateral arrangements in whatever ways they can work out. Though the thrust of this principle is clear enough, it is not easy to see how it can be applied and how far it can be carried. This brief sketch has already mentioned three important limitations: the gain to the members from some features of Comecon; the Community's inner logic as a bloc; the limits of intersystemic cooperation whether bilateral or via GATT. No one should need to be reminded that Moscow sets the bounds for separate action by the smaller countries, though it does not do so uniformly or sometimes without cost to itself. What is perhaps most important from a global or systemic point of view is that the East-West nexus (and certainly the subordinate part of it that concerns the balance of the smaller countries' relations to the outside world and the U.S.S.R.) is only one feature of Comecon and is more likely to be shaped by other forces than to be itself the dominant shaper. Among these other forces shaping the future of Comecon and the choices its members make about working through it or along separate courses is whether the rest of the world is made up of blocs and regional groupings or is a multilateral world with most states acting as separate entities. (No doubt it is going to be mixed, but the proportions of the mix are important to the issues with which this essay has been concerned.) In turn, East-West relations generally—or So-

viet-American relations—will be only one set of factors determining what is done about blocs and multilateralism. How strong
a factor it will be is hard to say, but, up to a point, those who
have some choice in the matter ought to bear in mind the interest
of those who have very little choice—the small members of
Comecon.

In considering these matters, one should bear in mind that the
dilemma for members of Comecon is not just that of the advantages of integration against the disadvantages of Soviet dominance. It is also a question of their own national differences.
History and culture apart—though we cannot really set them
apart—this is a question of differences in the conduct of their
national economies. From a systemic point of view, the similarities of socialism must seem greater than national differences.
But in terms of the evolution of systems, and especially the
efforts to satisfy different needs and to find new and better ways
of doing things, a certain national freedom of action is vital. One
result is diversity. From the point of view of the international
system, the ability to accommodate such diversity is a virtue.
Up to a point, Comecon can help in that process; beyond that
point, it inhibits experimentation and enforces uniformity. The
tradeoffs with Comecon's other advantages can only be made
by the members and they are limited in their choices (one less
than the others). Outsiders cannot settle these matters, but they
can have some influence on them. One avenue of influence that
avoids some of the political disadvantages of Western national
(or Community or collective) action is the international economic
system.

What would not be desirable from a Western point of view—
or a systemic one either—would be the addition to Comecon
from time to time of countries from the Third World. These
accretions are not true memberships fully comparable to that of
the existing European states. They are more like the adhesion
of Mediterranean and African countries to the Community. There
may be some advantages to the individual countries involved,
but there is little to be said for the practice in systemic terms
unless there are no better roads to development. Whether the
West can do much about it other than provide more neutral

alternatives is another matter. Perhaps one has to entertain the possibility that a less developed country (LDC) might be associated with more than one group. If not, either the accretion should reflect clear-cut adherence to a socialist system (as in Cuba and Vietnam) or it may have to be seen as the kind of dividing up of the Third World that our ninth assumption (Chapter 1) took to be only a limited phenomenon. If it is so, it might mean that East-West cooperation is not a good enough prospect for the 1980s to warrant an essay even as long as this one.

On the margin of the Comecon questions, but of particular interest in connection with the smaller countries, is the matter of future economic cooperation within Europe. Here many salient issues have a more important geographic dimension than is true of trade generally: transportation, communications, electricity supply and other energy issues, environmental questions, and so on. Many of these matters are trade-related, but a strong case can be made for saying that they should be dealt with by countries occupying the European peninsula in whatever combinations are functionally relevant. No doubt some will be on the agenda for Comecon-Community discussion. Though many are dealt with on a national basis within the Community, they might be easier than trade for Comecon to handle on a common basis. Historically, the Economic Commission for Europe (ECE) has been the natural home for work on a number of these questions. The Helsinki agreement has given them a further push, sometimes within ECE and sometimes outside. In both these settings, however, the Soviet Union and the United States tend to get involved, and that does not necessarily make for progress. The interesting question is whether ways can be found of diminishing (or eliminating) the role of both superpowers and what the results of that would be for the effectiveness of the work that was done without them and for the interests of the smaller countries.

FIVE

North-South Issues

The intersection of North-South and East-West issues involves too wide a range of matters to be properly discussed here. A few somewhat disparate comments will point a direction.

The history of the intersection is more ambiguous than is always remembered. The entry of the U.S.S.R. into aid and trade for development in the period after Stalin's death undoubtedly led to much wasteful cold-warism in the Third World and some harmful military assistance, but it was also a stimulus to Western economic aid. Though the rivalry persisted for a long time and was often pronounced, there developed in a few places a certain amount of accommodation and symbiosis that had interesting possibilities. By the late 1960s, there was a fair amount of evidence that the Russians, like the Westerners, had learned a good bit about the difficulties of development and the frustrations of "influence," while Third World countries had learned something of the limits of Moscow's socialism, planning, and world outlook.

Our view of what may happen in the 1980s is confused by two present uncertainties. First, whether the Third World will again become some kind of battlefield between the two "camps." Second, the high ratio of rhetoric to action in dealing with LDC economic concerns obscures our view of Soviet intentions and capabilities. When the agitation for a new international economic order began, it was at first easy for Moscow to take positions without being required to perform. As time passed, however, the developing countries began looking for more material results.

Rivalry with China must have added to the feeling in Moscow that Soviet performance would have to be improved.

In facing these issues, the Soviet Union had both advantages and difficulties. It can more easily guarantee levels of purchases from LDCs than market-economy countries can. In principle, it is also easier for a planned economy to minimize dislocation from increases in imports, but it is not necessarily easier to increase imports if it means cutting down domestic production. Some cases of the reexportation of LDC products to third markets suggest another set of difficulties.

While the Soviet market is very big, it is not always very dynamic. Growth is not greatest in the things the LDCs export. Though the U.S.S.R. finds it easier than market economies to accept payment in goods, it is also more reluctant to pay in convertible currencies except for relatively scarce raw materials. Payment in its own currency amounts to barter. While sometimes LDCs can find advantages in adopting the kind of technology used in socialist countries, those countries are importers, not exporters, of some of the more glamorous kinds of technology that LDCs want.

To a degree, the socialist countries are in competition with LDCs for technology-based "investments" by Western LDCs. The composition of exports of communist countries to the West is more like that of LDCs than of industrial countries, so the two are competitive in another sense as well.

While the sharp focus in North-South issues is inevitably on the U.S.S.R., the smaller countries should not be left out since they are sometimes well equipped to play a part in development and have indeed done so. Technical assistance, human capital, planning, and some other lines of activity are among their strong points. China, too, is a factor in several different ways. Playing the double role of communist and underdeveloped country, it at once challenged the Soviet Union for influence in the Third World and depicted Moscow as aligned with the capitalist countries. China provided economic and military aid to a number of countries even when its contacts with the outside world were most limited. How the great shift in Chinese policy that began in 1978 and that promises to expand ties with Japan, Europe, and the

United States will affect China's policy toward the developing world is far from clear.

A common strand that ties together North-South issues with those that have been discussed earlier is the place of organizations and the agreements embodying them in the international economic system and the place of socialist countries in these organizations. Before turning to this subject—which cuts across most of the issues already discussed—let us recapitulate what has come out about national and systemic differences.

The simple idea of a socialist, centrally planned economy is modified when countries give some independence of decision to enterprises, make use of the price system, and permit some activity by foreign entrepreneurs on one basis or another.

There are important issues for which systemic differences are not crucial. The willingness of the communist countries to engage in international cooperation in dealing with these matters and the importance of their doing or not doing so differs significantly from country to country. Both systemic and other conditions are altered by differences in national economies, factor endowments, salient problems, and all the other elements that make one country different from another.

SIX

International Institutions and Organizations

Organizations based primarily on cooperation among market economies—notably GATT and the IMF—present problems that have been dealt with at length in the text. It seems worth underlining several propositions and questions. Membership in these organizations is not, as such, a solution to intersystemic problems and, therefore, should not be regarded as a major objective of Western policy. However, conditions approximating those of membership can be achieved by some socialist economies. The fact that individual socialist countries can join these organizations when others do not—and even make special terms—is a desirable feature of the system. One troublesome question is whether any serious damage is done, in principle or in practice, to the organizations in question or to trade rules and relations when points are stretched to make possible the membership of the socialist countries.

One might think of these organizations as having a special socialist "chamber" or a "chapter" in their rules that recognizes the difference between that kind of membership and the membership of market countries. An argument for this is that frank recognition should be given to the problems already mentioned, while against it is the case for giving weight to national differences. Also to be taken into account is the fact that improving the rules on state trading—an important part of the problem—is a matter relevant to other countries as well as those we have been discussing.

The difference between the Soviet Union and the smaller countries is inescapable. The range of conceivable accommodations for the latter is wide, but Soviet membership in GATT or the IMF would change those organizations. (It is not just a matter of the size of the economy and its organization; the Soviet Union would be concerned with status, voting rights, and its position as a great power—as it was at Bretton Woods.)

With regard to new organizations that might be formed to deal with food, energy, technological transfer, raw materials, and so forth, a wholly different set of considerations applies. Systemic differences are far less important. The membership of the Soviet Union and other socialist countries would often be quite desirable for the objectives of the organization, provided it could be had on terms that did not undermine either the principles of the agreement or their chances of operation. Here the question of a separate chamber or separate terms might look rather different from the GATT case. Moreover, if special arrangements did have to be made to accommodate different trading practices, it could be argued that one should try to set up some rules but then work out a body of practice that would be far more meaningful than what was done in GATT about state-trading principles. The general principle noted earlier that cooperative arrangements should not be held back by foot-dragging in the East would certainly apply here. This leads to further questions as to whether nominal membership from the beginning, even if it is ineffective for a period of time, is preferable to getting matters under way and waiting for later decisions from the East. In part, this is a question of not delaying matters when they are ripe for action and, in part, one of emphasizing that all members must take obligations seriously.

A special case may arise in agencies concerning North-South matters that are negotiated in the first place by the Western countries. It is presumably no accident that the Soviet Union was not in on the ground floor, for example, in the Conference on International Economic Cooperation (CIEC). This itself may be a barrier to Soviet interest in joining. If not, the essence of the matter will be whether the Soviet Union can fit in without endangering any new arrangements that might be made.

UN agencies are, of course, an entirely different matter. It must be taken for granted that the Soviet Union will usually be present. Whether from the point of view of the West this in itself makes UN agencies undesirable places to deal with important issues probably depends on cases. There is a further question with regard to the extent to which declaratory policies in UN debates are to be disregarded or taken seriously as damaging the chances for East-West cooperation.

The special problems of intra-European economic cooperation concern the position of ECE, the possibility of setting up new post-Helsinki agencies, and what can be done without Soviet or American participation.

The OECD, NATO, and other Western organizations have been omitted from the discussion for the same reasons that problems of Western policy generally, and specifically the coordination of national policies, have been omitted. The questions here are familiar ones that revolve around such issues as whether security controls should be dealt with only in NATO, credit coordination via OECD, and so on. Is there any reason not to apply to East-West issues Miriam Camps's recommendation about the use of OECD to prepare issues before negotiating about them in other forums?[1] Might a distinction have to be made between national policies toward the East and the participation of communist countries in broader efforts? A different kind of question is whether the Yugoslav case means that other socialist countries should be allowed (or encouraged) to associate themselves in one way or another with OECD activities. Whether there is any real interest in the East in doing this is an open question, as is Moscow's willingness to permit it. The question is connected with the ECE issue and related matters. Without much analysis, my own feeling is that while occasional ad hoc arrangements might make sense, anything that looks like a move toward full membership for some or all of the Comecon countries is probably undesirable.

[1]Miriam Camps, *"First World" Relationships: The Role of the OECD*. Paris, Atlantic Institute for International Affairs; N.Y., Council on Foreign Relations. 1975.

Slightly different from membership in organizations is the question of the involvement of the Soviet Union and Eastern countries in negotiations on issues that might result in the creation of new organizations, or at least in changes in institutional behavior. Here it is in general desirable at least to feel out the area in advance to discover how much interest there is in the East and then, if there is interest, to be receptive to the idea of engaging in negotiations provided there is no reason to believe that such a step will seriously imperil the objective.

It can be taken for granted that the U.S.S.R. will insist on recognition of its position as a superpower. Thus, any departure from the one-nation, one-vote principle will almost certainly lead to a demand for something approaching equality between Soviet votes and those of the strongest Western powers. This is not a problem with regard to a limited number of international economic issues but is a major difficulty with regard to any serious effort to formalize differences in strength and interest, unless it is accepted that the U.S.S.R. is always an exception that can be accommodated without vitiating the formula as it applies to other countries.

With regard to the small countries, a key question is their ability to belong to organizations in their own right whether other communist countries belong or not. To the extent that East-West issues are given weight, this becomes a strong argument for more multilateralism in the international system.

The question of when Comecon as such should be a participant in international organizations and negotiations is a matter that will be decided largely within that group. However, there are a certain number of situations in which Western behavior can have an important influence. It seems generally desirable to avoid situations that strengthen the pressures for solidifying the bloc. All in all, the arguments used in this paper suggest that a pluralistic approach to international trading arrangements is desirable.

Enough has been said about the difficulty and occasional undesirability of engaging the U.S.S.R. in international economic cooperation to make it clear that any thinking about this subject must also be accompanied by ideas about how any arrangement deals with outsiders. This is a particular problem for the United States in its key relations with the two major communist powers. Bilateral arrangements that parallel or supplement multilateral agreements look as if they would be the most serious possibilities, but the subject needs more attention.

SEVEN

Politics Again

Most of this essay has been written on the tacit assumption that the world of the late 1980s will see advances in international economic cooperation and the common handling of common problems. That is a reasonable enough point of view for those prescribing for a moderate world order. But it is only too clear that things may go in the other direction. In a world where cooperation is either minimal or limited to a few groups of countries for a few purposes and often directed against other groups, the moderate, step-by-step, and fairly relaxed prescriptions of this essay are likely to be irrelevant to the real questions of the place of the U.S.S.R. and the other communist countries in the world economy. If we reject some sort of *renversement des alliances,* with Moscow and Washington playing wary but cooperative partners who go as far as they can in many things together for their own benefit, the key economic issues are likely to center around friction between the two superpowers. Instead of asking how far one can draw the U.S.S.R. and China into economic cooperation, the question will be: How can we resist the efforts the U.S.S.R. will make to exploit the divisiveness in the rest of the world? How dangerous will be the competition among Western countries to make advantageous deals with the communist countries? What chance is there of a constructive solution for problems of the Third World (or of the global economy) if Moscow, Peking, Washington, and all other capitals is jockeying for profit or for a rather narrowly conceived conception of national interest?

We cannot pursue these possibilities. We have already left out far milder, nearer, and more likely hypotheses. This paper has been not so much Hamlet without the Prince as Macbeth without Banquo's ghost (or perhaps the Lady's dagger). The omission of any discussion of United States policy rules out such queries as whether the Western governments should try to follow common policies, to exert pressure on one or another of the communist countries, and to let "political" and "security" considerations shape their economic policy.

The result is another series of omissions. This must be one of the few papers on this subject that has said nothing about the coordination of Western export controls, the setting of common standards for export credit, and why agreements on these matters have been so fragile. There has been no discussion of whether long-term export credits for capital goods at some point become the equivalent of foreign aid, or whether public credit inevitably involves some degree of subsidy.

Not all of the omissions are primarily connected with economic warfare and political pressure. A discussion of the proper role of government in supporting private firms in dealing with communist governments or of arrangements to permit normal competitors to join forces in dealing with the Soviet monopsonist might also be seen as reflections of intersystemic difficulties. From another angle, the last of these points is seen to involve questions about the conditions of competition in market economies and whether the same rules apply to dealings with outsiders. The former question touches on the kinds of government-business relations that are or are not suitable to the international economy. Bilateralism was only briefly mentioned, but it is clear that our general prescriptions condemn it as a generally undesirable state of affairs, even when it results from competition among market economies for business with the East.

As we have not dealt with negotiations and said relatively little about the way the passage of time may affect relations, we have lost some of the flavor of politico-economic bargaining that is central to the evolution of East-West relations. But our prescription can accommodate this process. We have spoken of the step-by-step and the experimental. Almost none of the arrangements suggested are all-or-nothing affairs; they involve continuing processes that could usually be accelerated or decelerated according to circumstances. We have stressed the need to order things so that international cooperative arrangements open to the communist countries can also operate without them. We have warned that while nominal but ineffective participation is often tolerated, participation that distorts negotiations or prevents their conclusion is not. These conditions are sometimes difficult to fulfill, sometimes easy, and sometimes impossible.

Something that is inescapable in the discussion of East-West economic relations is linkage. Linkage is not just a negotiating tactic but a condition of effective cooperation and a natural element in relations among political units that pursue multiple ends. Everyone can be sensible about linkage in clearly defined circumstances, but it is hard to find useful generalizations that fit all cases. Maybe some rough distinctions will help. One can see four types of linkage:

(a) The inherent—some trade and payments arrangements cannot operate unless others also work.

(b) The economic balance—this is essentially the process of putting together a package of measures that are not inherently related but that make up a bargain that is acceptable and reasonably desirable because both sides benefit. Necessary when starting a process or working out basic arrangements, it becomes dispensable once the parties have confidence that their "loss" today will be offset by a "gain" another day. It is hard to dispense with this kind of linkage when the parties have different economic systems.

(c) The noneconomic but specific—the use of economic agreements to assure progress in other fields—disarmament, human rights, etc. This will often be desirable if workable but may fail either because the specific tying is unacceptable or because the bargaining power of the economic measure is not great enough. Formal and public links may be unacceptable where private ones are not.

(d) The noneconomic but general—this is essentially the crucial link between closer economic cooperation and détente. If serious disputes erupt over arms control or human rights or something like the invasion of Czechoslovakia in 1968 or other kinds of global behavior, it is neither politically plausible nor wise to expect the kind of close economic cooperation that would otherwise be desirable. Nor would it be politically prudent to add to the pressure for compromise on such matters when a strong position on other matters may be more important to the proper functioning of the system. So long as participation in international economic cooperation seems to be of more value to the communist countries than it is to the rest of the world, it will be hard to argue that a link between that cooperation and the general state of East-West relations is improper or irrelevant.

In considering these kinds of linkage, two further thoughts about East-West economic relations ought to be kept in mind. (1) While it has often been convenient to speak of "cooperation," the positive and formal relation that term implies is not the only way of achieving satisfactory East-West economic relations in the 1980s. Parallel or complementary action, tacit understanding, pursuit of a predictable and not damaging course, or simply refraining from doing certain things can all be positive. (2) To prescribe what is desirable is not to say that the failure to achieve it is intolerable or disastrous.

Appendixes

This figure demonstrates that the organizations of party, government, and soviets are parallel at the center of power (Moscow)

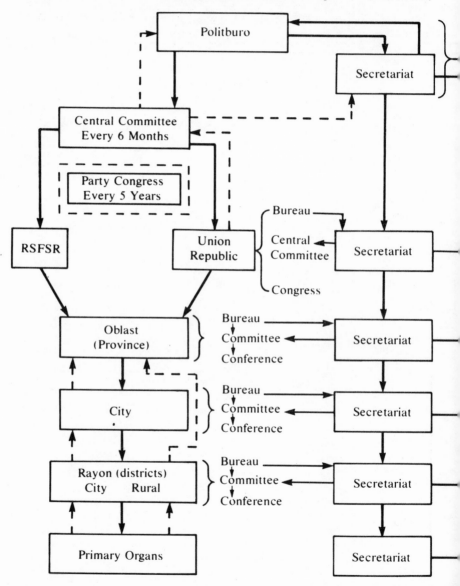

and at other regional levels. It also suggests that the party dominates the government and soviet organizations.

NOTE: Arrows indicate effective flow of decision-making power. Broken arrows suggest formal flow of power, often ineffective.

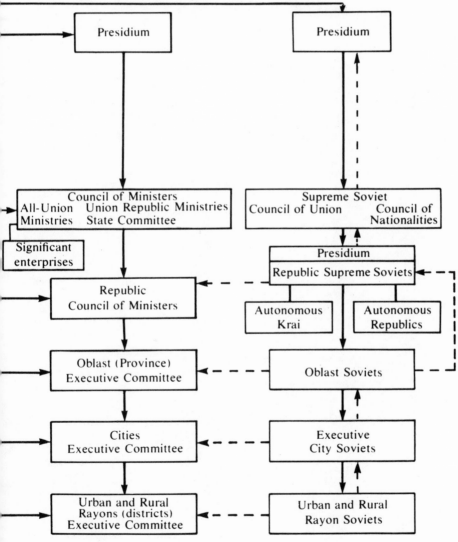

Central Soviet Leadership

This figure organizes the personalities of the principal party organs at the center of power—the Politburo and Secretariat—chronologically by age. It also lists some of the most important personalities in the Council of Ministers. Combined, these lists constitute the most important actors in the Soviet power structure.

APPENDIX TWO

Central Soviet Leadership

Politburo of the CPSU Central Committee

Full Members	Birthdate	Age Jan. 1980	Position before 25th Congress	Date Elected in Politburo
Pel'she, Arvid Yanovich	7 Feb. 1899	80	Chairman, Party Control Committee	Apr. 1966
Suslov, Mikhail Andreyevich	21 Nov. 1902	77	Secretary, CPSU Central Committee	Jul. 1955
Kosygin, Aleksey Nikolayevich	21 Feb. 1904	75	Chairman, USSR Council of Ministers	May 1960
Kirilenko, Andrey Pavlovich	8 Sept. 1906	73	Secretary, CPSU Central Committee	Apr. 1962
Brezhnev, Leonid Il'ich	19 Dec. 1906	73	General Secretary, CPSU Central Committee	Jun. 1957
Ustinov, Dmitriy Fedorovich	30 Oct. 1908	71	Secretary, CPSU Central Committee	Mar. 1965/Full Mar. 1976
Gromyko, Andrey Andreyevich	18 Jul. 1909	70	USSR Minister of Foreign Affairs	Apr. 1973
Cherneenko, Konstantin Ustinovich	24 Sept. 1911	68	Chief, General Department of Secretariat	Oct. 1977/Full Oct. 1978
Kunayev, Dinmukhamed Akhmedovich	12 Jan. 1912	67	First Secretary, Central Committee, CP, Kazakhstan	Apr. 1971
Andropov, Yuriy Vladimirovich	15 Jun. 1914	65	Chairman, USSR Committee for State Security (KGB)	Apr. 1973
Grishin, Viktor Vasil'yevich	18 Sept. 1914	65	First Secretary, Moscow City Party Committee	Apr. 1971
Scherbitskiy, Vladimir Vasil'yevich	17 Feb. 1918	61	First Secretary, Central Committee, CP, Ukraine	Apr. 1971

	Birthdate	Age Jan. 1980	Other Positions	Date Elected Current Highest Position
Romanov, Grigoriy Vasil'yevich	7 Feb. 1923	55	First Secretary, Leningrad Oblast, Party Committee	Apr. 1973/Full, Mar. 1976
Tikhonov, N. A.			First Deputy Chairman, U.S.S.R.	Nov. 1978/Full, Nov. 1979
Candidate Members				
Kuznetsov, Vasiliy	13 Feb. 1901	78	First Deputy Chairman, Presidium, USSR Supreme Soviet	Oct. 1977
Ponomarev, Boris Nikolayevich	17 Jan. 1905	74	Chief, International Department, CPSU Central Committee	May 1972
Solomentsev, Mikhail Sergeyevich	5 Nov. 1913	65	Chairman, RSFSR Council of Ministers	Nov. 1971
Rashidov, Sharaf Rashidovich	6 Nov. 1917	61	First Secretary, Central Committee, CP, Uzbekistan	Oct. 1961
Demichev, Petr Nilovich	3 Jan. 1918	61	USSR Minister of Culture	Nov. 1964
Masherov, Petr Mironovich	Feb. 1918	60	First Secretary, Central Committee, CP, Belorussia	Apr. 1966
Aliyev, Geydar Ali Rza	10 May 1923	55	First Secretary, Central Committee, Azerbaydzhan	Mar. 1976
Shevardnadze, E. A.			Council of Ministers	Nov. 1978
Gorbachev, Mikhail Sergeyevich	Feb. 1915		Chief, Organizational Party Work Department Party Secretary	Nov. 1979 Nov. 1979

	Birthdate	*Age Jan. 1980*	*Other Positions*	*Date Elected Current Highest Position*
Secretariat				
Suslov, Mikhail Andreyevich	21 Nov. 1902	77	Member, Politburo, CPSU Central Committee	Mar. 1947

Politburo of the CPSU Central Committee (Cont.)

Secretariat	Birthdate	Age Jan. 1980	Other Positions	Date Elected Current Highest Position
Ponomarev, Boris Nikolayevich	17 Jan. 1905	75	Candidate Member, Politburo	Oct. 1961
Kirilenko, Andrey Pavlovich	8 Sept. 1906	73	Member, Politburo	Apr. 1966
Brezhnev, Leonid Il'ich	19 Dec. 1906	73	Member, Politburo	Oct. 1964
Rusakov, Konstantin Viktorovich	31 Dec. 1909	70	Chief, Department for Liaison With Communist and Workers Parties	May 1977
Chernenko, Konstantin Ustinovich	24 Sept. 1911	68	Chief, General Department	Oct. 1977
Zimyanin, Mikhail Vasil'yevich	21 Nov. 1914	65	Editor, Pravda	Feb. 1976
Kapitonov, Ivan Vasil'yevich			Department	Dec. 1965
Dolgikh, Vladimir Ivanovich	1924	55	None; apparently has general responsibility for heavy industry sector	Dec. 1972
Ryabov, Yakov Petrovich	24 Mar. 1928	51	Has responsibility for Defense Industry	Oct. 1976
Gorbachev, Mikhail Sergeyevich	1932	48	Candidate Member, Politburo	Nov. 1979

U.S.S.R. Council of Ministers

Presidium

Chairman:

Kosygin, Aleksey Nikolayevich	21 Feb. 1904	75	Member, Politburo	Oct. 1974

First Deputy Chairmen:				
Mazurov, Kirill Trofimovich	Apr. 1914	65	1st Deputy Chairman	
Tikhonov, Nikolay Aleksandrovich			1st Deputy Chairman	Sept. 1976
Deputy Chairmen:				
Arkhipov, Ivan Vasil'yevich			Deputy Chairman	
Baybakov, Nikolay Konstantinovich			Deputy Chairman and Chairman, State Planning Committee	
Dymshits, Veniamin Emmanuilovich			Deputy Chairman	
Katushev, Konstantin Fedorovich	1 Oct. 1927	52	Chairman, Commission for CMEA Affairs	Mar. 1977
Kirillin, Vladimir Aleseyevich	NA*		Chairman, State Committee for Science and Technology	
Lesechko, Mikhail Avksent'yevich	NA			
Martynov, Nikolay Vasil'yevich	NA		Chairman, State Committee for Material and Technical Supply	June 1976
Novikov, Ignatiy Trofimovich	NA		Chairman, State Committee for Construction	
Novikov, Vladimir Nikolayevich			Chairman, Commission for Foreign Economic Questions	
Nuriyev, Ziya Nuriyevich				
Smirnov, Leonid Vasil'yevich			Chairman, Military-Industrial Committee	
Other Important Members:				
Andropov, Yuriy V.	15 Jun. 1914	65	Member, Politburo, Chairman, Committee for State Security	

301

Politburo of the CPSU Central Committee (Cont.)

Other Important Members	Birthdate	Age Jan. 1980	Other Positions	Date Elected Current Highest Position
Gromyko, Andrey A.	18 Jul. 1909	70	Member, Politburo, Minister of Foreign Affairs	
Ustinov, Dmitriy F.	30 Oct. 1908	71	Member, Politburo, Minister of Defense	

*NA = not available.

Index

About the Authors

LAWRENCE T. CALDWELL earned his M.A. and Ph.D. degrees from the Fletcher School of Law and Diplomacy, Tufts University, and in 1967 joined Occidental College in California where he now serves as Associate Professor of Political Science. Mr. Caldwell has also been Research Associate at the Institute for Strategic Studies in London, Visiting Professor and Director of European Studies at the National War College in Washington, D.C., and a NATO Research Fellow. His many articles and books include *Soviet Intentions in Africa* (forthcoming), *Soviet and American Relations: One Half Decade of Detente,* and "East European Integration and European Politics."

WILLIAM DIEBOLD, JR. is a Senior Research Fellow at the Council on Foreign Relations. He was educated at Swarthmore College, Yale University, and the London School of Economics. From 1940–43, Mr. Diebold served as a Research Secretary of the Council's War and Peace Studies. After working with the Department of State, the U.S. Army, and the Office of Strategic Services, he rejoined the Council in 1947 as a staff member where he has written extensively on a wide range of international economic issues. His recent work has concentrated on problems related to American policy toward the communist countries and on issues of structural change in the world economy. His latest book is *Industrial Policy as an International Issue.*

JOHN C. CAMPBELL has been a Senior Research Fellow at the Council on Foreign Relations in New York since 1955. After earning his Ph.D. in 1940 from Harvard University in modern history, Mr. Campbell joined the Department of State as an Eastern European specialist. During the next 15 years, he served in the Department's European Affairs section and on the Policy Planning staff. He was also a member of the staff of the United States delegations to the Council of Foreign Ministers, the Paris Peace Conference, and the Danube Conference. Mr. Campbell has written and edited numerous books, articles, and reviews on East Europe and the Middle East, including three volumes of *The United States in World Affairs* (1945–49); *American Policy Toward Communist Eastern Europe: The Choices Ahead;* and *Tito's Separate Road: America and Yugoslavia in World Politics.*

Date Due